# GENDER, IDENTITY AND THE IRISH PRESS
## 1922-1937
### Embodying the Nation

Front cover photograph depicts 'Queen Tailte' as portrayed by Nancy Rock at the Aonach Tailteann, *Irish Independent,* 13 August 1928, shelfmark 141. Reproduced by permission of the British Library.

# GENDER, IDENTITY AND THE IRISH PRESS 1922-1937
## Embodying the Nation

Louise Ryan

The Edwin Mellen Press
Lewiston•Queenston•Lampeter

**Library of Congress Cataloging-in-Publication Data**

Ryan, Louise.
    Gender, identity, and the Irish press, 1922-1937 : embodying the nation / Louise Ryan.
        p. cm. --
    Includes bibliographical references (p. ) and index.
    ISBN 0-7734-7298-3
    1. Women--Press coverage--Ireland--History--20th century. 2. Press--Ireland--History--20th century. I. Title.

PN5147.W58 R93 2001
070.4'493054'09415--dc21

2001042794

*hors série.*


A CIP catalog record for this book is available from the British Library.

Copyright  ©  2002  Louise Ryan

All rights reserved. For information contact

    The Edwin Mellen Press      The Edwin Mellen Press
    Box 450     Box 67
    Lewiston, New York     Queenston, Ontario
    USA 14092-0450     CANADA L0S 1L0

The Edwin Mellen Press, Ltd.
Lampeter, Ceredigion, Wales
UNITED KINGDOM SA48 8LT

Printed in the United States of America

For Finnian

# CONTENTS

| | |
|---|---|
| Acknowledgements | ix |
| Preface by Margaret Ward | xi |
| Chapter 1: Introduction | 1 |
| Chapter 2: Fashionable Bodies | 37 |
|     Section 1: The Modern Girl | 37 |
|     Section 2: Reach for the Skies – Adventurous women and the Irish Press | 69 |
| Chapter 3: Working Bodies | 91 |
|     Section 1: The Business Girl and the Woman in Industry | 92 |
|     Section 2: Emigrant Girls and the Absent Body | 109 |
|     Section 3: Woman, Citizen and Worker – the Constitution of 1937 | 126 |
| Chapter 4: Maternal Bodies: Family, Home, Motherhood and the Nation | 151 |
|     Section 1: Spinning Wheels and Country Cottages | 154 |
|     Section 2: Disorderly Bodies: Representations and Explanations of Domestic and Family Deviance | 167 |
|     Section 3: Mothering the Nation | 191 |
| Chapter 5: Rebellious Bodies | 205 |
|     Section 1: Representations of Republican Women in the Campaign for Irish Independence | 206 |
|     Section 2: Militant Women in the Post-Civil War Period | 221 |
| Chapter 6: Concealing Bodies: Newspaper Representations of Infanticide | 253 |
| Conclusion | 289 |
| Bibliography | 295 |
| Index | 301 |

# ACKNOWLEDGEMENTS

I first began researching this book in 1995. During the five years it took to complete I have enjoyed two sabbaticals from the University of Central Lancashire without which I would not have been able to devote so much time to reading the many volumes of newspapers involved in this project. In May 2000, I began a two year leave of absence in order to take up a research fellowship at the Irish Studies Centre, University of North London. This has afforded me the opportunity to develop some of the research ideas that have grown out of this book.

When I commenced work on this book I was not sure what shape it would take. Confronted with a mind-boggling array of material, I followed pathways that seemed interesting and fruitful. It has not been possible to explore all the many aspects of women's experiences as reported in the press during the 1920s-1930s. In focusing on just six key areas I have attempted to illustrate at least some of the topics that were regularly discussed in the newspapers of the period. Early on in the research I took the decision to focus on issues that have been under-researched. As I read the newspapers one of the first issues that really forced itself on my attention was infanticide. In the autumn of 1995 I spent a great deal of time at the county library archives in Cork reading gruesome accounts of infanticide and concealment in the *Cork Examiner*. When I came to write the chapter for this book in 1999 I was pregnant and, for the first time, I began to empathise with how all those young women must have felt as they concealed their pregnancies and went about their daily routines as normal. Because of that, the chapter I have written here is probably very different from what it might otherwise have been.

Over the last five years I have tried out various sections of this book as conference papers and they have no doubt benefited from the helpful comments

and suggestions received. In addition, I have cajoled busy friends and colleagues into reading chapters. I am particularly grateful to Breda Gray, University College Cork, Wendy Webster, University of Central Lancashire, Heidi MacPherson, University of Central Lancashire, Lisa Smyth, University of Warwick and Isobel Ni Riain, City University, Cairo. I would also like to thank Mary Hickman, University of North London and Liam Harte, St. Mary's University College.

Most of the research for the book was carried out at the British Library and the British Newspaper Library, London. I never cease to be impressed by the kindness, cheerfulness and professionalism of the staff there. I am grateful for the permission of the British Library to reproduce five photographs: *Irish Independent,* 13 and 24 August 1928 (shelfmark 141), *Irish Press,* 12 March 1936 (shelfmark 234), *Irish Press,* 1 and 3 October 1936 (shelfmark 237).

I owe a big debt of gratitude to Eugene O'Brien who read the proofs with great care and thoroughness and wrote lots of encouraging comments. Any errors, however, are entirely my own.

Completing this book with a small baby in the house has made life complicated, exhausting and exciting in so many ways. I had never fully appreciated how difficult it was to be a working mother. Thanks to Margaret Ward for all her words of encouragement. It would not have been possible to complete this book without Donatus who played with Finnian and allowed me to get on with writing.

Louise Ryan,
University of North London and
University of Central Lancashire,
March 2001.

# PREFACE

This is without any doubt a ground-breaking collection. Louise Ryan has, throughout her career, combined to telling effect the insights of the sociologist with the meticulous attention to detail of the historian. In the field of Irish women's studies her work is unique.

The scope of this new work *Gender, Identity and the Irish Press, 1922-1937: Embodying the Nation* is ambitious in that the author ranges freely throughout her defined historical period, gathering evidence to illuminate her discursive analysis and adding layers of carefully nuanced testimony to build up a comprehensive picture of the 'nation' through diverse images of womanhood. The use of provincial newspapers is a most welcome addition to feminist historiography, while her dissection of competing political tendencies in the national papers reveals sophistication in its appraisal of the interplay between the role of the media and competing political discourses. This approach will be of great benefit to students of media studies as well as historians and those engaged in women's studies.

While there have been several recent studies of the formation of the Irish State, they have been notably free of any serious gender content. This work in its deconstruction of national rhetoric, images and symbols, challenges the narrative

approach of many historians while adding colour and depth to previous analyses. It is a work which commands serious attention by scholars and students alike.

Margaret Ward,

Belfast, 2001.

# CHAPTER ONE:

## GENDER, IDENTITY AND THE IRISH PRESS, 1922-1937: EMBODYING THE NATION

**Introduction:**

> Ireland, like other sites of colonisation, was gendered female and this rhetorical act engendered a range of further possibilities and strategies within the register of colonial discourse. (Sharkey 1994:5)

According to Sharkey, nationalist myths and symbols need to be located within reactions to the particular context of colonialism. She argues that it was colonisers who first popularised feminised images of Ireland. Thus conquering and conquered masculinities were defined in relation to the female body of Ireland. Gendered narratives of rape, mastery and rescue, commonly used in colonial discourses, shaped nationalist rhetoric and symbolism. In colonial discourses the unruly female body represented the unruly land and its unruly people. Alternatively in nationalist discourses the passive, abused female body symbolised the violation of the land and the populace. The female gendering of Ireland has led to a plethora of womanly representations - Erin, Hibernia, Cathleen, Roisin Dubh. In the blurring of boundaries between representations of the people and the country, these allegorical women stood for both Ireland and Irishness (Innes 1993).

The use of such powerful and evocative female icons had particular consequences for the ways in which Irish women were described and represented. Sharkey claims that there is a 'notable coincidence' in the metaphors applied to the country and those applied to women (1994:16). The slippage between the emblematic woman and real women simplifies and contains women within male-defined projects : 'Erin suggested all that was feminine, courageous and chaste about Irish womanhood' (Innes 1993: 17). But just as the allegorical Erin represented Irish womanhood, so too Irish womanhood embodied Erin giving life to idealised femininity. In addition to the nation and the land, women have also been used to represent Irish culture, identity and traditions. 'By dressing and behaving "properly", and by giving birth to children within legitimate marriages' women embodied and reproduced 'the symbolic and legal boundaries of the collectivity' (Anthias and Yuval-Davis 1993: 28). However, as has been argued at length elsewhere (see Gray and Ryan 1997: 517-534), "woman" did not simply represent the idealised qualities of national identity. Within nationalist and religious discourses "woman" also signified national weakness, vulnerability and susceptibility to corrupting foreign influences. Thus, "woman" simultaneously represented both the essence of traditional Irish virtue and morality as well as the threat of immorality and sexual impurity. Through her body, allegorical woman symbolised the strength, purity and uniqueness of Irishness as well as its weakness, fragility and culpability. Such images are particularly apparent in the period from the establishment of the state in 1922 to the Constitution in 1937.

## *The Free State:*

> for most of its history, the Republic was considered a country where both politics and social attitudes were frozen in the 1920s. (Mark Ryan 1994: 91)

Following the Anglo-Irish war of independence (1919-1921), the establishment of the Free State in 1922 created a need to define not only political boundaries but social and cultural ones as well. The contentious partition of the island into the 26 county Free State and the northern 'six counties' which remained part of the United Kingdom, was viewed by many in the south as a victory for northern unionism and British intransigence. As Ryan (1994) has argued, nobody in Ireland had ever fought for a 26 county nation-state. According to Maurice

Goldring, this new state faced a crisis of legitimacy. In the wake of the bloody Civil War, the new middle class leaders of the state 'had to justify their power to their own people, to the world and maybe first of all to themselves' (1993: 18). In asserting their legitimacy as leaders and their authority as rulers, the new Free State government embarked on a policy of law and order. Such policies had very significant consequences for women who formed the focus for particular pieces of government legislation, perhaps most significantly the Constitution of 1937.

In discussing the early years of the newly established Free State, Maryann Valiulis argues that Irish politicians from across the political spectrum saw women only in domestic terms. 'Women were mothers. Women were wives. Women minded the hearth and home' (1995a: 118). A series of repressive legislation quickly instituted the traditional role of Irish womanhood despite the objections of women's groups. For example, in 1925 the Civil Service Amendment Act restricted women's promotion through the ranks of the civil service, while the Juries Act 1927 limited women's participation in jury service. In addition, the 'twenties also witnessed the banning of divorce and the censorship of information on contraception. In their campaign to restrict women's participation in society, political parties received the full backing of the Catholic Church :

> Ecclesiastical leaders legitimated and sanctioned both the limited vision of women's role in the state as well as the restrictive legislation which politicians proffered. The prelates agreed that women should be denied access to the public arena. (Valiulis 1995a: 118)

The Catholic Church played a very specific role not only in defining Irish identity but also in helping to implement the government's law and order policies. According to Terence Brown, 'crucial to the institutional and popular achievements of the Church...was the role played by Catholicism in confirming a sense of national identity' (1987: 28). Religion helped to distinguish Irish cultural identity and lifestyle from Englishness and thus had formed part of the impetus for Irish political independence. However, following independence, the Catholic hierarchy expressed concerns about declining morality in Ireland. Foreign cultural influences and years of war and political unrest were blamed for the corruption of Irish virtues.

Jim Smyth argues that despite the range of economic and political crises facing the Free State in the 1920s, the Catholic Church focused their attention very narrowly on the prevalence of immorality, immodesty and indecency (1993: 51-54). Irishwomen were especially criticised for their 'sinful' behaviour. Women, who should have been the guardians of traditional family values, were accused of immodest dress, loose morals and blatant disregard for authority. But why did both the Catholic Church and the government find it necessary to impose legal restrictions on Irish women in particular? It could be argued that such a focus on women's immorality proved a convenient distraction from the realities of poverty, unemployment, poor housing and high infant mortality. As Valiulis suggests:

> The government compensated for its inability to control much of what was happening around it by asserting its power vis a vis restrictions against women. In this, the government's response was typical of post-revolutionary societies which often consolidate their power by enacting measures against women. (1995a: 127)

Similarly, Gerardine Meaney claims that in the post-colonial context, with male leaders determined to assert their authority, women were targets for many of the new controls and restrictions introduced immediately after independence. Women's bodies were widely perceived as vessels of sin and temptation, hence the rapid introduction of legislation to control these bodies :

> Anxiety about one's fitness for a (masculine) role of authority, deriving from a history of defeat or helplessness, is assuaged by the assumption of sexual dominance. Women in these conditions become guarantors of their men's status, bearers of national honour and scapegoats of national

> identity...The Irish obsession with the control of women's bodies by church, state boards of ethics and judicial enquiries, has its roots in such anxieties. (Meaney 1993: 233)

In analysing the female embodiment of the Irish nation, this book examines a range of female images, some of which were idealised: – representing the good woman; but most of which were demonised: – representing the bad, evil or disorderly woman. I argue that both sets of images were used in the nation-building project to represent aspects of Ireland and Irishness. By analysing newspaper representations of women, I seek to access the most common place and widely accessible of all gendered images of nation and nationhood. Newspapers are particularly important in analysing the process of nation-building because, as Benedict Anderson (1993) has argued, the print media has facilitated the emergence of national consciousness and the dissemination of national symbols and meanings. The printed media provided a means through which the national community could be imagined (1993: 44).

*Newspapers Narrating the Nation:*

> Historians are adept at using media sources as evidence or as primary data, but rarely examine the ways in which newspapers and the broadcast media orchestrate and construct their messages...The manner in which newspaper stories, for example, are structured in distinctive ways by journalistic codes and conventions that make them different from, say, religious sermons, folklore, legal discourse or indeed pamphlets and other literary forms is seldom given adequate attention. By the same token, the fact that the different mass media are not just neutral observers but are major participants in politics in their own right locked into competition with other powerful ideological agencies such as the churches, educational institutions and the family is also rarely attended to. (Gibbons 1996: 10-11)

This book seeks to take up some of the challenges laid down by Luke Gibbons. I argue that newspapers played a key role not only in reporting the project of nation-building but also by actively participating in that project. In addition to being widely available to the general public, newspapers, unlike, for example, novels, plays and poetry, claimed to be impartial and objective in their representations of Irish people and society. However, while newspapers are useful in analysing the powerful gender ideologies underpinning the political and religious structures of the State, my research probes a little deeper. An examination of the national and provincial press uncovers a variety of conflicting and competing discourses. In fact, I argue that newspapers provide an insight into the complex and multifaceted nature of attitudes and opinions in the Irish Free State. As Caitriona Clear has recently argued, it is important not to assume 'a homogeneity of opinion on women which just did not exist' (Clear 2000: 5). Hence, in my view, the press offers a fascinating and under-researched insight into the many layered constructions of Irishness in the early years of the Free State.

In *Narrating the Nation* (1994), Homi Bhabha argues that to study the way in which the nation is spoken about and written about reveals the active process of constructing what is usually taken for granted as given, as handed down from the past, ancient and traditional. Martin Conboy (1996) suggests the national newspaper is important as a function of the communality of the nation - its culture, narratives, memories, shared images, etc. In addition, the newspaper also serves as a source of analysis for that particular society:

> The nation, as an object of study, is as elusively complex as the ways in which it is defined discursively. The text of the newspaper and the newspaper's cultural project as narrator, educator and entertainer of a society make it a particularly important site for the scrutiny of this kind of subtle discourse. (Conboy 1996: 197)

In the early decades of Southern Irish independence, newspapers were the dominant form of media communication and played a key role in supporting, defining and explaining the newly created Irish Free State to their readers. The press was additionally important in the Irish case because of the very high rate of literacy

(Lee 1988). Newspapers disseminated messages from politicians, regularly reprinting political speeches, usually reinforced through editorial comment. Newspapers also helped to disseminate the teachings of the Catholic Church: sermons, lenten pastorals and various speeches were regularly reprinted in great detail in both national and provincial papers. The main national daily during the 1920s was the *Irish Independent*, this was joined in the 1930s by the *Irish Press*. While the *Irish Times* was also a national daily, it had limited circulation among the urban middle class, upper class and Protestant communities. As well as the national dailies, I also draw upon the provincial press from the three southern provinces of Munster, Leinster and Connacht. There were scores of weekly provincial newspapers representing virtually every town-land in the state. Therefore, it has been necessary to limit my research to some of the more widely read papers. I have selected the largest provincial paper the *Cork Examiner*, unusually a daily paper, and the *Limerick Leader*, published trice weekly, one of the more outspoken, fervent cultural nationalist newspapers. In addition, I have selected five weekly papers. The *Kerryman* was based in Tralee but circulated throughout Kerry, Clare and North Cork. The *Connacht Tribune* and its sister paper the *Connacht Sentinel*, were based in Galway but with a wide circulation throughout Mayo and the West of Ireland. I have also chosen to examine the *Sligo Champion* and the *Wicklow People*. These papers were chosen partly at random but also because they circulated in large sections of the countryside. Though not claiming to be completely exhaustive, together, these papers do cover most of the country outside of the metropolitan centre of Dublin and, of course, the North of Ireland.

My analysis of newspapers from the 1922-1937 attempts, in part, to illustrate the dominant discourses in the Free State. As Conboy argues: 'Different newspapers adopt different tones but a common focus of national interest is often in evidence' (1996: 197). Strict censorship and the marginalisation of the republican movement after their defeat in the civil war, meant that the dominant discourse held considerable sway supported as it was by the main Churches and the press (Brown 1987). Maurice Goldring (1993) indicates that the press formed part of a series of relays and transmissions that actively sought to contribute to the formation of Irish national community and identity. In many ways, the newspapers were clearly aware of this role. For example, on 2 January 1925, the *Irish Independent* editorial stated the policy of that paper: 'to foster a strong spirit of sane nationalism, to help in guiding the people's thoughts towards the problems of practical politics and...to serve the nation by honest and fearless criticism'. However, my study of newspapers also attempts to illustrate the other discourses that existed alongside, and in opposition to, the dominant voices.

This study of gender and national identities in the Irish press in the 1920s-1930s is divided into six chapters. The remainder of this chapter is devoted to a case study of Queen Tailte. I analyse the use of this symbolic female image which was 'revived' in the early 1920s, and which came to embody a particular representation of the Irish nation and Irish cultural traditions. I suggest that Tailte reveals more about the attitudes of the 1920s-1930s than 'she' does about an ancient past.

Chapter two is divided into two sections. The first section examines newspaper coverage of the flapper or 'modern girl'. I argue that this was a highly contested and deeply controversial symbol of womanhood. Within nationalist and Catholic discourses of the period, the fashionable flapper with her shingled hair and knee-length dress embodied vice, immorality, sexuality and disobedience. As the polar opposite of the idealised, virtuous, innocent, Irish *cailín* [girl], the flapper was constructed as un-Irish, foreign and pagan. Through her embodiment of foreign fashions and lifestyles, she symbolised a threat to Irish identity, traditions and ultimately to the nation itself. This chapter draws upon the national and provincial press of the 1920s in particular to analyse the various representations of the flapper in both rural and urban society. I suggest that the flapper embodied the many complexities and contradictions of the Irish Free State because 'she' was simultaneously condemned and promoted in the press. While Catholic leaders loathed this elegant sinner, commercial interests used 'her' to sell a wide array of products and lifestyles. These divergent images and viewpoints begin to question the assumed hegemony of traditional Catholic and nationalist dogma.

The second section of this chapter argues that the ambiguities surrounding the modern girl or flapper are nowhere more apparent than in representations of female adventurers – particularly pilots – which were in abundance throughout the 1920s-1930s. This section focuses on press reports of the daring successes of women pilots such as Amelia Earhart and Amy Johnson who embodied the spirit of adventure of the period. However, Ireland was not without its own 'home grown' female fliers. The colourful Lady Heath visibly demonstrated many of the contradictions of newspaper coverage of the modern woman and her role in the Irish Free State.

Chapter three focuses on the working woman and is divided into three sections exploring newspaper representations and debates on the role of the working woman in the Irish Free State. Section 1 focuses on representations of different types of female worker. The single, white collar, professional worker was frequently celebrated in the press, especially in the women's pages. She embodied many of the qualities of the fashionable flapper and occupied a world of bachelor flats and bed-sits, wore lovely clothes and enjoyed a carefree lifestyle. The industrial woman worker was not only far less glamorous but she also posed a threat to traditional gender boundaries. By entering the industrial sector, she undermined her femininity, threatening the jobs and status of male workers. The third kind of working woman was the domestic servant. This working woman constituted the majority of the female workforce, outside of agriculture. However, during the 1930s she became embroiled in heated debates about training, domesticity and the emigration trail to Britain. Section 2 focuses in more detail on 'the emigrant girl'. During the 1930s many thousands of Irish women flocked to English cities to work as domestic servants. This not only fuelled concerns about female employment at home, but also highlighted fears about the plight of young, vulnerable girls facing the many hazards of life in cities like London and Liverpool. Such was the growing concern that, in 1936, the *Irish Independent* commissioned a study into the experiences of 'the emigrant girl'. Section 3 analyses the role of newspapers during the debates on the draft constitution of 1937. The constitution, which had several articles specifically devoted to the rights and responsibilities of women in the State, indicated the growing tensions around female employment outside the home. But newspapers did not merely report on the constitutional debates. I argue that they were active players in those debates. For example, while the *Irish Press* vehemently supported President Eamon de Valera and his constitution against all critics, the *Independent* used feminist concerns about women's rights to attack the President and undermine the constitution. The press debates raised questions not only about the role of women in the constitution but also about the role of women in the nation as a whole. Central to these debates were the thorny issues of women's employment, emigration and the idealised position of the Irish mother in the home.

Chapter four is divided into three sections and examines in more detail representations of women, home, motherhood and the nation. Family is a key site for the biological reproduction of the nation. Family also represents continuity of tradition, language, religion and identity. The trope of family frames women's relationship to the nation. Women as mothers become conflated with the nation as mother (mother Ireland) and the Catholic Church as mother (mother Church). This is a well-rehearsed argument. However, my research on the Irish national and provincial press suggests a more complex and multifaceted picture. Woman was not simply represented as the good, idealised mother but was also symbolised as the bad, inadequate, absent mother. In section 1, I examine the diverse images of motherhood and home symbolised in the dichotomous construction of spinning wheels and cosy cottages on the one hand and urban slums on the other. Family, home and mothering were circumscribed by class, morality and location. But that is not to imply a simple dichotomy of urban decay versus rural idyll. Notions of rural poverty, backwardness and lawlessness were clearly evident in constructions of the 'wild west'. These images suggest more complex constructions of Irish motherhood. Section 2 focuses on press reports of disorderly bodies, domestic violence and family deviance. I examine how violence and deviance were explained and contained within the framework of a nationalist and Catholic discourse that promoted family values. Section 3 elaborates on the discussion of motherhood and the nation by analysing the press notices and obituaries of three mothers who died in 1932. The death of Mrs. Margaret Pearse has been discussed by several writers (see Valiulis 1995a). However, by comparing reports of her death with those of two other women from the period, I analyse the complex processes of exclusion and inclusion at work in creating national heroines and mothers of the nation. I argue that official representations of national mothers rely upon certain characteristics and operate to exclude women who do not comfortably fit with national myths and ideals.

Chapter five follows on the discussion of women who cannot be easily incorporated into the national myth by examining representations of Republican women. This chapter is divided into two chronological sections. The first section examines newspaper representations of women's involvement in the war of independence (1919-1921) and civil war (1922-23). While women activists have been largely excluded from histories of this violent period, they were widely depicted in the contemporary press. As rebellious bodies, these women transgressed traditional gender boundaries actively participating in militarism. However, while militant women successfully maintained a relatively low profile during the war of independence, by the civil war they were being singled out for special, negative attention. Variously depicted as furies, die-hards and dangerous hysterical women, female Republicans were used by politicians, Church hierarchy and the press to highlight all that was violent and irregular about the Republican movement. Section 2 concentrates on the period after the end of the civil war. Throughout the 1920s-30s, Republican women continued to play ambiguous roles: the defenders of the true Republican tradition, dangerous traitors and thorns in the side of the Free State government. Once again it is apparent that newspapers did not merely report the activities of these women but sought to frame them within conventional narratives of hysterical, unruly, wayward womanhood. On occasion, newspapers launched very personal attacks on these 'disorderly', 'unfeminine' women.

Chapter six focuses of newspaper reports of infanticide and further develops the themes of this book. I use the press, not merely to show that infanticide was rampant in the Free State, but also to illustrate the context in which it occurred. It is apparent that cultural nationalism, political conservatism and the power of the Catholic Church combined together to create the circumstances in which women's bodies became the contested sites of national good and national evil. I suggest that concealed pregnancies, abandoned babies and infanticide illustrated the complex relationship between women's bodies, deviant sexuality, sin, regulation and gendered national discourses. Through their unwanted pregnancies, young women embodied the evils of sex, while their dead babies embodied lost virtue and innocence. This chapter examines press reports of the uncovered bodies of dead infants, the arrest of suspicious young women and the partial and often confusing accounts of court proceedings. I suggest that newspapers played a role in not merely reporting cases of concealment and infanticide but also in explaining, interpreting and containing these tragic events.

Developing on the concepts introduced above, this introductory chapter will now analyse in more detail the use of symbolic woman in national discourses. I will discuss the re-imagining and reconstruction of ancient traditions in the modern Irish Free State through a case study of the 'revival' of the Tailteann Games and the press representation of the central female icon of Queen Tailte after whom the games were supposedly named. The 're-discovery' of this ancient motherly figure, and the many conflicting legends which surrounded her, illustrate the processes through which Irishness, the manly Gael and idealised Irishwoman were being negotiated and defined in the 1920s-1930s.

*The Symbolic Woman:*

> newly independent Ireland was endowed with a repository of myths, images and motifs, literary modes and conventions cultivated to a degree that might indeed have been the envy of most emerging states in this century of infant, fragile nationalisms. The antiquarian literary and cultural activity of the preceding one hundred years had offered Irishmen and women a range of modes of thought and feeling that could confirm national identity and unity. (Brown 1987: 79)

According to Terence Brown, the 'imaginative assets' generated by the late nineteenth century Literary Revival were particularly important in affirming 'the heroic traditions of the Irish people, directing their attention to the mythological tales of their past, to the heroes and noble deeds of a vanished age' (1987: 80). Writers such as Lady Augusta Gregory, W.B. Yeats and John Millington Synge revived or reinvented the ancient Celtic folklore of brave warriors such as Cuchulain and beautiful, iconographic figures such as Deirdre (Innes 1993):

> When such literary antiquarianism had managed to suggest a continuity of experience between past and present, a powerful propagandist weapon had been forged. (Brown 1987: 80)

The impact of these mythological figures and symbols can be seen throughout the early years of the twentieth century: not just in the plays and poetry of the literary set, but in militant nationalist rhetoric and visual representations. For example, the 'cult of Cuchulain', who heroically sacrificed himself in battle, bravely fighting to the end despite his fatal injuries, had a particular resonance for many in the nationalist military movement (Innes 1993). The connection between the Celtic hero and the Republican uprising of 1916 is visibly represented by the statue of the dying Cuchulain which has been erected in the General Post Office on O'Connell Street, Dublin, the military headquarters of the uprising.

While there were a number of male heroes who represented the warrior spirit of the past, the majority of images, motifs and symbols in Irish nationalist iconography were female (Innes 1993, Sharkey 1994). These female figures represented Ireland as a nation as well as simultaneously embodying national characteristics. For example, the *Shan Van Vocht* embodied national sacrifice and suffering; *Roisin Dubh* embodied national purity and integrity; *Erin* and *Hibernia* represented national vulnerability. These female icons were evoked by poets, playwrights, politicians and revolutionaries (Innes 1993, 1994). Thus these womanly symbols were portrayed as passive, silent and suffering, in opposition to the active strength, courage, heroism and martyrdom of the men they inspired. But this use of female symbols is certainly not unique to Irish nationalism. A range of studies from nationalist campaigns in many different countries indicates the extent to which nationalism is underpinned by a gendered ideology (McClintock 1993, Katrak, 1992, Mosse 1985, Radhakrishnan 1992, Thapar 1993). In this context a comparison with India may prove particularly fruitful.

In analysing the impact of these gendered discourses in India, Shakuntala Rao (1999) argues that the use of female iconography to represent a nation marginalises and silences the complexities of real women's experiences. Women are subsumed within nationalist rhetoric which privileges the imaginary woman over real women. 'While a nation could represent itself as woman, for example, in Nehru's constant references to India as *Bharat Mata* or Mother India, women within the nation could not represent themselves, their own identity, or their Indianess' (Rao 1999: 319). In other words, women did not actively participate in the process of symbol making, instead women were the bodies on to which symbols were mapped:

> These are passive symbols because they require the woman to remain voiceless, discourseless, and displaced from the constitutive processes of the symbol-making....One could be at the centre of a discourse...without having the power to define one's centrality within the borders of that narrative. (Rao 1999: 319)

In the early decades of the twentieth century, Indian nationalism and Irish nationalism shared many similar characteristics; both were influenced by their struggles against British colonialism and attempted to define true Indianess and true Irishness in opposition to the perceived characteristics of Britishness. Thus both nationalisms involved, to some extent, a rejection of the modernism, materialism and secularism of British society. Both drew heavily upon a sense of national tradition and heritage which was strongly influenced by religion. This involved the 'deliberate construction of a pure indigeneity' (Rao 1999: 326). As Hobsbawm (1992) has argued, nationalist legitimacy relies heavily upon 'an invention of tradition'. Or, to borrow Rao's phrase, national identity draws its validity from reimagining, reconstructing and rewriting the pre-colonial and premodern. In particular contexts this process is shaped not just by nationalism but by religion. This is especially relevant to India and Ireland where contemporary Hindu and Catholic ideology and imagery were imposed on pre-Hindu and pre-Christian pasts. Nevertheless, both countries were also anxious to define themselves as progressive, modern and enlightened and thus engaged in a complex process of negotiating a problematic path of religious traditionalism coupled with a home-grown style of modernity. In Ireland and India, these negotiations of modernity and tradition were partly facilitated by a gendered discourse which located 'woman' in the role of repository of national heritage, religion and tradition (Katrak 1992, Radhakrishnan 1992, Thapar 1993, Nash 1993, Innes 1993, Meaney 1993, Gray and Ryan 1997). This is particularly apparent, in an Irish context, in the representations of Queen Tailte.

## *The Celtic Queen and the Manly Gael: the revival of Aonach Tailteann 1920s-1930s*

According to legend, Aonach Tailteann – or Tailteann festival – had been initiated by Lugh Lamh Fhada (Lugh of the long hand) in honour of his step-mother Queen Tailte. It was claimed that the festival of games, music and dance began in the ancient period and continued until the Norman invasion of the twelfth century. Their revival in 1924 marked the return to independence after centuries of occupation. The games represented continuity with Ireland's ancient and glorious past. Modelled in part on the Olympics, the festival was timed to coincide with those games, for example, in 1924, 1928, 1932. For the newly established state, this was an opportunity to host a large, modern, international event which celebrated Irish heritage and cultural, as well as sporting, traditions. Thus the games embraced both the ancient and the modern in an attempt to define the identity of the nation and, perhaps more significantly, of the 'race'.

On 20 August 1927, the *Kerryman* newspaper reprinted an article from the Irish-American paper National Hibernian:

> The Tailteann games are to Ireland what the Olympic games were to ancient Greece. Nothing that the Irish people could do in a political way has rivalled what the Tailteann games will do eventually to knit the nation into unity. Only among such a people as the Irish could there have existed through more than two thousand years the games and sports which are a symbol of a race. (*Kerryman*, 20 August 1927)

In addition, the article claimed that the games would help to unite the scattered Irish peoples from across the world so that, in time, they would look to 'Ireland as the Motherland'. The games provided an opportunity for 'Irishmen' throughout the world to come together in celebration of Ireland. The Tailteann games had 'risen from the past to be a beacon for the future'. In this sense the games simultaneously represented continuity with past traditions and a bright hope for the future of the country. Newspaper articles such as this provide a valuable insight into constructions of Irish national/ cultural identity; the celebration of traditions as well as looking forward to the bright prospects for the future. But in this case, as in so many cases, newspapers offer diverse and fascinating accounts of events which provide a range of possible interpretations of national events such as Aonach Tailteann. The newspapers of the time reveal the many complexities and contradictions inherent in the process of nation building. For instance, while some papers celebrated the success of the games, others condemned them as badly organised and a waste of money. It is worth emphasising here that I am using newspapers as sources which provide a plethora of images, information and analyses not as accurate testimonies of specific historical events.

Of all the papers, it was the Dublin-based, national dailies – the *Irish Independent* and the *Irish Times*, and later the *Irish Press* – which devoted most coverage to the festival. For example, the games of 1928 received widespread coverage. Between 11-26 August 1928, the Tailteann games were held in Dublin (although some events were staged outside the city, for example, the rowing events were held on the river Lee in Cork). On 4 August 1928, the *Independent* gave lengthy coverage to the Aonach Tailteann which was heralded as the return of the Gael. This 'return' had a double significance. On the one hand, it represented the return to Ireland of Gaels from all over the world; emigrants and the children of emigrants. On the other hand, the notion of 'return' represented the re-establishment of Gaelic pride, identity, tradition after centuries of suppression, a return to past glories and self-confidence. The *Irish Times* cited the Director of the games, Mr. J.J. Walsh speaking at the Tailteann Banquet in Dublin on the eve of the opening ceremony: 'Aonach Tailteann was nothing new. Rather did it go right to the root of Celtic history...Tailteann of Tara was the beacon of light of a distinct and vigorous civilisation'. He went on to add that the revival 'was proof of the tenacity with which their race had clung to the ideal of a distinctive place in the family of ancient peoples' (*Irish Times*, 13 August 1928).

The national dailies highlighted and celebrated the symbolism of the festival. The festival was named after the ancient Celtic queen Tailte and her image was strongly associated with the revived games. The papers carried photographs of the actress, Nancy Rock, who played the part of Queen Tailte in the pageant that marked the opening of the festival. On 4 August 1928, the *Independent* carried a photo of her wearing 'traditional' Celtic clothing; a long dress and cloak tied with a large Celtic brooch, her hair plaited into two long braids reaching her waist, she was adorned in bangles and other jewellery rich in Celtic design and symbolism. On 13 August, the *Irish Times* and *Independent* carried a whole series of photos from the opening ceremony of the games. The *Irish Times* described the event under the headline 'Tailteann Games: Opening Ceremony at Croke Park, 20,000 Present'. 'The most appealing note was struck by the tableau of Queen Tailte, attended by Chieftains and maids, presented by the players who are to take part in the production of *The Vision of Queen Tailte* at the Theatre Royal on Sunday night. Miss Nancy Rock was an impressive figure in the part of the Queen'. There was a close-up photo of Miss Rock/Queen Tailte in profile pose. She was wearing a head-dress and enormous earrings in a Celtic design which obscured her face. She was draped in a cloak fastened by a large brooch.

The *Independent* also carried similar photos of the procession and pageant. Included amongst the photos was a large picture of a procession by men and women 'wearing ancient Irish costume'. In the foreground of the photo were two rows of women walking across the packed arena, all dressed like Queen Tailte, with long braided hair, they carried very tall spears which towered over their heads. The men were in the background wearing short tunics and carrying shields and spears. There was a separate photo of Queen Tailte (Nancy Rock), 'after whom the games are called'. This time she was standing with an Irish wolfhound by her side, she was again dressed in 'traditional' Celtic clothes, but it is noteworthy that she wore rather modern, 1920s-style, high heeled shoes (*Irish Independent* 13 August 1928).

Nancy Rock's portrayal of Tailte goes back to the first revival of the games in 1924. On 12 August 1924, the *Irish Times* carried a photo of Miss Rock who was to play the part of Queen Tailte at the Theatre Royal in Dublin. On the following day, 13 August, the *Times* published a review of the production under the heading 'Queen Tailte: A Vision Play'. Written by Major Lawlor of the National Army, the play was based on a reconstruction of the life of Tailte shown through a series of tableaux. Between each tableau, a *seanchaí* (storyteller) narrated the story of Tailte, her husband Eochaidh, last of the Firbolg kings of Ireland, and her stepson Lugh Lamh Fhada. 'Miss Rock looked every inch the Queen'. The play was directed by her mother, Mrs. Rock, and most of the participants were members of the Rock school of dance and drama. The review was generally positive but it questioned the ability of several of the younger girls in the group to accurately portray elderly noblemen and kings.

From her first appearance as Tailte in 1924, Nancy Rock seems to have become a central figure of the festival. This striking young woman came to embody the ancient Queen but in so doing she both shaped and was shaped by notions of the glorious past. As discussed at the start of this paper, the deliberate re-imagining and re-constructing of a pure and ancient indigeneity, free from all colonial/foreign influences, was a central part of nationalism. The figure of Queen Tailte embodied ancient Ireland. Her hair, clothing, jewellery and even the wolfhound, locate her in the distant past, or at least a particular representation of the past. Unlike, the short skirt wearing, bobbed haired, cigarette smoking flapper who embraced modern decadence and foreign fashions, Queen Tailte embodied all that was good and pure in Irish society. However, the photo of Miss Rock wearing modern high-heeled shoes represents a jarring note. However, in so doing, it also symbolises the many inherent contradictions in this image of Ireland, Irishness and Tailte herself.

## *Tailte: Gaelic Mother or Celtic Goddess*

In fact, on closer examination it seems that the Celtic queen was a very ambiguous character. On the 2 June 1928, the *Sligo Champion* provided some more background history to the origins of Aonach Tailteann:

> Aonach Tailteann was instituted by Lugh Lamh Fhada, a prince of the Tuatha de Danaan. The festival was in commemoration of Queen Tailte, a Spanish lady wife of Eochaidh, king of the Firbolg. (*Sligo Champion*, 2 June 1928)

This history locates the festival deep in the mists of ancient Celtic legend, in the time of noble warriors and warring tribes when Ireland was ruled by scores of rival kings and armies. However, what is most noteworthy about this short paragraph is the fact that it describes the famous queen as 'a Spanish lady' – not Irish at all. The identity of Tailte remained a matter of speculation. Interestingly, it was in the *Irish Press*, founded by de Valera's political party Fianna Fail in the early 1930s and arguably the most Catholic and nationalist of all three main dailies, that an alternative reading of Tailte was provided in 1932. In a special feature article, Seamus MacCall explored the possible origins of Tailte and offered a more analytical and critical perspective than most other sources at that time:

> Aonach Tailteann is the oldest of several great festivals which were periodically celebrated in Ireland. It is also the newest. It began in some period to remote to define with certainty. (The *Irish Press* 20 June 1932)

In this opening paragraph, MacCall is suggesting his awareness of the extent to which Aonach Tailteann is 'new' and hence reconstructed in the modern period. He is wary of asserting any precise starting date for the festival. However, he offers the view that the festival shares many similar characteristics with ancient

Greek festivals. Indeed, he pushes this comparison further than other commentators had done:

> The 'rationalised' tradition tells us that the first Aonach Tailteann was an 'assembly of lamentation' ordained by Lugh in honour of his foster mother Tailte.

MacCall repeats the story that she was the daughter of a Spanish king. But then he begins to cast serious doubt on this 'rationalised' version of events. His research could not uncover any such Spanish king or any such Tailte. MacCall suggests that the notion that she was from abroad, across the sea, a foreigner, is really an indication that she was other-worldly, that she was not from this world:

> Tailte or Tailtiu was no mortal but a goddess whose known attributes clearly indicate that she was patroness of agriculture, or in other words a goddess of fertility....Lugh, her supposed foster son, was even more certainly the old Irish sun god, whose 'long arms' were to be seen in the sun's rays.

MacCall goes on to make the argument that the festival, which traditionally took place in August, was also known as *Lughnasadh*. It may well have had its origins in a sort of harvest festival 'in which the first ripening was symbolised as a meeting of the sun god and the goddess of fertility'. As is the case with similar Greek festivals, the gods were honoured by displays of games, dances and contests. MacCall draws on a number of classical texts and, although he is strongly influenced by interpretations of Greek mythology, his analysis of Celtic symbols and myths is very convincing. Clearly Tailte was a highly complex and ambiguous figure. On the one hand, her previous incarnation as a sexualised goddess of fertility might well suggest that she was an unsuitable icon for a Catholic nation. But, on the other hand, the success with which she was reconstructed as a safe, motherly symbol suggests a very deliberate, self-conscious process of nationalist re-appropriation and reinvention of the past.

This reinvention was framed by the ambiguity of Celticism versus the Gaelicisation of Irish society. Clearly, Celtic myths and legends were part of a pagan folklore which pre-dated Christainity by several centuries. However, in the eyes of the Catholic Church 'paganism' had very negative connotations, for example, everything that was foreign, dangerous, threatening, and emanating from decadent places such as Paris, London and Hollywood. In addition, the Celticism of the ancient legends and mythologies which had been revived as part of the Anglo-Irish literary movement in the early twentieth century became associated with the specific project of that Anglo-Irish elite group. This was resented by many in the Irish-Ireland movement who wished to reconstruct Ireland's past as Gaelic as opposed to just Catholic, and in the Irish language as opposed to the English medium usually associated with the Anglo-Irish literary set. Thus the Celtic/Gaelic dichotomy represented a conflict not only in terms of language and religion but also in terms of the particular identity of Ireland's past and its implications for Ireland's future (Nash 1993). It is apparent that Aonach Tailteann was predominantly represented as Catholic/ Gaelic although the myths and symbolism upon which it was based could equally be termed pagan/ Celtic.

Some of these tensions are hinted at in the *Irish Times* editorial of 4 August 1924:

> Persons who lay stress on the Gaelic element in the racial origins of the Irish people take the old Aonach Tailteann as standing for a tradition of Gaelic culture....there are, of course, large numbers of Irish people to whom the Gaelic tradition has never made very strong appeal. They, however, with their share of Irish imagination and idealism, have appreciated the purpose of the promoters of a revived Aonach Tailteann, and the festival now enjoys the sympathy...of *Irishmen* of every class. (emphasis added)

This quote simultaneously represents the inclusiveness and exclusiveness of the ideology underpinning the festival. The ambiguity of the Celtic versus Gaelic symbolism allows for the inclusion of all of those who share an interest in Irish history and culture even if they disagree about the precise origins of its traditions. However, this quote also underlines the masculinity of the festival and in so doing highlights the ways in which women were both excluded and celebrated within the revival of Aonach Tailteann. As has been argued above, the process of nation building and defining national identity was highly gendered. The masculine strengths of national manhood were constructed in opposition to the dependency, fragility and purity of national womanhood. Particularly in Gaelic-Catholic iconography, the Gael was an exclusively male figure who represented the best aspects of Ireland's past glory and future aspirations. The corresponding female role was that of the idealised mother, devoted, selfless and desexualised (Nash 1993: 47). It is surely no coincidence that while the Gaelic man was to test his manhood on the sports field, woman as depicted by Queen Tailte was constructed as loyal wife and mother – or in the case of Tailte, step-mother to Lugh Lamh Fhada.

This imagery of motherhood was used repeatedly by the press in describing the significance of the festival. It is apparent that the entire festival of games, Irish songs and dance took on a cultural and national importance far beyond the particular event itself. On 11 August, the *Independent* carried an article entitled 'In the Name of an Irish Queen'. The sub-heading read: 'Tailte takes her children to her bosom. 6,000 in Review. Old Glories Revived':

> The sons of the scattered Gael have come home again. They have crossed the seven seas at the bidding of the land from which their sires have sprung. They have come in the name of an Irish Queen, and today mid the regal splendour of far-off days, and the pristine glory of a Golden age, she will clasp them to her bosom in joyful, loving welcome. (*Irish Independent*, 11 August 1928)

This quote is rich in gendered symbolism. Queen Tailte represents Ireland, a motherland from whom 'sires' had 'sprung', now clasping her long lost sons to her welcoming bosom. Thus the Gaels are all represented as men, while the land/nation is female. This motherly symbol embodies continuity with past glories, heritage and tradition. If the legend of Tailte originated in the fertility goddess Tailtiu, as MacCall suggested, then her reappropriation as mother Ireland seems oddly appropriate. However, that process of her reinvention also indicates the extent to which she was sanitised and transformed from powerful Celtic goddess to the weaker and more passive mother of the Gael.

*The Manly Gael:*

The gendered symbolism of the festival was reinforced in an editorial in the *Independent* a few days later:

> Few races have a stronger sense of historic continuity than the Irish, and through long centuries not least of the aims of the national struggle was to restore contacts that had been ruthlessly severed by the laws, as well as by the sword of the invader. There have been few happier inspirations than the decision that the emergence of a new Ireland should be followed by the revival of Aonach Tailteann. The festival dates back almost to the dawn of history....the tradition embodied in the games is expressive of emotions and ideals that make as strong an appeal to the Irishman of today as they did to his ancestors (*Irish Independent*, 13 August 1928).

Although the British invaders tried to sever all connections with traditional Irish language and culture, the revival of the festival ensured the continuity of a distinctive Irish national identity. However, this symbolism continues to be gendered in the sense that the spirit of the games appeals to Irishmen. The Irish race is thus not only constructed as distinct, unique and ancient but also as masculine. The festival aimed to include Irish competitors from around the world and was especially keen to attract Irish-American athletes. Indeed, participants were reported as coming from Canada, New Zealand, Australia and parts of Britain, as well as the USA. But there was concern that perhaps not all of these were of Irish descent. Later in the month, when the games were completed, the *Independent* editorial again returned to the topic:

> The revival of Aonach Tailteann after a lapse of seven and a half centuries was a bold and ambitious undertaking....The changes wrought by time could not be undone; and so the promoters had the delicate task of devising a scheme that would fit into the modern order of things without doing violence to the essential character of the ancient festival, and to preserve the racial solidarity of which Aonach Tailteann was once a living proof....If the games are to fulfil their purpose the organisers must see that only those of Irish descent participate. (*Irish Independent*, 27 August 1928)

It is not clear if this editorial referred to one particular athlete or to a group of athletes who had participated in the 1928 games. However, it is very clear that the *Independent* viewed the games as a showcase for Irish talent and an opportunity to assert racial solidarity free from any foreign, that is non-Irish, interference. However, it is apparent that not everyone agreed on the games racial exclusivity. In 1932 when the third revival was held, the *Irish Times* devoted an editorial to the question of who should be allowed to compete:

> The games of 1932 promise to surpass in all respects the festivals of 1924 and 1928....in the present games – it was not possible to observe the rules strictly in the two preceding festivals – every competitor is Irish or of Irish descent. The surprise is that, under such a limitation, the entry has been so large and has come from so many quarters of the earth. (*Irish Times*, 30 June 1932)

However, the editorial adds a note of caution. While generally supporting the rule, the article speculates on the possibility of embracing 'a selected few of the great foreign athletes whom Ireland sees all too seldom'. Their inclusion would make the games no less Irish in character. Thus, for the *Irish Times* at least, foreign athletes, especially very great ones, should be invited to attend the games. In any case, few foreign athletes attended the games in 1932. This was not merely as a result of the Irish descent rule but also because, unlike 1924 and 1928, the

Olympic games were not being held in Europe and thus most international athletes were not available to travel to Europe in the summer of 1932. However, the games did coincide with another event in Ireland that may have helped to boost the attendance. In 1932, Ireland played host to the Eucharistic congress which saw bishops and cardinals from around the world attending numerous religious ceremonies across the country. Many of these turned out to watch the opening ceremony on 29 June.

Once again, the *Irish Independent* and the *Irish Times*, now joined by the newly established *Irish Press*, reported vivid descriptions of the elaborate opening ceremony and parade of athletes. As in previous games the image of Queen Tailte (portrayed once again by Nancy Rock) continued to be very much in evidence:

> Something of the historic glory of the court of Tailte, Queen of Ireland, was revived in Croke Park, Dublin, yesterday afternoon, at the opening ceremony of the third revival within recent years of the games, first organised in 632 BC by Lugh Lamh Fhada, in honour of his foster mother, Queen Tailte. (*Irish Times*, 30 June 1932)

This quote is interesting firstly, because it reiterates the notion of 'historic glory' so often mentioned in the previous reports of Aonach Tailteann. Nearly a decade after their initial revival, the games are still repeatedly described as a symbol of continuity with the ancient past. Secondly, that past is now being recorded very specifically in terms of the date 632 BC. Considering that the *Irish Times* had earlier described the central characters as 'fabled' (13 August 1928), it is curious that an exact historical date is now being accorded to the commencement of the games. Thirdly, although Tailte is here being described as foster mother rather than step mother, she is nonetheless being contained within her mothering relationship to Lugh: he remains the active founder of the games, she is merely the muse, the passive source of inspiration.

In anticipation of 'Ireland's Great Sport Festival', the *Irish Press* published a special feature article on 28 June 1932. Across the top of the page were the photos of eleven sporting heroes, all male, who were expected to participate in the games, these included boxers and hurlers, both Irish born and of Irish descent. Beneath them was a picture of a bronze statuette of Queen Tailte, holding a laurel wreath in each of her outstretched hands. She was wearing a long flowing gown and a cloak fastened over one shoulder.

The lengthy article which accompanied these photographs reinforced the gendered imagery. The games were described as important in strengthening 'moral fibre' and so enhancing 'chivalry' and 'manhood'. The games were not only a display of national distinctiveness but celebrated the traditions of 'a virile race'. The fact that scores of women competed in such events as swimming and the vigorous game of camogie (a female version of hurling), as well as in the cultural events of dancing and singing, was not represented at all in either the images or the words of this article.

The opening ceremony of 1932 was presided over by Eamon de Valera, the Republican leader who boycotted the original revival in 1924, having recently been elected president of the Free State. De Valera was accompanied on the viewing stand by his eminence Cardinal MacRory, leader of the Catholic Church in Ireland. This led to a rather interesting and unspoken anomaly:

> The crowd beheld a young man clad in skin garments leading a large Irish wolfhound....massed bands of Irish pipers, with the Black raven standard at their head, led the members of Tailte's court into the arena. The glory that was Ireland, a young giant with sun tanned limbs, Lugh Lamh Fhada, preceded them. All the splendour of their court robes was revealed as Queen Tailte, her hand-maidens, druids and warriors extended their right arm in salute to Cardinal MacRory. (*Irish Times*, 30 June 1932)

The image of 'Celtic' royalty extending a salute to the head of the Catholic Church reveals many of the underlying tensions and contradictions in the revival of such ancient pagan myths in a modern, Catholic democratic state.

In the case of all three revivals being discussed in this chapter, the national press devoted a great deal of daily coverage to the wide range of events at the festival. There were regular reports on the traditional Irish singing and dancing competitions as well as more unusual events like the pipe band competition. Traditional Irish games such as handball, gaelic football, hurling and camogie shared the programme with athletics, swimming, gymnastics, boxing, rowing, cycling, chess and the marathon. The press reiterated the games' great importance to the nation. As has been discussed by other researchers, sport played a particularly significant role in constructions of Irish national identity (McDevitt 1997). Revived games such as hurling and Gaelic football produced an image of Irish masculinity based on order, strength and virtue (McDevitt 1997: 263). These games, organised by the nationalist Gaelic Athletic Association, served the dual purpose of giving Irish men a form of self-expression which was perceived as entirely distinct from British sporting activities, and of helping to counter British stereotypes of the Irish as lazy, disorderly and unskilled.

The importance of sports in the education of young Irish boys was emphasised by General O'Duffy, head of the Civic Guards, the Free State's police force (*Garda Siochana*), when he presented prizes to boys at a Dublin school. The *Irish Independent* carried the story under the headline: 'Boys urged to be more like Irish Heroes of Old' (14 June 1932). He said that in the past too much attention was given to the development of the mind, while the development of the body was completely ignored. He was very glad that this was now beginning to change and 'in line with the spirit of the Church they were going to develop the body and the mind'. O'Duffy 'held up to the boys the exploits of Finn,

Cuchualain and Ossain of old, and told them to typify in their lives the valour and chivalry of the Red Branch Knights'. (*Irish Independent*, 14 June 1932)

This sentiment was echoed in the editorial on the same day:

> General O'Duffy has rightly emphasised the danger of racial deterioration if physical culture be neglected in schools. In these days of easy travelling, of cinemas and dancing, wireless, and card parties, there are great temptations to avoid exercise. (*Irish Independent*, Editorial, 14 June 1932)

In this editorial the points made by O'Duffy are used to illustrate the dangers of racial deterioration. The easy living of modern times threatens to undermine the traditional strength and fitness of Irish manhood. It is surely no coincidence that these views were being expressed in the same month as Aonach Tailteann was about to commence. Those games represented the very best of Irish masculinity and the efforts at racial regeneration and rejuvenation. Once again the image of ancient Celtic warriors is used to appeal to young boys, their chivalry and valour serving as native and traditional role models for the youth of modern times. However, that Celtic imagery is safely contained within the discourses of modern Catholicism. While invoking Celtic heroes, O'Duffy reinforces the view that the education of Irish boys is the proper domain of the Church.

The Catholic Church's views on sport were clearly stated in an article that appeared in the *Cork Examiner* in July 1928 in the regular weekly section: 'Catholic News of the Week'. The article emphasised that sport teaches discipline, teamwork and the importance of rules. 'The youth learns to curb his character and passions'. Physical training brings the body under control and this leads to the 'greater honour and glory of God'. At a time when the Church was obsessed with the sexual immorality of young people, the value of sport in regulating behaviour was important for both sexes:

> The hockey fields, tennis grounds and gymnasiums have brought out the better development of young girls, so important to her in afterlife for the bringing up of healthy children. (*Cork Examiner*, 14 July 1928)

Thus sport was a healthy pursuit for young women which took their minds off clothes, dancing and cinema. In addition, sport prepared women for their true role in life – motherhood. While women did participate in Aonach Tailteann, most of the focus of attention in the press was on male competitors; the masculine Gaels represented the spirit of the games. The most prevalent female image was Queen Tailte herself who passively embodied Ireland and Irish traditional culture, rather than actively representing female participation in the games. Thus, as argued at the beginning of this chapter, women are usually not served by womanly symbols. Instead, female icons frequently silence and exclude women from public nationalist discourses. Thus the imaginary woman (Tailte) is privileged over real women (the competitors).

As mentioned earlier, the games were modelled on the Olympics and it was fortunate that the games coincided with European Olympic years in both 1924 and 1928, enabling athletes to attend both events. The importance of Irish participation in the 1928 Amsterdam Olympic Games was repeatedly emphasised by newspapers like the *Irish Independent*. On 5 June 1928, the *Independent* editorial made a passionate plea for the need to support Irish athletes so that they could train for, and attend, international sporting events:

> That Ireland has the manhood, the muscle and the grit to regain *her* former position of pre-eminence none can doubt. But we live in a different world from that of the last generations...The athlete must condemn *himself* to scientific and persistent training. (*Irish Independent*, 5 June 1928, emphasis added)

Again this is a very gendered image which equates Irish sporting success with Irish masculinity, while Ireland, the country, is gendered female. This quote also implicitly addresses negotiations of modernity and tradition. Although it is not clear when Ireland achieved a former position of sporting pre-eminence, there is, once again, an appeal to the glorious past and traditional masculinity. Nevertheless, there is also an acknowledgement of the needs of modern times: scientific training and the proper funding of athletes. On 31 July 1928, the *Independent* reported the great sense of national joy and pride in Ireland's first ever gold medal at the olympics. Dr. O'Callaghan won first place in the hammer throwing competition. Much was made of the raising of the tricolour and the playing of the Irish national anthem in such an international arena. Clearly a sporting success such as this helped to place the newly established Free State on the international map not just as an independent country but as a nation to be proud of.

*A Jarring Note:*

Nevertheless, it would be simplistic to imply that sport was unproblematic in Ireland or that the Irish press presented a united voice on the subject. While the *Irish Times*, *Independent* and *Irish Press* were obviously supportive of Aonach Tailteann, the same cannot be said of other papers. For example, on 17 January 1928, the *Connacht Sentinel* reported the growing tensions around the forthcoming festival. Apparently the Tailteann committee was in strong disagreement with the Gaelic Athletic Association [GAA] which demanded a controlling voice on the organising committee. The article argued that such tensions threatened the success of the event. Similar concerns were voiced in the *Wicklow People* on 21 January 1928. In providing some background details to the festival, the report says that the revival was first proposed in the early 1920s but had to be postponed twice due to 'the disturbed state of the country' – this presumably is a reference to the civil war. When the games were finally held in 1924, they were boycotted by 'Mr. De Valera's party' (Sinn Fein). Thus, according to the *Wicklow People*, 'they were little better than a failure'. The ambitious plans for the 1928 festival were considered to be 'impractical'. The paper also throws some light on the tensions within the organising committee. The supporters of the

GAA were in conflict with other interest groups such as Rugby supporters. 'Many of those who represent other games on the committee have no sympathy with Irish-Ireland ideals'. (*Wicklow People*, 21 January 1928) The GAA represented a very Catholic, nationalist view of Irish culture (McDevitt 1997), this would not have been shared by those involved in more 'Anglo-Irish' pursuits such as Rugby. This difference of opinon was not merely about sport but about defining the identity of the new nation-state. While a Celtic queen may have been a rather inclusive symbol for such a cultural festival, it is apparent that the underlying tensions represented highly contested views of tradition, identity, culture and exclusivity.

There are clearly some questions about the extent to which ancient symbols were successfully evoked in the newly established Free State. For example, Terence Brown claims that by the 1920s, the impact of Celtic symbolism was waning. In the aftermath of the civil war and in the harsh realities of economic reconstruction, romantic images seemed less applicable: 'There was a general sense that the heroic age had passed' (Brown 1987: 81). He argues that the Celtic symbolism of the festival failed to capture public imagination perhaps because of the harshness of modern life or the scepticism of the scientific age or simply because of the 'mediocre dullness of the new democratic Irish state' (1987: 83).

Meanwhile, the provincial press continued to focus on the controversies surrounding the festival of 1928. On 18 February, the *Wicklow People* reported that the government had given the organising committee a loan of £2,000 to be paid back out of net profits. The press-report pointed out that the 1924 games made a huge loss and so it was very unlikely that the current loan would be repaid. However, on the 14 August, the *Connacht Sentinel* reported that the festival had made 'an auspicious start'. Now that the 'foreign' teams had arrived from USA and elsewhere, 'things should go very merrily to the end':

> Despite all the initial difficulties encountered both in 1924 and now, the games have been firmly established as a feature of our national life. As time progresses they should prove a real hosting of the Gael at which all that is best in the race – physical, intellectual and spiritual – will find worthy expression. (*Connacht Sentinel*, 14 August 1928)

The *Wicklow People* continued, however, to be very negative about the festival and described the opening ceremony as 'disappointing'. It reported that all the Cumann na nGaedheal government ministers stayed away although members of Mr. De Valera's party were represented, which was a complete reversal of 1924. However, the report also stated that a crowd of 20,000 turned up to watch the opening hurling match between Ireland and the Irish-Americans (18 August 1928). The Galway-based *Connacht Sentinel* continued to give regular, positive reports on the progress of the games, although there are clearly situated in Dublin, very far removed from Galway. Reports of the games appeared in the section of the paper entitled 'From Dublin Town'. 'The games continue to draw fairly good crowds' (21 August 1928). The report went on to say that the performances in the athletics were 'of a very high standard...both the Americans and Canadians were very strong teams'. However, the *Sentinel* did find it necessary to mention some criticisms of the festival, particularly in relation to levels of organisation and management:

> One dislikes to strike a jarring note in connection with the affair, but it must be confessed that the arrangement left a good deal to be desired. (*Connacht Sentinel*, 21 August 1928)

The *Wicklow People* had no such qualms about striking a jarring note. While praising the swimming events as an 'outstanding success', the paper was very critical of 'the athletics which dragged out for four days' and was a 'fiasco'. 'Only four thousand people attended the last day's athletics'. This report also suggested some reason as to why the games received so much criticism in the *Wicklow People* and very little publicity in other provincial papers. Apparently there were tensions between members of the press corps and the organising committee. Journalists felt they were not getting proper access to events, in some cases this had led to 'heated arguments' (25 August 1925).

Although Aonach Tailteann was represented in the national dailies as a nationwide celebration of Irish sport and culture, the reports, or lack of reports, in the provincial press suggest that the festival may have been perceived as something which took place in Dublin, largely attended by Dublin people and was of little interest to those in the provinces. Overall, it would seem that the games were not as successful as had been originally hoped. This may explain why the planned games did not go ahead in 1936.

## *Conclusion:*

This rather lengthy discussion of press reporting on Aonach Tailteann 1924, 1928 and 1932, reveals many aspects of the ways in which the Irish press engaged with and reinforced particular representations of Ireland and Irishness in the early decades of the Irish Free State. I began by quoting Terence Brown's claim that the Celtic symbolism associated with such events as Aonach Tailteann failed to inspire widespread public enthusiasm in the harsh economic climate of the 1920s-1930s. However, while it is possible to suggest that Celtic imagery appealed to only a small minority of people, it is important not to underestimate the complexity and multifaceted nature of those myths and symbols. I have suggested that ancient legends and iconography provided a site for a range of competing discourses. Gendered symbols of national culture, tradition and identity reveal the processes through which the nation was imagined and depicted. Images of virtuous masculinity and motherly femininity overlapped with Catholic and nationalist iconography of Irish identity. Continuity between the 'glorious past' and a stable, successful future was embodied especially in female allegories of Ireland and Irish womanhood.

However, the discussion of Aonach Tailteann also suggests that representations of the nation and nationalist programmes of nation-building were by no means straightforward and unproblematic. The press did not speak with one monolithic voice. Newspaper reports indicate the tensions that existed between various interest groups and political parties. Perhaps these tensions suggest why ambiguous symbols like Queen Tailte were so useful as they helped to smooth over tensions and divisions, simultaneously representing a very general notion of past glories and future possibilities. As the rest of this book will demonstrate, the Irish press drew on a wide array of ambiguous female symbols to embody various aspects of the nation. These symbols can be read in numerous ways to reveal the many tensions and competing priorities of the newly established Irish Free State.

# CHAPTER TWO:

## FASHIONABLE BODIES

### Section 1: The Modern Girl

*The Modern Girl*

(extract)

Her feet are so very little
Her hands are so very white
Her jewels so very heavy
And her head so very light

Her colour is made of cosmetics -
Though this she'll never own
Her body is mostly cotton,
And her heart is wholly stone.

She falls in love with a fellow,
Who smells with a foreign air;
He marries her for her money,
They are a well matched pair.

John Marcus O'Sullivan
The *Kerryman* newspaper, 18 August 1928.

*Introduction:*

In the newly established Irish Free State of the 1920s, the flapper or 'modern girl' was a highly contested and deeply controversial symbol of womanhood (Ryan 1998a). Within 'Irish Ireland' nationalism and Catholic discourses the modern girl represented disobedience, vice, and immorality and was ultimately constructed as unIrish, foreign and pagan. Her embodiment of foreign fashions and lifestyles threatened to destabilise Irish identity and thus undermine the new nation. Dublin-based national daily newspapers regularly reported concerns about flappers. But such accounts tended to locate the modern, fashionable, independent young women in urban centres. This may be seen as reinforcing a dichotomy of modern, urban women versus rural, unfashionable, traditional womanhood (Ryan 1998b). This chapter sets out to question such an urban/rural dichotomy by examining the extent to which the archetypal flapper/ modern girl was discussed and represented in the provincial press, as well as in the national dailies, in the southern Irish Free State in the mid to late 1920s. This study of a previously neglected area of inquiry raises questions about not only the prevalence of the flapper archetype in rural Ireland, but also the construction of this symbol of womanhood in the context of Irish cultural and national identity. In addition, the chapter also examines the various ways in which this gendered and sexualised figure embodied conflicting notions of authority, freedom and pleasure. Press representations are complex and contradictory; advertisements, women's pages and feature articles indicate the range of perspectives and diverse opinions frequently celebrating women's independence and modernity. Such divergent viewpoints may begin to challenge the assumed hegemony of traditional Catholic dogma in Ireland at that time.

In an effort to understand the true extent of the flapper image in the country as a whole, I draw upon the provincial press from the three southern provinces of Munster, Leinster and Connacht. While choosing a fairly random sample of provincial papers, I have endeavoured to select those newspapers that not only had a wide circulation but also covered a significant spread of rural counties. The *Cork Examiner* was the largest provincial paper and was published on a daily basis (except Sunday). It circulated throughout the southern counties of Cork, Kerry, Limerick and Waterford. The *Limerick Leader*, published thrice weekly, was one of the more fervent cultural nationalists of all the newspapers. It was circulated in Limerick, Kerry and Clare.

In addition, I have selected five weekly papers. The *Kerryman* was based in Tralee but circulated throughout Kerry, Clare and North Cork. The *Connacht Tribune* and its sister paper the *Connacht Sentinel*, were based in Galway but with a wide circulation throughout Mayo and the West of Ireland. The *Sligo Champion* was circulated in the north west of the country. The *Wicklow People* covered Wicklow, Wexford, Tipperary and Waterford. While these papers did not cover the entire country, for example, certain parts of the midlands and the northern counties are not fully represented by this sample, nevertheless, together these seven provincial papers do cover a considerable area of the country outside of the metropolitan centre of Dublin and, of course, the North of Ireland.

In an attempt to make my study manageable, while at the same time aiming to include a good range of issues and topics, I have concentrated on the period between 1926-1928. Because the media was dominated by coverage of the armed struggle between 1919-1923 (see Ryan 1999), there seemed little point in analysing images of frivolous flappers in the early twenties. The mid to late twenties are important because this period represented not only an attempt to return to 'normality' but also a visible project of nation building and defining national cultural identity.

*The most 'popular myth of the twenties':*

In her book *Women and the Popular Imagination in the 'Twenties*, Billie Melman argues that the image of the flapper 'haunted the popular imagination' (1988: 1). This image embodied many diverse and, indeed, contradictory notions of femininity, womanhood and sexuality – beautiful/unwomanly, silly/sophisticated, desexed/highly sexualised, infantile/ dangerous. 'The equivocal figure became the centre of a polyphonic debate of many voices' (1988: 1). Debates about the flapper were carried on in magazines, popular novels and most significantly in newspapers. While debates about defiant young women had occurred in previous generations, what marked the distinctiveness of the flapper debates in the twenties was the fact that they were so public, vocal and central, fuelled in no small part by the press. According to Melman (1988), the flapper occupied the particular social, political and economic setting of the 1920s. The structural and demographic changes following World War I heightened concerns about the behaviour and pastimes of independent young women. The spread of radio, cinema, mass circulating newspapers and the growth in consumerism, especially amongst women, helped to spread the stereotypical image of the fashionable, fun-loving flapper. But the flapper was very much a creature of her time. The image faded in the 1930s, as according to Melman, the austerity of that decade could not accommodate this ultimate consumer.

While Melman's research on flappers is very interesting and raises several important issues, it is, nonetheless rather narrowly related to the particular context of post-war Britain. I am interested in how the flapper may be understood in another, very different, social, cultural and political context. O'Shea (in Nava and O'Shea 1996) has argued that the experiences of modernism varied in different countries. Modernity was not a simple universal process; it took on varying national characteristics and flavours. The flapper, as a symbol of modernism, embodied not only those different national characteristics but also helped to frame the specific debates and concerns of particular national contexts. Anti-colonial, nationalist movements represent one example of how women may be inscribed within particular definitions of culture, identity and traditional values. Thus the Irish Free State of the 1920s provides a very specific case in point.

As mentioned in the introduction to this book, nationalism is a gendered project within which women have been ascribed particular roles and responsibilities (McClintock 1993). While it is important not to ignore the active and often violent roles which women have played, and continue to play, in nationalist movements (Yuval-Davis 1998, Ryan 1999), women's more usual roles have tended to emphasise passivity and dependency. As Anthias and Yuval-Davis (1993) have theorised, women are represented as symbols of the nation, as mothers of the nation, as transmitters of cultural traditions and as boundary markers between nations.

While there are obvious similarities with concerns about the frivolous, jazzing flapper in Britain, it would be simplistic to assume that debates about the flapper were identical in all social contexts. The particular religious, social, cultural and political context of the Irish Free State informed the specific constructions and interpretations of the flapper. Unlike Britain, there was no 'flapper vote' in 1928 because universal suffrage had been achieved in 1922. There was no concern about the 'superfluous woman' as men outnumbered women in most geographical regions. The Great War was less of an historical watershed than the campaign for Irish independence. The deep divisions caused by the Civil War (1922-23) meant that creating a shared sense of national cohesion and national identity superseded any concerns about changes to the class structure:

> As a new nation, the Free State sought to assert its legitimacy by defining a unique culture and identity which marked Irish people apart and distinct from British people. (Gray and Ryan, 1997: 520)

Nevertheless, Irish culture in the 1920s was greatly influenced by British forms of entertainment and media, as well as by the growing enthusiasm for Hollywood films (Brown 1987). As Maryann Valiulis has argued 'the reality of independence certainly paled in comparison to the dreams and expectations of nationalist Ireland' (1995a: 126). The government and the powerful Catholic hierarchy attempted to define their authority by restoring traditional order. This carefully constructed notion of 'traditional' Gaelic, Catholic Ireland was one in which women were to play a very specific role. Part of this nationalist project was an attempt to distance Ireland from the unflattering and degrading stereotypes that had formed such a core aspect of the colonial experience (Valiulis 1995a). Therefore, there was a strong emphasis on the cultural purity, virtue, integrity and honour of the nation. Women were to embody these virtues and become 'the badge of respectability' of the new nation-state. Thus Irish women, in particular virginal young women and married mothers, were ascribed the thankless task of representing the purity and uniqueness of Irish national culture and identity (Innes 1993, Meaney 1993).

However, women did not simply represent national goodness, innocence and virtue. As I have argued elsewhere (with Gray 1997, 1998), women who deviated from traditional feminine roles were used to symbolise national weakness and susceptibility to foreign corruption. To borrow Meaney's phrase, women became the 'bearers of national honour' but also the 'scapegoats of national identity' (1993: 233). Women's weakness and susceptibility to foreign influences made them conveniently flawed boundary guards in need of constant monitoring and policing by men. Irish male political and religious leaders asserted their own masculine authority through their attempts to police and contain women's sinful and wayward bodies. 'Deviant' women embodied the decadence that threatened not only to undermine masculine authority but also to destabilise the fragile culture of the Irish nation-state. I will argue that it is precisely in this nationalist context that the Irish flapper needs to be located and understood.

### *Religion and the 'Virtue of Woman':*

One of the most vocal attacks on the 'modern girl' in Ireland came from the Catholic Church. But, in fact, the Church's criticism of modern fashions and lifestyles extended beyond Ireland. The Pope played an active part in the campaign against the 'modern girl'. While all newspapers gave frequent coverage to religious leaders, some papers carried regular columns devoted to religious news and events. The *Wicklow People* had a weekly column entitled 'Catholic Notes' and the *Cork Examiner* had a regular feature entitled 'Catholic News of the Week'.

For example, on 20 December 1926 the *Cork Examiner* reported on the Pope's 'scathing condemnation' of women's dress. The Pope urged a 'crusade' against 'immoral fashions and the irreverent manners of modern women'. He said that there was a need for Catholic men to occupy themselves 'with this very grave question of feminine fashions'. The Pope described the fashions as 'harmful', bearing the 'seed of countless catastrophes'. He asserted, not only the potential threat to social order posed by modern women, but also the need for Catholic men to exert control over 'deviant' women.

Significantly, while the Catholic hierarchy in many countries attacked modern fashions and lifestyles, in Ireland this was done within a cultural nationalism that constructed all evil influences as being imported from abroad and essentially alien to Irishness. Such foreign influences represented a threat to Irish culture, traditions and ultimately to national identity and sovereignty. Jim Smyth has suggested that while the Free State was beset with a range of economic, political and social problems, the Catholic Church focused attention narrowly on morality (Smyth 1993: 51). The opinions of Catholic leaders were given widespread coverage in the press through the regular reprinting of sermons, lenten pastorals, pamphlets and public lectures. The speeches of lay lobby groups usually found their way into the press also. On 13 October 1926 the *Irish Independent* carried a lengthy report on the annual conference of the Catholic Truth Society, an influential lobby group which campaigned for increased censorship. In his conference address Judge O'Brien attacked the *key problems* in Irish society: 'grave crimes', 'intemperance', 'the painting and scanty dressing of young women', and the 'plague of immoral literature' coming into Ireland from abroad 'like a cloud of locusts'. He was particularly anxious about the 'women of Ireland, hitherto renowned for their virtue and honour' who were now smoking cigarettes and drinking alcohol.

On the 18 June 1928, the *Independent* reported that Dr. Mulhern addressing a confirmation ceremony said 'of all the ways in which modesty was sinned against none was greater than in respect to dress'. 'Modern dress fashions were largely modelled on those created by pagan minds in foreign countries' said the paper paraphrasing the Bishop, 'and they were totally unfitted for a Catholic country such as Ireland'. The Bishop went on to say that he would like to see 'dress fashions designed in Ireland for Irish people'. He concluded that 'Irish girls always looked well until they began to make geegaws [fools] of themselves'.

The clothes worn by modern young women were frequently blamed for leading men to sin. For example, the *Wicklow People* on 15 May 1926, carried a report by a prison doctor who claimed that modern fashions 'had a direct bearing upon crime incitation no matter how innocent the wearing may be....when man's emotions are aroused he can't control himself'. In exposing so much of her flesh, the modern young woman was not merely a danger to herself but represented a threat to all decent society. On 20 October 1928, the *Wicklow People* published a sermon given by Father Degen in which he addressed the topic of modern fashions:

> Worship of the body takes the place of religion in women who are inordinately vane. The mortal soul is treated as non-existent, and nothing is recognised as sinful except dowdiness. In the case of some women their ambition appears to be to drag men's hearts about on a string. (*Wicklow People*, 20 October 1928)

The elevation of the body above the soul is an exact reverse of Catholic doctrine and so this image of women who worship their bodies but neglect their souls not only constructs them as vane but also as anti-Catholic and doomed to eternal damnation. As Mica Nava has argued, there was a growing suspicion that women derived a libidinous pleasure from 'the physical adornment and nurturing of the self' (1995: 11). But women who took such pains over their physical appearance not only endangered their own souls but were also a danger to men. They teased men and broke their hearts. This image of modern women was very common and will be explored in more detail later. For now let us continue with Fr. Degen. In attempting to explain this phenomenon he turns to mothers:

> What is your ideal of womanly perfection? Would you really prefer your daughters to imitate the daring sartorial suggestiveness of the modern flapper rather than the modesty, sweetness and gentleness of our Blessed Lady? (*Wicklow People*, 20 October 1928)

It was common for the flapper to be set up in direct opposition to the modesty of Mary the mother of God. 'The flapper was juxtaposed to the young girl who was innocent and vulnerable. Ecclesiastical discourse thus defined women in the traditional Madonna/Eve split – a dualism which is an integral part of catholic teaching' (Valiulis 1995b: 172). Flappers were constructed as wild and uncontrolled daughters but also as poor prospects for later marriage and motherhood. On 11 August 1928, the *Wicklow People* published an article on the 'modern young woman' which focused on her many faults and failings. While men would wish to marry 'a modest, intelligent girl,' 'a sensible, virtuous girl' with 'feminine charm', who would wish to marry 'a control defying, 'good time', 'can anybody come?' flapper'. Here the flapper is seen as frivolous, wilful, superficial and lacking in the feminine virtues of modesty and good sense. This image of the immodest and wayward flapper underpinned many sermons and religious pamphlets throughout the Irish Free State in the 1920s. On 7 May 1928, the *Cork Examiner* reported on a sermon by Dr. Roche, the Bishop of Ross:

> In modern times a bit of the spirit of paganism and love of pleasure are prominent features even in the life of good Catholics. It manifests itself particularly at present in regard to female dress. This failing is worldwide. It is not confined to one country or to one parish, or to one class of people, but the disease is prevalent in every land....our people have been caught in this snare of fashion, and in our towns and in the country too, at present, many of our young girls are dressed in a manner that is to men an occasion for sin. (*Cork Examiner*, 7 May 1928)

Bishop Roche highlighted the Church's fears about the 'love of pleasure' which was linked to paganism and so was in opposition to Catholicism. He also laid all the blame for modern paganism firmly on the shoulders of young women; women were the carriers and the transmitters of this 'disease', men were helpless victims. Interestingly, this quote also establishes the prevalence of modern fashionable girls in every area of Irish society, in every parish – town and countryside – and in every social class. Bishop Roche suggested that the flapper was not confined to urban centres. This point is certainly borne out by the provincial newspapers in my study.

On 6 March 1926 the Galway based weekly newspaper, the *Connacht Tribune*, carried an eye-catching headline 'Flappers and Shawls'. This headed a column of local court reports only one of which had any connection with the bold headline. In the trial of a woman for non-payment of bills, the prosecuting barrister asked if she had bought a coat for her daughter. She said no, to which he replied 'what does she put over her blouse, is it a shawl? Very few of the flappers now would be content with a shawl (laughter)'. On the 24 April 1926 the same paper carried an equally dramatic headline 'Armed Amazons'. This referred to a dispute over land rights in county Galway. Having arrested several men from the area, the Civic Guards were attacked by 'a party of women and girls mostly of the flapper age, armed with sticks and carrying baskets of stale eggs'. In both of these articles, the term flapper is used very generally to refer to young women. In the first article it refers to clothing and fashion but in the second it is vague and may or may not refer to age and physical appearance. However, what the articles do suggest is the extent to which the term 'flapper' was in common use in the Irish provincial press in the late 1920s. While these two particular references to the flapper were fairly innocuous, the more usual connotations were extremely negative. Concerns with flapper immorality and immodesty usually focused on her clothes. Her short skirts and sleeveless dresses symbolised not only her vanity and immodesty but also her modernity and, hence, her threat to traditional femininity.

*Pagan Fashions:*

On 2 May 1928 the *Limerick Leader* newspaper reported that notices had been posted outside Catholic Churches in the town of Ennis prohibiting the wearing of: 'dresses less than 4 inches below the knee, dresses cut lower than the collar bone, dresses without sleeves sufficiently long to cover the arm as far as the wrist, and dresses of transparent material'. This notice was not unique but was part of an orchestrated attempt on the part of Church leaders and nationalist organisations to rid Irish society of 'immodest fashion'. In 1927 the Modest Dress and Deportment Crusade was founded in Limerick. This had the backing not only of the Catholic hierarchy in Ireland but also received messages of support from Rome. Churches in Italy were also attempting to bar women wearing 'inappropriate dress' (Valiulis 1995b). Newspapers such as the *Limerick Leader* also supported the Crusade. On 11 June 1928 the *Leader*'s editorial addressed the topic of female fashion:

> [Short] feminine garments...are not so numerously or brazenly evident in Limerick now as they were a year or two ago. This gratifying evidence of a return to decency and sanity is largely attributable to the modest dress crusade....The craze for nudity was catching on to a disgusting extent all over Ireland. In this new movement for decency Limerick has so far played a prominent and laudable part....Those who still flaunt in the streets the unbecoming habiliments that are more suited to the bathroom than to a public thoroughfare are now very few and are steadily growing less in number. (*Limerick Leader*, 11 June 1928)

On 6 April 1928, the *Irish Independent* reprinted a long letter from the Modest Dress and Deportment Crusade that had originally been published in the 'Irish Catholic'. The letter likened the crusade to 'an army' and claimed that those who had joined this army were:

> superior in moral courage, in refinement of mind, and in independence of character to the vulgar crowd that fills our streets and by its servility to foreign fashion brings a blush to the cheek of those who love Ireland. (*Irish Independent*, 6 April 1928)

This is an interesting statement that established members of the Modest Dress and Deportment Crusade as true patriots of Ireland. Those who embrace foreign fashions are servile to foreign influences. They are represented as a mindless, vulgar crowd who lack independence of character and moral courage. They are unpatriotic. As with so many other critics of modern fashions, this letter constructs foreign influences as not merely unIrish but also as producing a mindless slavery. True freedom can only be achieved by rejecting foreign influences and remaining loyal to Irish, Catholic traditions. 'If we are free…we must have liberty to choose our own ideals. Why should anti-Christian leaders of fashion prescribe the rules of etiquette?' In analysing this statement it become apparent that the problem with foreign fashion was not simply that it was not Irish but that it was not Christian or, more precisely, was not Catholic. Interestingly, the writer linked the spread of foreign influences from urban centres to the provinces with the higher education of young women:

> One would imagine that higher education would tend to culture…How comes it then that girls who go from the country to the city to receive high education so often return vulgarians, with English slang on the tip of their tongues; a cigarette between the tips of their fingers and their frocks well above the tips of their knees? How then can we expect girls from the provinces to repudiate pagan influences? Can nothing be done to induce the leaders of fashion in Dublin to adopt a more modest attire at public functions? (*Irish Independent*, 6 April 1928).

It is significant that the writer condemns the educated young women's slang as 'English'. Therefore, Dublin acts as conduit for transmitting negative, foreign influences from England to the Irish countryside. In both urban and rural areas it is women, through their clothes, speech and lifestyle who embody these outside threats to traditional native modesty and freedom. Thus the notion of insiders and outsiders becomes blurred. Women who should embody the purity and modesty of insider, native cultural identity, become the link with outsider, foreign immodesty and impurity. This suggests the duality of women's role as the simultaneous embodiment of national purity and national weakness. The complex and multifaceted gendering of this process was illustrated by a report in the *Sligo Champion*.

On 7 April 1928 the *Sligo Champion* carried an article entitled 'A National Campaign for Modesty'. In supporting the MDDC the report began: 'Readers of the *Sligo Champion* who have not already heard of this new national movement will no doubt be glad to have news of it'. It is described in dramatic terms as 'a big push' to save the country from 'demoralising and denationalising influences'. The use of the term 'denationalising' locates the modest dress crusade in the particular context of national identity and national sovereignty and goes beyond the narrow focus on modesty and decency in dress. At this moment in history Ireland 'should prove that she is truly "a nation once again" and show her independence of foreign ascendancy'. The 'tyranny of fashion' is presented as a threat not just to decency but to the 'traditions of our land':

> It is a movement to ensure that 'Dark Rosaleen' shall, as the poet predicted, 'reign a queen' while the other nations of the world are grovelling in the paganism called the new civilisation which is merely a glorification of the animal nature of man and wholly opposed to the spiritual heritage of our race. (The *Sligo Champion*, 7 April 1928)

This quote is very revealing and suggests the relationship between nationhood, tradition, heritage, race and sovereignty. Irish independence can only be maintained if the uniqueness of Irish culture is preserved from modern, foreign, pagan influences. This sets up a dichotomy of native purity and tradition versus outside impurity and modernity. These images are gendered in several ways. Firstly, this dichotomy is mapped onto the bodies of women – the pure, native girl versus the immodest flapper. Secondly, Ireland, as a nation, is also represented by a female symbol 'Rosaleen', who is a beautiful, pure and innocent Irish girl. Thus women become inscribed within images of Ireland and images of Irishness. Women embody the essence of Irish cultural tradition as well as the potential susceptibility to foreign corruption. Therefore, it is essential that Irish womanhood is safeguarded from all moral corruption so that ultimately Ireland 'herself' can be preserved from foreign assimilation.

But where did all these foreign fashions come from and who was responsible for them? In all the newspapers modern fashions are presented as deeply alien, coming into Ireland from aboard. All the negative aspects of modern living, the so-called jazz age, were associated with foreign influences but the main sources of influence varied. Usually disreputable cinema influences came from Hollywood, salacious magazines and papers came from England, jazz was described as African, immodest fashions came from Paris. In its regular feature 'Catholic Notes', the *Wicklow People* frequently explored the problems and sources of modern fashions. For example, on 15 May 1926 'Catholic Notes' pointed out that 'vulgar fashions' were dictated by the 'underworld of Paris'. The exact make-up of that underworld was more fully explained in 'Catholic Notes' on 21 January 1928: 'The women of Ireland will be pleased to hear that the designers of their dresses and the fashions are Jews and Freemasons from Paris and other great continental cities.' These were aiming to 'deChristianise society'. 'What is to be said of Catholic women in Ireland who co-operate in this infamous design by slavishly following every mode decreed by these tyrannical fashion-makers?'

The insidious nature of these Parisian styles can be seen in a report published in the *Connacht Sentinel* on 28 February 1928 under the intriguing headline 'Parisian Style Frocks: Ceilidhe Fashions Criticised'. The Irish language movement, the Gaelic League expressed its concern about the clothes which women wore to traditional Irish dances or 'ceilidhe'. The League was determined to promote Irish dances and Irish music in opposition to foreign cultural influences. However, it was frustrated to discover that even when young women did turn up to such events they brought modern fashions with them: 'Ladies Irish costumes are scarcely ever seen; all the cailini [girls] are attired in the very latest Parisian fashions'.

In a report carried in both the *Connacht Tribune* and the *Sligo Champion*, 18 February 1928, Archbishop Gilmartin of Tuam was quoted as saying:

> We do not want to make you all monks and nuns. We do not want to ban your innocent recreations. All we want is that you would restrain yourselves from sinful excess, and not allow yourselves to become slaves to pagan fashions and sinful pleasures. We want you boys and girls to remake the beautiful Ireland of the past – an Ireland of brave, clean boys and pure girls; an Ireland of happy marriages and happy homes. (*Connacht Tribune* and *Sligo Champion*, 18 February 1928)

Thus 1920s fashions were constructed as being not only foreign and corrupting to Irish Catholic society, but also as tyrannical and oppressive, standing in opposition to freedom and independence. Both the independence of women and of the nation were undermined by the dictates of modern fashions. True happiness and freedom lay in the past, in heritage and tradition and not in the fashions and lifestyles of modernity. This argument presents a complete reversal of the usual way in which 1920s fashions were viewed, namely as liberating for women by representing women's newly found political, educational and economic opportunities (Wilson 1985). Coupled with the demise of constricting corsets, loose fitting clothing and shorter skirts facilitated women's greater mobility and freedom of movement.

But it was not just the Catholic Church who represented women as the slaves of foreign fashion influences. On 11 June 1928, the *Independent* carried an editorial entitled 'The Slaves of Fashion'. This article highlighted the link between women's dress and the decline in the woollen industry. Manufacturers of woollen materials were said to be suffering greatly because women preferred silk and artificial materials. In addition, the length of women's garments was proving a concern for textile manufacturers. 'Short skirts are blamed for throwing half the tweed looms idle in Scotland'.

## *Sartorial Civil War: Letters to the Editor*

In July 1926 a heated debate about the 'modern girl' broke out in the letters' page of the *Irish Independent*. Over the course of this debate some 18 letters were published. On 7 July 1926 there were two letters criticising the 'modern girl'. The first, from 'Mannered Boy', declared 'One cannot help condemning the modern girl for her unseemly behaviour at times'. Commenting upon a group of girls at the seaside scantily clad in sleeveless dresses, smoking cigarettes, he wrote 'they are a disgrace to their sex'. The other letter similarly commented upon the phenomenon of girls smoking. 'The modern girl is suffering from a high notion of her own importance, with the inevitable result that her manners and general behaviour are not, in her opinion, subject to the approval of the opposite sex'. This was an opinion that the letter writer clearly did not share. On the 8 July 1926 four letters were printed in the *Irish Independent* in the continuing debate on the 'modern girl'. One letter writer protested: 'I am rather hard on those who shed their femininity in their attempt to be masculine'. All of these letters use the 'modern girl' archetype to suggest disorderly behaviour and the challenge to traditional gender roles.

Some of the letters, however, reveal that not everyone viewed the 'modern girl' as necessarily negative. A number of the women who wrote to the paper clearly identified with the archetype in a self-affirming way. On 14 July 'Saucie Sue', professing to be a modern girl, reported that three young men on a tram recently would not get up to offer their seat to an elderly lady. 'Sue' despite being a cigarette smoking, short dress wearing girl, did give up her seat for the old lady. Two other letters were also printed on that day; a 'masculine man' declared that this was 1926 not the nineteenth century. Things had to change. He added that young men were probably more badly behaved than young women. Finally, 'Hibernian' expressed the opposing view. He declared that men liked *'womanly'* women not cigarette smoking, cocktail drinkers. He concluded that 99 men out of 100 secretly loathed such 'silly creatures'.

This series of letters suggests the range of opinion that existed on the 'modern girl'. Clearly, many complained about her immodesty and immorality, her rejection of traditional femininity. It was her drinking, smoking, short dresses, lifestyle, in essence, her thorough modernity which proved so distasteful. On 23 July, a letter was published in the *Independent* that placed the concerns about the 'modern girl' very much within the dichotomy of traditional Irish womanhood versus modern, foreign lifestyles. Entitled 'Advice to Irish Girls' it read:

> Irish girls have been honoured for their simplicity and natural modesty, and they should think long before they barter their natural birthrights for the foibles of the moment....The sooner our Irish girls realise the wanton foolishness, bordering on wickedness, of playing with attributes God gifted unto them, the sooner they will ascend to the plain of respect they now so foolishly desert for pastures less fair. (*Irish Independent* 23 July 1926)

In asserting that women stood to lose their *'natural'* birthrights and privileges by abandoning traditional femininity, this letter, like many others, drew a clear line between natural, traditional, Irish femininity and the contamination of *'unnatural'* foreign influences. As Kandiyoti (1996) has argued, for women within nationalist contexts, 'the modern' is always perilously close to the foreign and alien. Thus the 'modern girl' was not just failing in her patriotic duty to maintain culture and tradition, but in so doing was threatening the very order, stability and continuity of the nation.

In July 1928, the debate about women's fashions again erupted in the letters' page of the *Irish Independent*. On the 12 July a total of 10 letters on this topic were published. The first letter, written by a man named Patrick Power, said that 'it is certainly not a man's business to interfere in such a matter as women's dress'. He argued that men had no right to infringe the liberty of those who are 'already sufficiently restricted nowadays'. A similar point was made by another man who signed himself 'F.T.': 'I would not allow a girl to interfere as to my mode of dress, and hence it would not be for me to dictate theirs'. A third man wrote his letter under the heading 'Sartorial Civil War'. He claimed that some critics would not be happy until there were 'Civic Guards, assisted by tailors, meeting female tourists at Dun Laoghaire or the Border, armed with red tape measures or batons marked off in inches'. In similar good humour, a letter signed by 'Logician' raised the issue of male kilts. Kilts, worn by men and boys in 'pipe bands and other similarly attired bodies in this country', often displayed 'absolutely bare knees'. These should be lengthened to the required three inches below the knee. Boys' shorts and bathing costumes should also be adjusted 'provided bathing is still to be permitted'.

However, several of the letters echoed the views of the Catholic Church in condemning female fashions. For example, one letter entitled 'Most Glaring Ignorance' pointed out that short skirts 'have been condemned by the Pope who is infallible'. The women who persisted in wearing them were merely 'dupes of fashion'. In a similar argument, 'Catholic Layman' claimed that the Pope and Bishops had every right to condemn female fashions and a Catholic layman also had the same right, provided he was in consonance with Church teachings.

Several women contributed letters to the debate, for example, 'Veronica' claimed that 'virtue begins within' and it was impossible to judge a girl's virtue by the length of her skirt. She concluded that 'I am still of the opinion that no mere male has the right to criticise a girl's dress'. But not all the female correspondents were supportive of modern fashions. One letter, signed 'A University Graduate', was entitled 'Don't Mind the Feather Headed'. 'It is time we Irish girls and women admitted the truth about this fashion of the too-short skirt'. This skirt 'is neither modest nor a comfortable garment'. Girls have been too willing to give in to the pressures of foreign fashions. 'It is all a question of moral cowardice'. 'Let each sensible girl do her share in banishing what she helped to establish' (*Irish Independent*, 12 July 1928).

These letters reflect and reinforce the images of women's fashions that were being discussed elsewhere in the press and in the pulpits. The issue of 'freedom' appears to have been a particularly contested concept. Some of the letters, like the sermons of Bishops and priests, associated fashion with slavery. Women who followed the dictates of fashion were dismissed as 'dupes'. They were guilty of the 'most glaring ignorance'. Women who condemned foreign fashions such as the too-short skirt were described as 'sensible'. It took courage to reject the pressures of fashion and assert true moral virtue and modesty. Other letters asserted women's right to freedom of dress and to resist the pressures to conform to the dictates of male commentators. It is noteworthy that while several letters strongly defended the right of Church leaders to criticise women's dress, no letter directly challenged the Church. Instead letter writers used humour to highlight the nonsense of a fashion police who would harass tourists at the border or stipulate the length of traditional kilts.

On 2 August 1928, the *Independent* returned to the subject of women's hemlines with a special feature article entitled 'The Short Skirt: Is there a happy medium?' Nora Tynan O'Mahony claimed that 'everywhere one hears it still under discussion'. She began by arguing that 'no one wants women to go back to the cumbersome and ugly skirt fashions of our mothers and grandmothers...impeding every movement, dragging the poor back and limbs':

> A moderately short skirt, it must be admitted, looks always neat and tidy; gives a delightful sense of freedom in walking, at play...and now that women have become so enthusiastic about games...it is probable that the short skirt has come to stay. (*Irish Independent*, 2 August 1928)

However, Tynan O'Mahony went on to draw a careful distinction between the moderately short skirt that looked neat and permitted ease of movement and the too-short skirt. 'Skirts above the knee or even knee-length skirts, are to my mind ugly and abominable'. She concluded by warning women 'not to forget that men like reticence; far more perhaps than they like powder and paint – and legs!' Like the letters discussed above, this article focused the fashion debates around the specific issue of the short skirt. The knee-length hemline in the 1920s flapper represented the most dramatic change in women's fashions for centuries (Wilson 1985). As Tynan O'Mahony's article indicates the transition from the long, flowing skirts of the previous generation to the short skirts of 1920s had been rapid and somewhat startling for many people. The fact that women's knees were being debated in the Irish press for much of the mid to late 1920s reveals not only the intensity of feeling on this subject but also the extent to which the issue was deemed to be central to the nation's cultural and religious identity. Tynan O'Mahony acknowledged the advantages of shorter skirts particularly in the light of women's changing lifestyles and the growing enthusiasm for sport. Therefore, she did not advocate a return to 'cumbersome' clothing. Interestingly, she based her critique of the knee-length hemline not on the usual moral considerations or religious teaching but on the tastes of men. Men were more likely to be influenced by female reticence in make-up and in clothing. This argument suggested that men would be put off a young woman by her use of too much make-up and by the display of too much leg. It is likely that this argument was calculated to appeal to young women who were keen to impress rather than alienate potential suitors.

*Conflicting Images:*

Thus on first reading it would appear simply that Irish national and provincial newspapers were united in their condemnation of modern fashions and modern flappers, seeking instead to elevate traditional womanhood to her rightful place as pure embodiment of a pure nation. However, this reading ignores some of the wider complexities around the image of the fashionable modern girl. The women's pages of the newspapers provide several alternative readings of modern womanhood. The *Irish Independent*'s women's page was entitled 'the Ladies Page'. Here the latest Paris fashions and Hollywood hairstyles were discussed alongside cookery recipes. There were usually several pictures of fashionable women in short dresses, sporting bobbed hair. In addition, the lifestyle of modern women was frequently highlighted. On 28 September 1926, the Ladies Page contained an article entitled 'The Modern Girl's Education'. This drew largely on an interview with an actress, Violet Vanbrugh, who argued that modern girls were very different from their mothers and so needed a different type of education. She described modern girls as 'independent and self-reliant'. But she added that they needed to show respect to their elders. All girls should learn how to run a home but should also be taught useful skills that would enable them to earn a living – ' if the necessity arose'.

The women's page in the *Irish Times* was entitled 'Woman and her Home' and usually featured equal measures of fashion, recipes and household tips. The very title of the section – Woman *and her Home* – suggests its focus and content. The 'modern girl' was regularly discussed, with particular attention being paid to fashion and hairstyles. On 16 January 1926 the fashion section of 'Woman and her Home' was devoted to a polemic piece by M. Gaillard Palmer entitled 'The Shortest Skirt.' She condemned the newest, even shorter length in female dresses as impractical and unflattering:

> For goodness sake, let us try to get back to something approaching the normal in skirt lengths than the skittish, school-girlness of the articles of apparel we today dignify by the name of 'skirts'. (*Irish Times* 16 January 1926)

'Woman and Her Home' carried an interesting short story on 9 January 1926 which featured a conversation between a young flapper and her mother. While the mother reflects on how much simpler and less expensive life was in her youth, her daughter declares: 'I'm sure I don't know how you existed when you were young Mother'. The daughter went on to outline the drawbacks of youth in the previous generation:

> It must have been deadly: no cinema, no broadcasting: you had not even a motor car, nothing but a push bike. Then think of your dances...- no Tango, not a Foxtrot or Two-step...Those trailing skirts were the limit, and every morning you had to stick a couple of dozen hairpins in your hair. Poor mother! The shingle was hidden in the future...And if you wanted to smoke a cigarette it was in fear and trembling of being found out. (*Irish Times* 9 January 1926)

The mother retorted that she was happy in her youth and needed no sympathy from her daughter. Although short, this story is quite clever as it manages to encompass all the key elements of the 'modern girl' archetype – shingle, short dress, cigarettes, modern dances, cinema and motor cars. It also demonstrates, through her mother, nostalgia for the simpler lifestyle of the past. The piece represents the clash not only between the generations but also between modernity and traditions.

As well as the two national dailies, two of the provincial papers in this study had regular Women's Pages – the *Kerryman*'s 'Women's Chat' and the *Cork Examiner*'s 'Woman's World'. These concentrated mostly on fashion advice, reviewing the latest from Paris, London and Hollywood. There were also handy dress making patterns, advice on hair and skin care, diet and hobbies. There were also regular references to 'the modern girl', usually described in positive tones. However, what is particularly significant about both these two particular Women's Pages is that they were syndicated from England. All the reference points and examples were English, Ireland and Irish matters were never mentioned. In some ways this means that the Women's Pages of both the *Examiner* and the *Kerryman* are of little use in providing an insight into representations and debates on the modern girl/ flapper in the Irish Free State. The fashion, diet and hobbies features are not framed by Catholic or nationalist concerns for Irish traditional womanhood. But in my view, this adds to their appeal. Readers could gain information about the latest fashions, the newest hairstyles and the most up-to-date dance craze free from religious or traditionalist overtones. Hence these features are interesting because they provide a very different set of representations of the flapper than those usually propagated in the rest of the press. In this way, the Women's Pages begin to suggest some of the complexities and contradictions that underpinned images of the modern woman in the Irish press.

On 13 August 1927, the *Kerryman* carried a fashion report under the sensational heading 'Trousers for women'. Designers were refusing to shorten women's skirts any further despite the continuing pressures from women themselves. So in an attempt to solve the 'skirt length controversy' designers were proposing a compromise in the form of trousers which would look like 'plus fours' drawn into the leg well below the knee. Later that month, on 27 August 1927 'Women's Chat' again returned to the topic of women's reluctance to return to more constricting dress. Designers were reported to be making:

> considerable efforts to bring back the waist-line to its normal place but apparently nothing will induce women to look at boned corsets. These instruments of torture are being shown but as yet no one will buy anything more substantial than a band of woven silk elastic. (*Kerryman*, 27 August 1927)

According to Mica Nava (1995), there were many conflicting views about the consumer in the 1920s. As consumerism became increasingly feminised, opinions were divided about the powers of the consumer versus the powers of commercial and fashion industries. It is clearly apparent in the two articles cited above that the female consumer is being constructed as both powerful and as determined to get her own way. In both of these reports the designers are not presented as 'heathens' setting out to 'de-Christianise' women. Instead women are presented as assertive customers demanding the right to shorter and looser clothing than the designers would prefer. Such images stand in stark contrast to those propounded by the Catholic hierarchy and the traditionalists. These alternative constructions are particularly apparent in an article published in the *Kerryman* on 3 September 1927. Written by a 'London Physician', the article addresses clothing and good health:

> Most of you wear too many clothes; the girls have more sense than the men....Let the blessed air of Heaven get to the skin and keep it sweet and pure ...The ill-ventilated skin is never healthy. (*Kerryman*, 2 September 1927)

This is a rather unusual justification for the 'half-naked' fashions which so offended the Catholic bishops. The health of modern young women was again discussed in 'Women's Chat' on 24 September 1927 in a feature entitled 'Taller Women'. Citing research from the University of London it was reported that women were now on average 2 inches taller than 20 years previously:

> The fact that girls are taller, stronger and healthier than in times gone by is evidence that their present day, much criticised, modes of dress and habits of life are an altogether beneficial change from the old conditions which so restricted the activities and ambitions of women. (K*erryman*, 24 September 1927)

However, the Women's Pages were sensitive to the many criticisms made against the 'modern girl' and did not always attempt to justify them. On some occasions feature articles were critical of some of the excesses of modern life styles. On 15 June 1928, the *Cork Examiner*'s 'Woman's World' carried an article entitled 'When Girl's Smoke':

> The girl who smokes habitually is the exception who proves the rule. We hear a lot about the modern girl's cigarettes and cocktails; but it is merely a perverse desire to be ultramodern – really to shock the older people. (*Cork Examiner*, 15 June 1928)

For every girl who smokes, the article claims, six do not. Most modern girls realise that 'the cigarette habit can grow, and how, once formed, it can dull the complexion and teeth, besides staining the fingers'. The article concludes by saying that 'the majority of us prefer chocolates to 'fags' and so long as our men friends buy 'sweets for the sweet' we shall not ask for cigarettes'. Apart from the obvious attempt here to distinguish between the 'ultramodern', who border on the perverse, and the sweet modern girls, this article also situates the writer as a modern girl herself. This was common in the Women's Pages where features were frequently penned by 'A Modern Girl'. Thus both the reader and the writer are assumed to be modern girls and to share in a sense of what is acceptable, modern and fun. In that way, the Women's Pages adopt a chatty, friendly tone rather than an authoritative, judgmental tone. Only on rare occasions, like that cited above, is the ultramodern girl condemned for over indulgence in alcohol or cigarettes. The dominant image to emerge from these pages in the *Examiner* and the *Kerryman* is one of a healthy, clean, unrestricted, independent, happy modern girl. Her clothing, dancing, motoring, bobbed hair, confident, assertive personality all symbolised her vitality and independence. However, as discussed in the previous sections, it was precisely these features which represented her defiance and moral corruption in the eyes of religious leaders and traditionalists.

*Selling the Modern Girl:*

While the majority of provincial newspapers in this study did not have a 'women's page', that is not to imply that these papers represented a one-dimensional, monolithic, wholly negative view of the 'modern girl'. All the newspapers carried advertisements for fashion, films, dancehalls, motor cars and cigarettes that can be read as selling the modern life style. It was not uncommon for modern girls to be condemned on one page and then celebrated in advertisements on another page in the same newspaper. These tensions are apparent in relation to cigarettes.

On 28 July 1928 the *Sligo Champion* published a poem by regular contributor Randall McDonnell: 'The Girls of Sligo' (extract)

> ....So Free from Fashion Sway
> Dress Always in a Modest Way
>
> ....Unlike their sex in Dublin town
> They have no Tobacco tricks
>
> O the acme of perfection
> and the pink of etiquette
>
> Who ever met a Sligo Girl
> who smoked a cigarette.

This poem constructs Sligo girls as pure, modest and natural, untouched by modern fashions. They are very different from the women of Dublin City. It is questionable if young Sligo women would have found it quite so flattering to be described as unfashionable and most unlike city women. However, this urban/rural dichotomy draws upon the stereotypical image of the West of Ireland as representing the true source of native tradition (Nash 1993). But it is apparent that not every one shared such a viewpoint.

Just one week later on 4 August 1928, the *Sligo Champion* carried an advertisement for Gold Flake cigarettes, noting that they were Irish made (not foreign imports). The advertisement featured a bobbed haired modern girl playing tennis in a sleeveless, very short dress cut several inches above the knee. The image celebrated youth, health and vitality. Her clothing and cigarette symbolised her thorough modernity, her freedom and her enjoyment of pleasure. This image was very common not only in cigarette advertising but also in a wide array of products. The use of such an image to sell Irish made goods suggests the tensions between various interest groups within Irish society: the drive for commercial success versus the perceived threat to traditional order and authority. Regardless of the concerns expressed by the Catholic hierarchy, the female body was used to sell a range of diverse products. In some cases its link with the product in question was merely tangential. For example, on 28 August 1928, shortly after the debate in its letters' page about short skirts, the *Irish Independent* carried an advertisement for Lux soap. The drawing showed a woman wearing a fashionable cloche hat and a slim fitting knee-length dress on the golf links with a group of friends. She was delicately carrying a golf club in her hand. In the same month that it published the poem celebrating the traditional values of Sligo girls, the *Sligo Champion* carried a drawing of a young woman scantily clad in a swim suit – revealing her arms and legs – in the act of diving off a high board. The caption read 'prices dive deeper at our summer sale' this was for Henry Lyons + Co, Sligo (*Sligo Champion,* 7 July 1928).

Advertisements were aimed at the large cross section of the population. In accordance with the increasing feminisation of consumerism (Nava 1995), women were frequently targeted as consumers, not just for domestic essentials like washing powder but also for more luxury goods. On 31 March, the *Sligo Champion* carried a front-page ad. for the new Raleigh, all-steel bicycle accompanied by an image of a young woman in a knee-length dress riding the bike. Ladies' models were priced from £6, 9s. 6d. or 12s 3d on monthly payments. But women's mobility was apparently only limited by the size of their bank balances. On 23 June 1928, the *Champion* carried an advertisement for the Citroen car. The image portrayed a woman seated at the steering wheel while two fashionably dressed women stood outside chatting with her through the open window. One woman had her leg resting nonchalantly on the running board of the car. All three looked young, modern and relaxed. The car prices ranged from £220 to £295.

Car advertisements were frequently aimed at women, a fact that suggests women's growing financial independence in the 1920s-1930s (Daly 1995, Ryan 1998a+1998b). On 3 July 1926 the *Connacht Tribune* published an advertisement with the caption 'Ford Cars – Ladies First: it is the easiest car in the world to drive'. The image showed a woman laden with shopping about to climb into the driver's seat. On the following week, 10 July, the paper carried a similar ad for the 'greatly improved Ford – two seater' which cost £140. The image showed a young woman driving alone through open countryside, in the background was a thatched cottage that firmly located the scene in rural Ireland. But it wasn't just car manufacturers who aimed to capture the female market. On 2 October 1926, an advertisement appeared in the *Tribune* for Pratts petrol stations (owned by the Irish-American oil-company). The accompanying sketch showed a woman driving a car and the caption read:

> The discriminating lady motorist always runs on Pratts. She knows that Pratts will minimise engine trouble, give her easier running, a more comfortable sense of security and double the pleasure of her motoring.
> (*Connacht Tribune*, 2 October 1926)

This advertisement very deliberately appealed to the female consumer who was constructed as being very rational in her choice of petrol. Just as there was disagreement about whether or not women were powerful consumers, there were also diverse views about the extent to which women were rational or irrational consumers (Nava 1995). A woman chose Pratts petrol because it would minimise engine trouble – she was rational. However, she was also pleasure seeking. Pratts petrol would double the pleasure of her motoring. Again we see, in sharp contrast to the teaching of the Catholic Church, commercial interest groups directly appealing to notions of female pleasure in promoting their products. Thus the 'modern craze for pleasure' is not only recognised but also actively promoted.

Undoubtedly the products most explicitly aimed at women were clothes. All the newspapers in my study carried regular fashion advertisements. The accompanying drawings (rarely if ever photographs) portrayed the typical flapper fashions so despised by the religious leaders. Dresses were usually knee-length, and in summer frequently sleeveless, eveningwear in particular had necklines cut below the collarbone. The mannequins had bobbed hair, wore high-heeled shoes and displayed all the accessories of modern girls. For example, the *Connacht Tribune* regularly carried beautifully illustrated advertisements for the latest fashions at Moon's department store in Galway (25 September 1926, 30 June 1928). Even the *Limerick Leader*, a fervent supporter of the Irish-Ireland traditionalists, carried regular front-page fashion advertisements for the Limerick store La Moderne. On 19 March 1928, just two days after publishing a lenten pastoral castigating 'pagan influences' corrupting Irish girls (17 March), the front page of the *Leader* announced that La Moderne now had 'copies of the latest Paris models in most fashionable silks for Spring 1928'.

But to my mind one of the most interesting and incongruous aspects of the *Leader*'s advertisements related not so much to fashion as to that other great 'pagan influence' the cinema. Judging from the newspaper advertisements it would appear that three different films played in Limerick every week. Films were usually shown twice nightly at 7.00pm and at 9.00pm. The posters, reproduced in the newspaper, were very dramatic and often rather suggestive. For example, on 7 November 1928 the film 'Fire' was advertised featuring a semi-naked, semi-conscious May McAvoy being rescued by a fireman. The titles of the films often evoked contemporary images of fun and fashionable living, for example two films showing on 28 July 1928 'Jazz Mad' and 'Dance Magic'. These films were advertised just one week after a fiery sermon by Fr. Mangan appeared in the *Leader* in which he addressed the 'agents of Satan':

> the pictures in the cinema that night after night are working havoc on the souls of Catholic boys and girls....Pictures that are full of impure suggestions – that portray the lowest passions of men and women, that openly advocate immodesty and every manner of uncleaness. (*Limerick Leader*, 23 July 1928)

The 'impure' suggestions and low passions are made fairly explicit in the advertisement for one of the many desert romances of the '20s. On 29 October 1928 the *Leader* advertised Bebe Daniels starring in the film 'She's a Sheik':

> She loved a man who loved another, but she was used to having her way. She kidnaps him – takes him into the desert – and tames him. (*Limerick Leader*, 29 October 1928)

Newspapers are commercial enterprises that aim to cover their overheads and make a profit. In addition to maintaining their share of regular readers, they are also dependent on advertising. This meant that the newspapers were helping to publicise and sell a wide array of consumer goods and entertainment, while, at the same time, publishing the condemnatory outpourings of the Catholic church and traditionalists like the Gaelic League, Catholic Truth Society and the Modest Dress and Deportment Crusade. This incongruity within the press is very illuminating and suggests the many tensions and contradictions which underpinned Irish society. The conflicting images of the flapper or modern girl that emerge from these newspapers suggest the ways in which this archetypal female image came to represent both the positive and negative aspects of life in the 1920s. The fact that this controversial female image was as common in the provincial papers as in the national dailies is interesting and indicates the ways in which concerns for tradition, authority and national stability were played out in rural Ireland just as much as in the capital city.

*Conclusion:*

This section has argued that while the flapper of the twenties may appear to be a very general symbol, it is important to locate her within the cultural specificities of particular social contexts. Drawing on notions of gendered nationalist discourses, I have attempted to locate and analyse the flapper within the specific setting of the Irish Free State. Judging by the Irish provincial and national press, the flapper archetype was very powerful and pervasive throughout the twenty-six counties. The Catholic hierarchy in particular seemed to have been very attached to this female image and may have helped to enhance its notoriety. A wide range of signifiers distinguished the 'flapper/ modern girl' – her smoking, drinking, clothes, bobbed hair, motor cars, and her love of dancing and cinema. In different contexts any one or all of these features could be emphasised. The flexibility of this image meant that it could be applied to affluent, cocktail drinking sophisticats or to working class girls with a flare for fun. Without much need for further definition or clarification 'she' was used to represent sin, disorder, defiance and degeneracy. Such a useful symbol could not be left to dwell only in the metropolitan centres like Dublin or London. Thus, I argue, it is simplistic to locate the flapper within a narrowly defined urban/rural dichotomy that constructs 'urban' as essentially degenerate and 'rural' as essentially pure. 'Her' transition of this dichotomy suggests the complexities and contradictions faced by rural Ireland in the early decades of independence. The flapper's existence in local, rural communities demonstrated that the threats of modern excesses and the 'craze for pleasure' were everywhere; evil, sin and temptation were all around us. By giving into her lust for pleasure, amusement and sinful excess, the modern girl embodied the fate of all sinners and served as an exemplar to all young Irish girls about the evils that waited to ensnare them.

However, it is also apparent in the provincial, as well as in the national, press that while the image of the modern girl was widely shared, interpretations of her varied somewhat. In particular sections of the papers, for example cinema posters, fashion features, car and cigarette advertisements, women's pages, etc, the modern girl appeared as a very desirable image. Her youth, flare for amusement, loosely fitted clothing, health and vitality all symbolised freedom and independence. In addition, as a young woman without dependants, frequently employed in paid work, she represented the ultimate consumer of luxury goods – clothes, cosmetics, accessories. Therefore, the flapper embodied the tensions between, on the one hand, cultural nationalists and the Catholic church working to minimise foreign tastes and fashions and, on the other hand, commercial interests and popular consumer demand which continued to promote and enjoy them.

In both of these conflicting sets of images the modern girl is defined by a break with traditional femininity. Her clothes and lifestyle are very different from her mother's generation. But her defiance of traditional mores can be interpreted either as liberating and freeing or corrupting and enslaving. The qualities that made her so appealing to advertisers and filmmakers made her an anathema to cultural nationalists and the Catholic Church. Constructed in opposition to the goodness and purity of the 'Irish cailín', the good wife and mother of future generations, the transmitter of Irish cultural and religious values, the modern girl symbolised threats to national culture, national identity and ultimately to national stability. In her Parisian short skirts and Eton bobbed hair, she visibly embodied all the dangers of foreign influences on the delicate and fragile essence of Irish womanhood and hence the newly established Irish Free State.

# Section 2: Reach for the Skies: Adventurous women and the Irish press

*Introduction:*

1928 was a remarkable year for several reasons. In some ways it represented the peak of the 'roaring twenties'. It embodied the spirit of thrills and adventure. Coming just before the stock market crash of 1929 and the ensuing international depression of the 1930s, 1928 was a year of optimism when the future seemed to hold endless possibilities and the sky was, literally, the limit. In April of that year, the Irish Free State discovered its own dashing, adventurous hero, a man who gained international recognition and helped to put the fledgling nation-state on the world map. Major, soon to be promoted to Colonel, James Fitzmaurice joined the growing numbers of pioneering aviators who set out in the 1920s to conquer the skies, engaging in dangerous rivalries to set new records of speed, height and distance. Fitzmaurice set out from an airfield near Dublin along with two German airmen to fly east to west across the Atlantic Ocean in the Breman aircraft. It has been suggested that the two Germans, fearing a cool reception in the USA, invited the dashing young Irish pilot to join their expedition in the knowledge that he would be very popular with the American people (Byrne 1980). The three men had initially planned to land in mainland USA but were forced to come down on Greenly Island off the coast of Canada. After several days, with the eyes of the international press corps upon them, the men abandoned their attempts to take off from Greenly. However, they had crossed the Atlantic and so were deemed heroes, receiving rapturous welcomes in cities across America. When they arrived back in Ireland they were the heroes of the hour.

The *Irish Independent* on 4 July 1928 reported that Fitzmaurice and his two German companions finally arrived back in Dublin. There were several photographs of the vast crowds who thronged the streets of the capital to welcome them back. These amazing scenes suggest the extent to which the aviators had captured the public imagination, helped in no small part by the regular coverage of their adventures in both national and local newspapers. The *Independent* devoted an editorial to the subject:

> Our hearts have always gone out to the men of our race who have kept alive the spirit of romantic adventure. Major Fitzmaurice...has illuminated a new world of enterprise and opportunity....It is for Ireland, especially young Ireland, to see to it that the new impulse is developed along lines that will be worthy of the Fitzmaurice tradition. (*Irish Independent*, 4 July 1928)

Fitzmaurice continued to work for the promotion of the aviation industry in Ireland arguing that the country's location on the Atlantic seaboard made it ideally suited for the trans-Atlantic passenger services which were inevitable in the future. The tall, good looking, army man, frequently photographed with his lovely wife and their photogenic little daughter Patricia, embodied all that was modern, courageous and successful in the new nation. The 'Irish Lindbergh' had been discovered and duly instated as a national hero. However, he became disillusioned with the lack of government support for aviation and spent much of his life in the USA. Returning to Ireland toward the end of his life, he lived in poor circumstances but received a hero's funeral when he died in 1965 (Byrne 1980).

But men did not have a monopoly on aviation. In fact, the 1920s saw a large number of female pilots who set out to equal if not surpass the records and successes of men. In June 1928, the young American, Amelia Earhart, accompanied by two male pilots became the first woman to successfully cross the Altantic. Several women had died attempting the dangerous journey. There was some disappointment that Earhart did not land in Ireland as had been initially planned but instead flew on to Britain. Nevertheless, she received pages of coverage in the Irish press.

On 5 June 1928, under the headline 'Atlantic Flight: Lady to Make Attempt Today', the *Independent* reported that Miss Amelia Earhart of Boston was to attempt to become the first woman to fly across the Atlantic. In describing this young adventurer, the paper informed its readers that she was 'feminine to her finger tips'. But Miss Earhart was not the only woman in pursuit of this coveted achievement. On 8 June the paper reported that two other women, the American Miss Mabel Boll and the German Miss Rasche, were also making preparations to fly the Atlantic. Thus a sense of excitement and tension was built up over several days as various rivals entered and dropped out of contention.

The risks involved in undertaking these long distance, hazardous flights were brought home to the reader throughout June 1928 with daily reports of the search for the airship 'Italia' which had been lost in its attempt to fly over the North Pole. On 11 June, the *Independent* reported that, after an eighteen-day search, radio contact had finally been made with the crew of the airship. However, on 14 June a lengthy feature described how the surviving members of the ill-fated crew were still stranded on the ice, as no ship was able to reach them. The dramatic nature of these reports can be gauged by the following quote: 'The wind howls its fury over the dreary wastes. Help is coming, nearer, nearer....It is a race for life, a race with Death' (*Irish Independent*, 14 June 1928). It was not until over one week later on 21 June that the discovery of the missing adventurers, led by the Italian General Nobile, was eventually reported. Several men died in this expedition, including some of those who had gone to rescue the crew of the 'Italia'. The regular reports in the *Independent* created a sense of anxiety; keeping the Irish reader well informed of all the dramatic twists and turns of this rather bizarre episode in aviation history. The story of the 'Italia' coincided with the Atlantic crossing of Amelia Earhart.

On 19 June, the *Independent* carried the banner headline 'I am the Proudest Woman in the World: Miss Earhart first woman to succeed'. The plane had taken off in Newfoundland, Canada, and landed safely in Wales. An entire page was devoted to the trans-Atlantic flight, there were several pictures of Miss Earhart and the seaplane 'Friendship'. Although Earhart had not actually flown the plane, the pilots were both men, and she was in effect merely a passenger, this in no way diminished the excitement of her being the first woman to cross the Atlantic in a plane. However, as she had not flown the plane, the focus of press attention was on her appearance and personality rather than her abilities as an aviator, although she was by this time an accomplished pilot. It is interesting to note that her male companions were virtually ignored in the newspaper reports. 'Bobbed hair and a bandeau' was the subheading of the *Irish Independent* report on 19 June. It described Earhart as a 'slip of courageous girlhood':

> Her bobbed hair was swathed in a brightly hued bandeau, and she was wearing breeches, stout leather boots and a long woollen coat with a fur collar. (*Irish Independent*, 19 June 1928)

In the 1920s, women's wearing of trousers proved very controversial. However, despite her masculine attire and her success in a very masculine world, Earhart's femininity was reassuringly underlined by the press reports. She was depicted as 'shy' and reluctant to have her photograph taken. But she was also described as 'giving a truly feminine touch to her hair'. Her smile was reported to be 'captivating'. Over the next few days she received several column inches and there were numerous photographs of her in the *Independent*. But, as we will see below, Earhart was to have an even more dramatic impact on Ireland and the Irish fascination with aviation in the early 1930s.

However, not all newspapers approved of women's participation in the dangerous sport of flying. On 31 March 1928, the Galway-based *Connacht Tribune* devoted an editorial to the topic of aviation under the heading 'Adventure and Progress'. This acknowledged the great strides that had been made in recent years, 'under the stress of the necessity of the Great War, the art of flying made the span within a few brief and crowded years of a whole generation of progress'. In reference to planned attempts to fly across the Atlantic from east to west the editorial stated: 'Up to now the pioneers in the adventure – a goodly band of brave men and foolish women – have perished somewhere in the waste of waters'. These wealthy, 'titled ladies seeking notoriety' had paid pilots to take them in their planes:

> The history of humanity is the history of brave pioneers going forth to achieve death or deathless glory...in these adventures man is always the pioneer. He is only accompanied by the woman as his helpmate when the exigencies of the case demand that he shall take her with him. As civilisation has developed, the woman has disappeared as a pioneering unit in the forward march. Her part is the no less heroic one of watching and waiting and it seems fitting that it should be so, and that her natural protector and guardian should go forth upon such hazardous adventures accompanied only by members of his own sex. (*Connacht Tribune*, 31 March 1928)

### *Lady Heath takes to the Air:*

Nevertheless, it is apparent that not everyone shared this point of view. If Ireland had found its own version of Lindbergh, it did not have far to look to find its own version of Earhart. However, unlike the dashing and rather wholesome Fitzmaurice, the 'famous Irishwoman aviator' was a far more ambiguous and controversial character. Lady Heath received constant attention in the Irish press; she embodied courage, determination and international success but she also embodied many of the qualities of the modern flapper and challenged traditional notions of Irish womanhood. On 2 April 1928, the *Cork Examiner* carried a short report from Reuters at Khartoum that the 'British airwoman', Lady Heath, was flying the length of the African continent from the Cape to Cairo and on to England. Clearly in the eyes of the Reuter's reporter she was a British woman and the *Ex-*

*aminer* did not contradict this statement. But the ambiguity of her identity was made clear in a short progress report published on 16 April. While the headline boldly states 'Irishwoman's Mediterranean Flight', the Reuter's reporter at Cairo said that 'the British airwoman took off here at 6 o'clock this morning'. Meanwhile her identity was further defined in a *Limerick Leader* article on the same day (16 April) which was headed 'Famous Limerick Airwoman'. The *Leader* had provided clarification of her identity in an article printed on 3 March 1928 also under the headline 'Famous Limerick Airwoman'. That article stated that she was born at Knockaderry House, near Newcastle West, Co. Limerick. This established her not merely as Irish but as a Limerick woman. In fact, she was born Sophie Mary Pierce Evans on 1896. Her many name changes reflect her many marriages. Her first marriage was to Mr. Elliott-Lynn and she was widowed at a young age (Lomax 1986). She was briefly married to Lord Heath and later married G.A. Williams (Byrne 1980).

On 17 May 1928, the *Irish Independent* carried the headline 'Irish Airwoman's Great Flight'. Having flown to Paris, Lady Heath was now on the last leg of her 10,000-mile solo flight from Cape Town to London. She was the first woman to fly the length of Africa. On the following day (18 May), the *Independent* reported 'Her Triumph' as she arrived in London. The image which emerges is one a very relaxed, stylish, fashion-conscious, young woman. The article reported that she ate chocolates and read a novel while flying and also managed to put on a pair of silk stockings while in mid-air. She added that it was possible for a 'lady' to apply face powder while flying a plane. Also reporting on her arrival at Croydon aerodrome, the *Kerryman* newspaper carried the headline 'Irish Airwoman's Triumph'. The article stated that prior to marrying Lord Heath, she was Mrs. Elliott-Lynn of Co. Limerick. In describing her physical appearance as she stepped out of her plane, the paper stated she was 'dressed for an afternoon call instead of the usual leather flying coat and helmet'.

In fact, the *Kerryman* had reported her marriage in the previous year:

> Mrs. Elliott-Lynn, the world's most famous airwoman, who is a native of Co. Limerick, was married to Sir James Heath, the wealthy iron master and colliery-owner, who is 75....Mrs. Elliott-Lynn, who is 30, was the first woman to loop the loop in an aeroplane, and the first to obtain a certificate entitling her to carry passengers. (15 October 1927)

In marrying a man 45 years her senior, she acquired a title and access to a significant fortune. Though, as was revealed later, her new husband was not prepared to finance all her flying expenses. On 17 November 1928, the *Independent* reported that Lady Heath was currently on a lecture tour in the USA. Her husband, 76 year old Lord Heath had publicly disclaimed any responsibility for her debts. The article also added that before she became a pilot, Lady Heath had been a successful athlete and held the world record for the high jump and for the javelin.

Sophie Pierce Evans was a complex woman. As 'a militant advocate of both women's rights and aviation' (Lomax 1986: 37), she campaigned for women's right to participate in various events in the Olympic games as well as for women's right to work as commercial pilots. In her tireless efforts to champion women's aviation she courted publicity and undertook a number of 'dare-devil stunts'. This earned her the nick-name 'Lady Hell of a Din' (Boase 1979: 47).

The glamorous aviator seems an unlikely choice as Irish heroine. Although she had been educated in Ireland, attaining a degree from an Irish university, she lived most of her life abroad, travelling extensively in Africa. In fact, she is usually referred to as a British woman by aviation historians (see for example, Boase 1979, Lomax 1986). Visibly embracing modernity and exotic modern lifestyles, she bore none of the hallmarks of traditional Irish femininity. But her appeal no doubt lay in her consistent achievements. The *Cork Examiner* once referred to 'Our Airwoman' as 'one of the most consistently successful and courageous of today's great fliers' (Editorial 30 August 1928).

On 11 July, the *Independent* reported that she had set a new altitude record at Rochester in England, achieving a height of more than two miles above ground level. This tireless adventurer was again in the news just two weeks later when she piloted a commercial flight from Holland to London with 15 passengers on board. The headline 'Irish Airwoman Leads the Way' indicates the sense of national pride in this intrepid young woman. The article reported that she was believed to be the first woman to pilot a commercial passenger flight. 'Lady Heath wore a neat brown costume, a leopard skin coat and a flying helmet' (*Irish Independent* 28 July 1928). Clearly, Lady Heath was a woman who thrived on danger and new challenges. On 5 October, the *Independent* reported that she had more than doubled her previous altitude record, attaining a height of over four miles above ground level flying alone in her Cirrus Moth plane. She cheerfully reported that she could have gone higher but her goggles froze and her engine cut out at 23,000 feet. This report was also carried in the *Limerick Leader* on 6 October.

In August 1928, Lady Heath confirmed her place in the Irish popular imagination by paying a visit to Ireland and flying around the countryside much to the amazement and awe of her many onlookers and admirers. On 24 August, the *Independent* reported that Lady Heath, flying her Moth aeroplane to Dublin, was forced to land on a golf links due to low cloud. She donated £600 to the newly formed Irish Aero Club so that scholarships could be given to student pilots including women. The photo depicted Lady Heath swinging the propeller of her plane surrounded by a group of curious on-lookers. A few days later on 1 September, the *Connacht Tribune*, despite its earlier misgivings about women pilots, reported that the 'Irish airwoman' had flown into Galway. On 8 September, the *Tribune* carried a photograph of Lady Heath in the western village of Claddagh. Dressed in her famous, knee-length leopard skin coat and wearing white stockings, Lady Heath embodied fashionable, adventurous modernity which seemed very incongruously situated beside a white-washed, thatched cottage, surrounded by women wearing traditional shawls and long skirts who seemed to embody tradition, heritage and links with the past.

An account of her journey in the west of Ireland was given more coverage in the *Connacht Sentinel* on 4 September, under the heading 'Pretty Thrilling'. On route to Galway, Lady Heath had landed her plane on a beach in Co. Mayo and subsequently got stuck in quicksand. Several local farmers and fishermen came to her rescue and it appears to have caused a local sensation. The unflappable Lady Heath seemed to have been completely undisturbed by the incident and, after minor repairs to the plane, continued her journey.

Her flying tour of Ireland was well reported in all the local papers. For example, the *Kerryman* reported with a sense of pride that while she had flown over her birthplace of Newcastle West, she had not landed there but instead proceeded to Kerry where she visited relatives (1 September 1928). The *Kerryman* referred to her as 'the courageous young airwoman'. Meanwhile, the *Limerick Leader* concentrated not on her failure to land in her birth county but instead quoted her in an editorial on being proud to be Irish. The editorial cited her as saying that Irish people should 'not forget that the fact of being Irish and of doing things a little differently from other people, was the greatest asset they had'. The editorial continued by stating that:

> a nation without sound patriotic instincts cannot have self-esteem, self-confidence or legitimate pride of race, and in the absence of these a country cannot possibly have the grit to make its mark in any direction.
> (*Limerick Leader*, 1 September 1928)

This editorial is interesting when considered along side the photograph of Lady Heath in Claddagh village (*Connacht Tribune*, 8 September 1928). As has been discussed earlier in relation to Aonach Tailteann, there was a strong interest in retaining and even strengthening the nation's links with the past. From past glories and traditions would come the sense of a unique national identity that represented Irish cultural distinctiveness, and political independence, from Britain. Female allegories, such as Queen Tailte, were frequently used to represent the past. As discussed in the earlier part of this chapter, young women who embraced modern fashions, lifestyles and morality were deemed disloyal to their culture and hence represented a potentially destabilising influence within the nation. However, it would be overly simplistic to construct a 'modernity versus tradition' dichotomy which inscribed women in narrow and one-dimensional roles. Lady Heath embodied many of the complexities around modernity, progress and technical advancement. In one way, as a modern, fashionable, fast living, young woman she epitomised all that was 'wrong' with the younger generation. In another way, she symbolised daring, courage and represented the future success of the Irish Free State in the international arena of commercial aviation. Nowhere were these contradictions made clearer than in the *Connacht Tribune*. In March 1928, the editorial of this paper had castigated women aviators. However, in an editorial on 29 September of the same year, it presented a completely contradictory view. This change of heart appears to have been prompted largely by Lady Heath who:

> has achieved excellent pioneering work for air services in the west of Ireland. The intrepid Irishwoman demonstrated that, equipped only with a light comparatively cheap Baby Moth 'plane, it is possible to fly all over Connacht, and, notwithstanding the natural ruggedness of the general terrain, always to remain within easy reach of a suitable landing place. (*Connacht Tribune*, 29 September 1928)

This editorial formed part of the on-going campaign to promote civil aviation in the Free State in general and, in particular, to build an airport in Galway. The *Connacht Tribune* frequently represented Galway as the most ideal site for a trans-Atlantic airport. Galway was the natural gateway to the USA. These facilities were vital if 'we are to keep abreast of modern progress' (29 September 1928).

As adventurers and highly successful aviators Lady Heath and Colonel Fitzmaurice represented the spirit of the twenties. In addition, as Irish people they represented the hopes and aspirations of those who wished the Free State to embrace modern technology and economic prosperity while simultaneously asserting a pride in the cultural distinctiveness of being Irish. Like the Olympic gold medalist Dr. O'Callaghan, they achieved recognition and won praise abroad, thus helping to locate the Free State in an international arena. While this was more complex in relation to Lady Heath who was frequently described as British rather than Irish, nonetheless, the Irish press took every opportunity to clarify her origins. Her birthplace in county Limerick was repeatedly mentioned as if to reaffirm her Irishness. Thus this short case study of Lady Heath suggests the complexity and fluidity of national identity as it moves across national boundaries.

*Difficult Feats of High Adventure:*

While the 1920s may be represented as the period of adventure, youthful recklessness and the frenzied pursuit of excitement, the 1930s are often represented as a more bleak and depressing decade. In the wake of the Wall Street crash and the ensuing global economic slump, culminating in the rise of totalitarian regimes, the 1930s frequently appear drab, lifeless and colourless in comparison to the glamour of the previous decade. For example, as Billie Melman has commented, in the austerity of the 1930s, images of fashionable, frivolous flappers began to fade from the press and public discourse (1988). However, Melman also warns against a simplistic dichotomy between the 1920s and 1930s as if the two decades had easily discernible and completely distinct personalities. She claims that there were several continuities of images and debates across the period from the late '20s to the early '30s. Although Melman was writing largely about the British situation, I think that her warning could also be applied to the Irish case. Clearly there is much that separates the 1920s and 1930s in Ireland. The change of government from Cumann na nGaedheal to Fianna Fail led to a dramatic change in economic policy with severe consequences. The rise of dictators and the gathering war clouds across Europe were ominous signs for the future. At a socio-cultural level there were marked changes in entertainment with the increasing popularity of 'talkie' films and the increasing availability of radio sets (Brown 1987). Developments in fashion brought very visible changes in women's physical appearance. The bobbed haired and boyish styles of the 1920s were replaced with the softer, more feminine styles of high waists and longer hemlines. Nevertheless, many of the concerns of the 1920s, the spirit of adventure and the pursuit of new thrills, continued well into the 1930s. This continuity is very visibly represented by the aviation achievements of Amelia Earhart.

On 20 May 1932, under the somewhat familiar headline 'Woman's Atlantic Flight', the *Irish Independent* reported that Miss Earhart, now Mrs. Putnam, had left the USA in her attempt to become the first woman to fly solo across the Atlantic. The short article reminded readers that she had been a passenger on a previously successful crossing of the Atlantic. Her current venture was being financed by her husband, a wealthy publisher. Earhart's intention was to replicate Lindbergh's historic flight on the fifth anniversary of his successful landing in France. However, a few days later on 23 May 1932, the *Independent* announced in banner headlines that Miss Earhart had been blown off course in a storm and had, in fact, landed in Co. Derry. Ironically, it had been widely hoped that her first successful crossing of the Atlantic in 1928 would land in Ireland instead of Wales and now, four years later, here she was landing in Ireland, albeit by accident rather than design. The *Independent* devoted all of page 7, the world news page, to her achievement under the telling headline 'Historic Ocean Flight ends in Ireland': there were several photos of Earhart, her plane and surprised local residents of a small village outside Derry city. The eyes of the world's press were on Ireland now as photographers and reporters as well as local dignitaries rushed to meet the famous airwoman.

The *Independent* which had achieved something of a scoop by having Earhart land on its doorstep, so to speak, proudly boasted that not only was she the first woman to fly solo across the Atlantic but she was the only person to have flown over the Atlantic twice. The lengthy report quoted Earhart as saying 'I had often heard of Irish hospitality, but the reception given me exceeded all by expectations'. She described the difficulties encountered on her hazardous journey. Apart from the storm that blew her off course, she also discovered that her fuel tank was leaking and it was this fact that prevented her from making any further efforts to fly on toward France. But true to her previous form, Earhart again made light of her achievements. 'I just did this flight for fun'. She added: 'Don't you think my husband is a good sport? He does not interfere in my flying and I do not interfere in his affairs.' The *Independent* also reprinted the contents of a telegram sent to Earhart by President Hoover:

> You have demonstrated not only your own dauntless courage, but also the capability of women to match the skill of men in carrying through the most difficult feats of high adventure.(*Irish Independent*, 23 May 1932)

Unlike the previous reports of 1928, there was little or no mention of Earhart's clothes or personal characteristics. These press reports present her as a serious and accomplished pilot. This change in reporting may be partly due to the fact that while she was a passenger on the flight and something of a novelty in 1928, by 1932 she had asserted her true capabilities as a pilot who deserved to be taken seriously. In addition, it is possible that there was an Irish dimension to this change in reporting. The fact that Earhart had landed in Ireland, albeit in the North rather than in the Free State, may have influenced the *Independent* in emphasising the enormity of her achievement rather than the style of her clothing or the charm of her smile. The *Independent* continued to show a keen interest in Earhart's success. On 26 August 1932 it reported her 'new record':

> Miss Amelia Earhart (Mrs. G. Putnam) the first woman to fly the Atlantic alone from West to East (she landed in Co. Derry) completed yesterday the first non-stop flight across the American continent by a woman. (*Irish Independent*, 26 August 1932)

She flew from Los Angeles to Newark in a time of 19 hours and 2 minutes. It is noteworthy that even in this short paragraph the *Independent* took the opportunity to remind readers that Earhart's historic solo flight had landed in Co. Derry. It is interesting that the paper repeatedly refers to the location as Co. Derry not Northern Ireland and certainly not Londonderry. Referring to the place as 'Co. Derry' suggested that this was part of the island of Ireland rather than part of the United Kingdom.

But by August 1932, the Free State had another aviation hero to celebrate. On 11 July 1932 the *Independent* announced that Amy Johnson and her fiancé James Mollison had flown into Baldonnel airport in Dublin. They were looking for a suitable location to commence a trans-Atlantic flight. This flight, to be undertaken by Mollison alone, would be unique in that he planned to fly to America and back again to Europe in a matter of days. In early August, Mollison and Johnson who had recently married and spent their honeymoon on a flying holiday, returned to Dublin to prepare for the mammoth crossing of the Atlantic in both directions. Finally on 19 August, after several weeks of preparations, the *Independent* reported that Mollison had flown off from Portmarnock beach in Co. Dublin. The entire photo page was given over to pictures of his plane on the beach and the anxious crowds who came to watch the spectacle. Amy Johnson was prominently featured in the photos. One picture showed Mollison and his new wife formally shaking hands as he was about to board his plane.

The following day the *Independent* carried lengthy reports on Mollison's flight and news of his safe arrival in Canada after a 30 hour journey. Although he had originally planned to fly to New York, he eventually gave up on that idea and decided to travel by land before commencing his return flight across the Atlantic.

Once arriving in New York, he immediately began to prepare for his next flight. In fact, on 24 August the *Independent* reported that he had taken off from New York. However, over the next few days he met with several delays caused primarily by poor weather conditions.

Nevertheless, he continued to be extremely newsworthy, with daily reports on his progress. On 26 August, the *Independent* reported that he was 'held up by weather' but added a new dimension to the story. It seemed that Mollison was becoming embroiled in a controversy about his wife's flying career. It was reported that he had prevented her from trying to fly across the Atlantic from East to West, something which no woman had done. Amy Johnson was reported as saying: 'It has been my ambition to fly the Atlantic ever since I started my flying career...I know my husband is dead against the idea, but I don't take his decision as final. I shall talk the matter over fully with him, and do my best to persuade him to let me make the attempt. If he definitely says no I shall fall in with his decision' (*Irish Independent*, 26 August 1932).

This story was reported on the same day and in the same column as the account of Earhart's successful flight across the American continent. The interesting juxtaposition of these stories about two famous women aviators not only emphasises the prominent role which women played in early aviation history, but also serves to highlight the different circumstances which framed these women's opportunities to fly. While Earhart's husband not only supported but also funded her dare-devil adventures, Johnson's husband refused her permission to undertake a record making flight. Rather like Lady Heath, whose wealthy husband publicly refused to honour her debts, female dependency on the support and finances of husbands framed the activities of even the most famous and adventurous of women.

On 1 September 1932, the *Independent* reported that James Mollison, after several failed attempts to begin his return flight across the Atlantic, finally agreed to give into the wishes of friends and advisors and abandon all hopes of completing the second leg of his record making flight. He agreed to return to England by boat. The fact that Mollison was forced, despite all his best efforts, to abandon his return flight highlights the unreliable nature of trans-Atlantic flight. Like Earhart who was aiming for France and ended up in Co. Derry, Mollison had not been successful in flying from Portmarnock to New York, being forced to land in Canada. Even in 1932 it was virtually impossible to predict where a flyer would successfully land. So long as it remained dangerous and unpredictable, flying was exciting and adventurous, but any hopes of a commercially viable and reliable trans-Atlantic service must have seemed a very long way off.

In the late 1930s the fascination with flight had not diminished even though it was now becoming much more common place. The quest for new records and new achievements continued right up to the end of the decade. In 1936 three women aviators made newspaper headlines in the Irish Free State. In May of that year Amy Johnson, now known as Mrs. Mollison, made a successful attempt on the record for flying from London to the South African Cape. Her achievement was given widespread coverage in the Irish press. On 8 May, the *Cork Examiner* carried the report 'London to Cape: Successful Trip by Mrs. Mollison'. Hailing the journey as 'one of the most outstanding of her achievements', the report claimed that she had now been established as 'Britain's premier airwoman'. The article praised her 'power of endurance and navigational ability'. A similar report was carried in the *Irish Independent* under the eye-catching headline 'Amy's Fine Feat' (8 May 1936). Knocking twelve hours off the existing record held by Tommy Rose, she made the journey in three days, six hours and twenty-six minutes. But clearly Amy Mollison was not satisfied with that achievement. On 16 May, the *Irish Press* reported that 'Mrs. Mollison takes three records'. On arriving back in London she had successfully achieved record times for the London to

Cape journey, the Cape to London journey and the combined return trip. The article reported that she was 'mobbed' by a 'vast crowd' at Croydon aerodrome.

The second woman to fly her way into the record books in 1936 was Beryl Markham. On 5 September 1936, the *Irish Press* reported that Mrs. Markham 'English society woman, and mother of a son of seven' had left England in her attempt to fly solo across the Atlantic from East to West, a feat that had never been accomplished by a woman. She was described as 33 years of age and 'plucky'. The *Cork Examiner* also described her as 'an English society woman' (5 September). Both reports stated that she had begun her flying career in Kenya. In fact, Beryl Markham had grown up and lived for much of her life in Kenya. It was there that she learned to fly and enjoyed a successful if rather hazardous career as a pilot (Markham 1988). The depiction of her as 'an English society woman' simplified her background and underestimated her flying achievements. The report in the *Irish Independent* also stated that she was 33 years old and had a young son. However, it described her as 'an experienced pilot' who was 'making her daring bid in a Percival Gull machine'. The *Independent* carried a photo of Mrs. Markham with her friends Mr. and Mrs. Mollison (5 September 1936).

Two days later, on 7 September, all three papers carried very detailed reports of Markham's successful arrival on the other side of the Atlantic. Although she had been forced to land off course in Nova Scotia, she had become the first woman to fly from East to West across the Atlantic. The *Cork Examiner* reported:

> Clad in a shirt and grey flannel trousers, Mrs. Markham arrived at her hotel in a car bedecked with Union Jacks and surrounded by a police escort. An eager crowd cheered...She had no hat and no luggage. A strip of adhesive plaster on her forehead was the only evidence of the injuries she sustained in the forced landing. (*Cork Examiner*, 7 September 1936)

In its report 'Atlantic Heroine', the *Irish Press* also commented on her style of dress – 'the tall slim airwoman, in her open necked man's blue shirt and grey trousers' (7 September). Meanwhile the *Independent* carried the headline 'New York's Great Welcome – Air Heroine's Arrival'. The paper reported that Beryl Markham was the first woman to fly solo across the Atlantic from East to West, Amy Mollison had made the journey with her husband in 1933. Markham had completed the 1,900 miles in 18 hours and 5 minutes. On arrival in New York she was greeted by 'cheering thousands' and given an official reception by Mayor La Guardia (7 September 1936).

The following month, October 1936, saw a third woman aviator making her name in the press. Jean Batten, a 26 year old New Zealander, beat the record previously held by Mr. Broadbent by flying solo from England to Australia (*Irish Independent*, 12 October). On 17 October, the *Independent* reported that Miss Batten had now arrived in New Zealand, thus setting a new record as the first person to fly solo from England to New Zealand.

The newspapers' fascination with the heroines of the air is reflected not only in the many detailed reports of their flying achievements but also in the attention paid to their private lives. Clearly, these women were the international superstars of this period. On 21 October 1936, the *Irish Press* reported that Amy Mollison was to part from her husband after their four-year marriage. She would henceforth be known by her maiden name – Amy Johnson. However, the drama between the Mollisons continued to prove newsworthy when James Mollison attempted to beat the record set by his wife in the journey from London to the South African Cape in December 1936. But, as the *Irish Press* reported, his plane went off course in bad weather and he failed to beat her record (3 December 1936). The competition to set records between Mr. and Mrs. Mollison, and between Miss Batten and Mr. Broadbent were, in effect, very exciting high-altitude battles of the sexes and made fascinating newspaper stories.

In its special feature, 'Outstanding Incidents of the Year', the *Cork Examiner* recalled some of the most significant events and personalities of 1936 by reprinting a two page spread of photographs. It is noteworthy that only three women were pictured. All three were aviators – Amy Johnson, Beryl Markham and Jean Batten (31 December 1936). This suggests the impact of women aviators not just in the year 1936 but throughout the 1920s-1930s. In a period of great adventures and daring heroes, these women were exceptional. The enthusiasm generated by their flying achievements extended from the streets of New York city, to Croydon aerodrome, to remote farms in Co. Derry. They wore unusual clothes; these were among the very few women ever photographed in daily newspapers wearing trousers, long leather coats and men's shirts. They lived dangerous, exciting lives. They travelled widely at incredible speeds. They seemed unflappable even in the face of great danger and physical hardships. These young women embodied the modern spirit of adventure and the modern optimism that anything was possible.

The great interest in flying adventures spanned the generations and the social classes of Irish society. Even the president was not immune. When Colonel Charles Lindbergh arrived in Ireland in 1936, one of his most enthusiastic passengers was Eamon de Valera. The *Cork Examiner* carried a photograph of the president, wearing a flying suit, climbing a little awkwardly into Lindbergh's plane (25 November 1936).

In 1937 the dangers of flying, particularly the hazardous, record-breaking flying undertaken by adventurous young men and women, were underlined by the news that Amelia Earhart was missing. On 6 July 1937, the *Irish Independent* reported that Miss Earhart and her navigator Captain Noonan, who were attempting to fly around the world, had lost radio contact. 'The greatest rescue expedition in the history of flying has been mobilised to comb the Pacific for Miss Earhart and her companion'. 57 fighter planes, a battleship, 4 destroyers and an aircraft carrier all took part in the search. This report not only highlights the shared sense of concern and urgency in the search to locate the missing airwoman, but also the extent to which aviation had developed in leaps and bounds over the last twenty years. The fact that an aircraft carrier and 57 fighter planes were involved in the search indicates the extent to which flight had become militarised. Beyond its potential for commercial commuter transport, aviation was being rapidly developed for the purposes of waging war. Perhaps the age of the spirited adventurer was coming to a close, the death of Miss Earhart one of the most famous adventurers, signalled the end of an era. There were daily reports of the continuing search for Earhart and Noonan. But after two weeks, on 20 July 1937, the *Independent* reported that 'Earhart Search Ends'. The lengthy report reminded the reader of her many great achievements. She was the first woman to fly the Atlantic in 1928. She became the first woman to fly alone across the Atlantic from West to East when she famously landed in near Derry in 1932. She was the first woman to fly across the American continent and she made a record flight across the Pacific in 1935. She was the first woman to fly solo from Hawaii to California. Earhart was 37 years old.

*Conclusion:*

The story of fearless aviators, especially trans-Atlantic ones, is very relevant to an analysis of the early decades of the Irish Free State. As this chapter has shown, in both the 1920s and 1930s, Ireland was involved directly and indirectly in several spectacular successes. Apart from Earhart who landed in Ireland, and Mollison who took off from Ireland, Irish people like Colonel Fitzmaurice and Lady Heath flew themselves into the record books. While their record time, speed, altitude and distance could all be easily beaten, their achievement in being 'the first' to successfully undertake hazardous journeys could never be undone. The media pre-occupation with flight did not limit itself to stories involving Irish people or involving Ireland. All pioneers were given generous coverage. But why was this the case? Firstly, it is explained by the general excitement of the period, science and new discoveries enabled men and women to undertake daring new challenges, and these sensational stories made excellent newspaper copy. Secondly, these adventurers were celebrities, though the celebrity won by people like Colonel Lindbergh brought its own tragedies. Earhart and Lindbergh were household names. When Earhart landed in a field in Co. Derry she was instantly recognised by local people who were familiar with her photograph in newspapers. Thirdly, the Irish Free State was a small, poor, fledgling nation on the edge of the European continent. Locating itself at the centre of aviation history provided a sense of importance and pride in the close association with so many great achievements and record making adventures.

But this process was not without its complications. On the one hand, national identity in the new state was firmly rooted in the past. Heritage, traditions, religion, ancient legends and symbols provided the hallmarks of cultural identity in the Irish Free State. But, on the other hand, the country also sought recognition as a modern democratic state. This delicate balancing act between loyalty to the traditions of the past and celebrations of modern developments is clearly demonstrated in the press. Newspaper editors, both national and provincial, clamoured for a modern airport so that the Free State could benefit from its location on the Atlantic seaboard and become an ideal location for air traffic to and from America. However, such views were often counterposed by calls to maintain the traditional, anti-material, and anti-modern basis of Irish society. As discussed at length in the first section of this chapter, the recklessness of modern living was presented as bad and morally corrupting for young people, especially young women. As will become apparent in later chapters, this conflict about the underlying nature and future direction of Irish society informed many debates in the press. These conflicts and contradictions are illuminating and give a valuable insight into the complex and multifaceted nature of life in the new nation.

# CHAPTER THREE:

## WORKING BODIES

*Introduction:*

> Today we have the anomaly of male preachers, writers and critics upbraiding modern women for their tendency to shirk the marriage bond and at the same time penalising marriage by dismissing them from their jobs the moment they are outside the church door. (*Irish Independent*, 27 January 1925)

This quote is taken from an article entitled 'No Women Need Apply' published in the Ladies' Page of the *Irish Independent*. The article highlighted the case of a typist who was sacked from her job because she had married. As will be discussed throughout this chapter, the 1920s-1930s witnessed several conflicting and competing discourses about the role of women in the Irish Free State. Discussions of female employment need to be placed within constructions of the feminine roles of domesticity and motherhood and the masculine roles of authority figure, head of household and breadwinner. In addition, in the Irish Free State, these concerns were compounded by the peculiarity of an extraordinarily low marriage rate, uniquely high rates of female emigration and rural depopulation in a predominantly agricultural society with a small industrial sector.

These issues are particularly apparent in discussions about female employment in the 1930s. Following the economic crisis of the late 1920s and early 1930s, the 'economic war' between the Free State and Britain (when Britain taxed imported Irish products in a dispute over the repayment of land annuities) and the resultant increase in male unemployment, the issue of female employment took on a particular political and economic significance. Culminating in the controversial measures in the Constitution of 1937 which threatened to reduce women's rights to paid work, the issue of female employment reveals the many competing interests and ideologies in Irish society.

This chapter is divided into three sections. The first section will examine various representations of the working woman especially the 'business girl', the 'married woman worker' and the 'woman in industry'. The second section will focus more specifically on the discussions of the 'girl emigrant' and the 'domestic servant' and finally, the third section will analyse the press debates around the constitution of 1937 and the particular representations of the 'working woman', 'woman within the home' and feminist activists.

## Section 1: The 'Business Girl' and the 'Woman in Industry'

In the context of the many modernising influences of the period, young women in the 1920s-1930s were experiencing new freedom as workers and consumers. Although the Free State had a relatively low level of female employment compared to its European neighbours, there was a definite increase in the numbers of women in paid work during this period (Daly 1995). In 1926, 48.6% of single women were in paid employment, while the European average at that time was closer to 60%. However, by 1936 the figure in the Free State had risen to 53.3%. Breaking this percentage down into specific age categories reveals that young women aged between 18 and 24 years had the highest rate of employment at over 60%, while the rate for women aged over 25 fell off dramatically to less than 40% (see Daly 1995: 103). However, these figures probably conceal the extent to which women were economically active in small family-run businesses, for example in shops, public houses and hotels. In addition, many single women worked on family farms where their contributions were often unpaid, taken for granted and officially unacknowledged. Many thousands of women worked in cottage based industries, for example, Daly (1995) estimates that in 1926 over 7,000 women worked as seamstresses in their own homes.

It is noteworthy that Irish girls had a very high rate of participation in education. Perhaps because of the dominance of agriculture with all of its demands on the boys and young men of the farming communities, girls were more likely than boys to stay on in education after the age of compulsory attendance. By 1930 the Free State had one of the highest percentage of female attendance in secondary school in Europe. This pattern continued in third level education. Only Finland had a higher percentage of female attendance in university than the Free State (Daly 1995: 107). Thus, given their high level of education, it comes as no surprise that Irish young women were rapidly gaining access to clerical and other white-collar jobs in the 1920s-1930s:

> The establishment of a native civil service brought increased openings for low-grade clerical positions, such as writing assistant and typist...The number of established female civil servants increased by 140 percent during the first ten years of the Irish Free State from 940 to 2,260. (Daly 1995: 107)

Young women had to pass several tests and examinations to qualify for these posts. Therefore, the successful ones tended to be well educated and were overwhelmingly from middle class families. Because civil servants, along with teachers and other state employees, had to retire upon marriage, all of these young women were, by definition, single. Thus, in cities like Dublin there was a perceptible increase in the number of 'bachelor girls' working in white-collar jobs, often sharing bachelor flats. They represented the apparently free and easy lifestyle of the modern flappers (Ryan 1998a and 1998b). However, the majority of young women who were economically active continued to work in a very different sector of the economy. Domestic service remained the primary employment opportunity for single, working class young women. In the early decades of the twentieth century domestic service remained the second largest area of female employment, after agriculture, with over 100,000 indoor servants in Ireland (Hearn 1993). Despite the stereotype of the large country houses employing many servants, most 'domestics' worked for middle class employers as the only general servant. Mona Hearn estimates that 80% of Dublin domestics worked in one-servant households (1993: 9). But it was not only in big cities like Dublin that domestic servants were employed in large numbers. Employment figures for County Galway in 1928 reveal that there were 2,443 female domestic servants in that county compared to 1,468 women working in professions such as teaching. However, the fact that over 11,000 women were registered as employed in agriculture, indicates the extent to which women in rural counties continued to work on the land (*Connacht Tribune*, 22 September 1928).

As Mona Hearn's research has shown, domestic servants were usually very young women. 24% of servants were aged between 15-19 years with a total of 47% aged under 25 years. Unmarried servants were preferred and were expected to leave service upon getting married. Living in their employers' home with a demanding work schedule, these young women had little leisure time and almost no privacy. Employers, often middle class and keen to assert their own position in society, demanded 'respectable', 'clean' and 'sober' servants (Hearn 1993).

However, as will be discussed in following sections, even this sector of female employment was to prove the site of lively debate in the 1930s. Newspapers reported various discussions which focused primarily around the training and reliability of domestic servants, the so-called 'servant problem'. In addition, close connections were drawn between domestic service and emigration to Britain. The image of the lone young woman from a humble family boarding the boat for England and a life of domestic service embodied a range of concerns about emigration. These young women were attracted by the offer of higher wages, as well as by the bright lights and excitement of life away from home. Anxiety about the respectability of these young women and the establishments where they were employed in England, fuelled debates about the safety – both physical and moral – of young emigrant girls.

*Bachelor Girls and the Professions:*

As mentioned above, one of the most common representations of the working woman in the 1920s-1930s was the young, single, urban, white-collar 'bachelor girl'. As has been discussed at length in Chapter two, this young woman represented the ultimate consumer. She was glamorous, fashion-conscious, an avid reader of glossy, imported magazines and regularly attended the cinema where she absorbed the latest Hollywood images of femininity. In this section, I will focus more closely on the ways in which the press represented this archetypal young woman as the embodiment of particular notions of female employment, careers and working patterns.

In the 1920s women made inroads into many occupations from which they had been previously barred or discouraged. The press regularly reported the success of pioneering young women. For example, on 21 October 1926, the *Cork Examiner* carried the heading 'The March of Women' which reported that for the first time a woman had appeared as a clerk to the court registrar in a Dublin courtroom. The short article commented that there was no longer any obstacle 'to the ascent to the Bench of any of the young lady barristers who, without any great encouragement to do so, continue the practice of the law'. While the achievements of these exceptional young women were often singled out for special attention and praise, that is not to suggest that the press was generally open-minded about the wholesale entry of women into male-dominated occupations.

The most sympathetic discussions of the professional, career woman were usually to be found in the Women's Pages of newspapers. For example, the *Kerry-*

*man*'s weekly woman's page 'Women's Chat' frequently contained positive references to the success which women were achieving in commercial clerical employment (4 February 1928), as well as the opportunities available to women in professions such as dentistry and medicine (3 March 1928). In March 1928, 'Women's Chat' addressed the large numbers of spinster women:

> The unattached woman nowadays is well groomed, dresses smartly, and not infrequently shows considerable ability in carrying out a career for herself....She is doing wonders in business, in sports and athletics, and generally appears to have made up her mind that if she is to overrun the earth she will do so in a capable and cheerful manner. (The *Kerryman*, 31 March 1928)

Although the women's pages in the *Kerryman* and its near neighbour the *Cork Examiner* were syndicated from Britain during the 1920s, such articles are important nonetheless because they provided Irish readers with positive and encouraging images of modern working women.

However, while single women may have been encouraged to pursue careers, the employment opportunities of married women were being severely curtailed. On 9 January 1932, the *Irish Independent* carried a report entitled 'Marriage Ban on Teachers: Women Who Wed Must Go'. The Department of Education had officially notified the Irish National Teachers' Organisation [INTO] that from 1 April women teachers who marry will 'cease to be eligible in any capacity in a National School'. On 1 April 1932, the *Independent* reported the reactions of the INTO under the banner headline 'Ban on Married Women Teachers'. The union's congress, meeting in Dublin, declared its uncompromising opposition to this new legislation. Several of the speakers were cited in the newspaper article, interestingly they were all male teachers. There were three main reasons given for opposing the ban; firstly, it would deter women from entering the profession, secondly, it would mean that those women who did become teachers would be merely 'birds of passage' who flew away after a few years, and thirdly, women had just as much right to get married as male teachers.

The ban on married women extended to other areas of state employment. On 18 April 1932, the *Independent* carried a very humorous report on the employment prospects for young women in the General Post Office [GPO]. The rather lengthy headline sets the tone for the article: 'The money is good – but not much – Government job at 5 shillings a week – Chance for our Girls'. The article began with a question: 'Girls, want a good job? The line forms to the right so please don't rush'. The government was advertising for female telephonists on a rate of 5 shillings per week. 'All you've got to have is a knowledge of Gaelic, English and mathematics, and a papa or a mama, or a guardian who is willing to swear that you are not the kind of girl who is likely to paint the whole world red on 5/- a week.' Of course, in addition to the academic qualifications and the character reference, there was the additional qualification that female employees should remain unmarried. 'The G.P.O. will not stand for any gold diggers wedding you and annexing that 5/-'. The article concluded in the same humorous tone encouraging all prospective telephonists to tell their young suitors: 'On your way kid, I'm quality, on your way'.

Behind this very sarcastic snipe at Government employment practices, there lies the more serious point that young girls who were expected to have good education and respectable characters were paid so little that it would have been virtually impossible for them to survive without the financial support of their families. Therefore, these jobs were limited to girls from affluent backgrounds. This point is illustrated very clearly in a series of articles, 'Careers at Home', published in the *Irish Independent* in 1936. Focusing on job opportunities available for men and women in the Free State, the series concentrated on a different career each week. The first instalment dealt with 'A Civil Service Opening for Young Girls' (29 January 1936). This factual column presented clear-cut information on the recruitment procedures, pay and promotion prospects for writing assistants which was one of the lowest levels of entry to the civil service. According to the article, about 20-30 vacancies became available twice yearly 'because of the rule that female civil servants must retire when they get married'. Upon marriage, women received a gratuity of one month's salary for every year of service but only if they had been employed for a total of six years.

Vacancies were aimed at 'girls' aged 16 to 18 years with candidates passing examinations in History, Geography, Irish, English, Mathematics, as well as handwriting tests. Salaries began at 17/- per week rising by annual increments of 2/- to a maximum of 34/- per week. In addition, there was a living allowance because most of the jobs were based in Dublin city. However, even with the living allowance, the article pointed out that in order 'to live in Dublin away from home, girls will probably require some help from their parents for a year or two'. Although it was not stated explicitly in the article, it is clear that positions in the civil service were not only limited to young women who had had the benefit of post-primary schooling, but also to those whose parents could afford to subsidise their earnings.

Throughout February 1936 the *Independent* not only ran its series of articles on 'Careers at Home' but also reported on a radio series hosted by Dene Fitzgibbon which was devoted to the discussion of careers for women. On 3 February, the *Independent* carried a lengthy report of the radio broadcast concerning women and librarianship. While women were clearly making great inroads in this sector, for example, 16 of the 20 county librarians in the Free State were female, the marriage bar meant that this career was only available to single women. On 17 February, the *Independent*'s review of this radio series focused on women's success in the area of commerce. The principal of Rathmines Technical Institute was quoted as saying that women had proven themselves 'as serious and highly efficient workers'. However, he admitted that the majority of women clerical workers 'were grossly underpaid'. On the same day, the series of articles 'Careers at Home' was devoted to the work of national (primary) school teaching. Of the 9,000 national teachers in the Saorstat, 4,000 were men and 5,000 were women. Both men and women had to undertake a 6 year training course which involved college fees of £22 per year, in addition, women had to qualify in the extra subject of needle work. This article also provided very clear information on the pay differentials between the sexes. While women began at £128 per annum and rose to a maximum of £246, men began at £140 and rose to £303. Thus the pay difference increased with seniority. Men were also far more likely than women to become principals (*Irish Independent*, 17 February 1936). The fact that lowly telephonists and writing assistants on modest wages, as well as qualified librarians and experienced teachers were all prevented from marrying illustrates the extent to which the state viewed employment and marriage as diametrically opposed choices for women.

But, clearly women were not limited to careers in the state sector. On 27 July 1932, the *Independent* carried a feature article by Josephine Bullen entitled 'Hotel Management by Women Fresh from the University'. Bullen began with the somewhat optimistic claim that 'we have almost forgotten the days when woman were constantly being reminded that her rightful place was in the home, so completely and effectively has she stepped out of it'. Few of the women graduating from university were prepared to settle down immediately to a life of marriage and domesticity. One of the newer occupations becoming available to educated young women was hotel management. Bullen linked the growth of tourism to a boom in the hotel business. Irish young women were particularly well suited to this area of work: 'to the confidence and *savoir-faire* a college training gives to women, the Irish girl adds a charm all her own. Nature has gifted her with a welcoming graciousness, a lively humour, and a spirit of hospitality that makes her a perfect hostess'. This feature article is interesting because it blends together two, seemingly competing, images of Irish womanhood. The well-educated, competent business woman is presented as essentially feminine and charming. Thus Bullen manages to successfully combine traditional notions of femininity with more modern attributes.

Bullen was not the only writer to attempt to blend seemingly competing aspects of womanhood. In her weekly *Irish Independent* column, 'Leaves from a Woman's Diary', Gertrude Gaffney regularly discussed aspects of female employment in the Irish Free State. On 11 November 1932, she focused on 'A Husband and A Career'. Examining career opportunities for women in Irish universities, she attacked Trinity College Dublin for its reluctance to appoint any women professors. 'Is it fear of feminine competition that is eating at the heart of this masculine stronghold? For it is only the presence of those from whom we have something to fear that we guard against'. University College Dublin, on the other hand, had 'been sane and reasonable in its attitude towards women'. It employed three women professors; Mary Hayden, Mary Macken and Agnes O'Farrelly. In addition, University College Cork also had three women professors. Gaffney then turned her attention to those women who had combined marriage and a university career. 'That marriage and a successful husband are no impediments to a successful university career is demonstrated by the fact that two women holding important positions in University College are wives of government ministers'. She was referring to Mrs. Sean T. O'Kelly who taught French and Mrs. Sean MacEntee who taught Irish language.

Gaffney was rare among journalists of the 1930s. Not only was she one of the few female journalists to have her own weekly column in a national daily, but she was an outspoken advocate of women's rights. Her column 'Leaves from a Woman's Diary' tackled a range of controversial issues and was very different from the weekly women's pages with their focus on recipes and dress designs. The issue of married women's working rights was something she returned to many times over the years. In January 1936 she wrote an article simply entitled

'Married Women in Employment'. This was a response to criticisms that married women were not efficient employees because their minds were always on their homes and family. 'Married women workers are on the whole far more efficient than many younger, unmarried women' Gaffney asserted:

> In this country when a married woman takes up a position outside her home, it is in 99 cases out of 100 through sheer economic necessity. Holding her job is of such vital concern to her that her entire energy is thrown into the effort to compete with cheap adolescent labour by doing her work better than her competitors can do it. (*Irish Independent*, 4 January 1936)

She praised the many married women throughout the country who were running very efficient businesses. The point that married women worked not out of ambition or choice but out of necessity was one repeatedly made by Gaffney and other feminist commentators in the 1930s. It is a point to which we will return later.

Like the women's pages in the other daily and provincial newspapers, the *Irish Press*'s women's page gave regular coverage to employment opportunities for women. In a very interesting article on 25 January 1932, the women's page discussed how the new bachelor girls or business girls were generating work for other women. Under the heading 'Stay-at-home-girls Make Money: Profit Giving Occupations', the article explored a range of occupations including the 'handy woman', the silver cleaner and the basket maker. A woman who could undertake such work found 'a ready market for her talents among go-out-to-work girls with small purses who yet like their homes comfortable and artistic'. The laundry lady was likely to find plenty of willing customers among business girls whose landladies objected to their washing clothes in their bathrooms. As the 'business girls' budgets' would not stretch to professional laundry services, there was an opportunity for the 'laundry girl' who 'washes out and irons the business girl's "pretties" at a modest price'. While this article suggests the extent of the phenomenon of urban business girls living on a modest salary in lodging houses and flats, it also indicates a class-based work experience. While the business girl lived in comfortable, artistic surroundings and wore pretty clothes, the 'stay-at-home girls' acted out the role of servants and laundry maids.

Although the 'bachelor, business girl' was regularly featured in the *Irish Press*, such articles were usually contained within the perimeters of the women's page which concentrated on fashion, food recipes and home improvements. For example, on the 5 March 1932 a feature on home decorations suggested that the 'bachelor girl' who lived in a bed-sitting room could vastly improve her surroundings by adopting some clever space-saving devices including a multifunctional sofa bed. On 1 October 1932, the women's page carried a feature under the self-explanatory heading 'Ways with Eggs for the Business Girl'. 'Eggs are a real stand-by in the business girl's diet....Where the business girl lives in a bed-sittingroom a gasring will cook most egg dishes, and their preparation gives off practically no cooking smells'. Recipes included simple dishes like eggs on toast but also more sophisticated meals like egg mayonnaise and poached eggs with shrimp sauce. It is no coincidence that this white-collar worker was always referred to as a business *girl*. The *Irish Press* women's page tended to assume that all gainfully employed women were young and single. There appears to have been an acceptance that employment and marriage were incompatible. This point was made very explicitly in a feature published in March 1932:

> Since women took to combining a profession with housekeeping there has been a notable decrease in the number who are prepared to devote a portion of each morning to household catering.... But women who combine work and housekeeping are still fortunately few in Ireland, where the majority of women realise that the work of wife and mother is wholetime when efficiently done. (*Irish Press*, 1 March 1932)

The use of the phrase 'still fortunately few' suggests that this article was not merely commenting on the low levels of economic activity among married women, but was expressing a clear opinion that this was precisely as it should be. In the 1930s, married women (excluding widows) had only a 5.6% rate of labour force participation (Daly 1995). The views expressed in its women's page were very much in line with those of the *Irish Press* editorial. For example, on 29 July 1932, the editorial focused on the topic of 'Female Labour'. The editor began by asking the question 'Are there too many women in trade and industry?' This was a question which, it was claimed, the whole country was discussing. In suggesting that this question should be answered in the affirmative, the editorial cited the well-known trade union leader Miss Louie Bennett. Addressing a meeting of the Irish Trade's Union Congress in Cork, she had said:

> I have no desire to put a spoke in the wheel of women's employment, but the modern tendency to draw women into industry in increasing numbers is of no real advantage to them. It is a menace to family life; and, in so far as it blocks the employment of men, it has intensified poverty. (Bennett in *Irish Press*, editorial, 29 July 1932)

The editorial firmly endorsed these views: 'Like Miss Bennett, we are no enemies to the employment of women in vocations to which they are suited; but we deplore the tendency to substitute cheap female labour for that of heads of families' (29 July 1932). An example was given from Galway City where, it was reported, young women who had completed a commercial course were ten times more likely to find a job than men who had completed the same course. The editorial suggested that this was largely due to the fact that women were cheaper to hire than men. According to the editorial, this situation was against 'natural human development' and had led to vast unemployment among men.

Thus there appears to have been clear differentiation between different types of women workers. While the young, single, white-collar or business girl was generally accepted as a phenomenon of the modern age, this lifestyle was judged by many in the press to be incompatible with marriage. But this view went beyond mere rhetoric or ideology. State legislation was passed to actually prevent women from combining marriage and employment in such sectors as the civil service, school teaching and even the post office. The other working woman who provoked consternation in many quarters, including among trade unions, was the industrial worker. Industrial work was deemed to be unsuitable for women. However, it is likely that the real explanation for such antagonism lay in the fear that these women would deprive men of jobs in factories.

*The Industrial Woman Worker Debates of 1936:*

In November 1936 Aodh de Blacam, an important figure in the Fianna Fail political party, addressed the annual convention of *Muintir na Tire* (People of the Land), an influential organisation of agriculturalists and countryside interest groups. The national press gave generous coverage to de Blacam's speech, in particular his assertion that the Irish people 'might live to curse the day' when factories began employing women. He claimed that 'with the exception of the cinemas', factories which employed women:

> were the greatest evil that had come to this country and in the towns where women were engaged in this work the old Irish character had gone, homes were being disrupted and womanhood was being denaturalised and turned into something it was never intended for. (de Blacam in *Irish Press*, 9 November 1936)

A very similar report of this speech was also printed on the same day in the *Irish Independent*. A few days later, both newspapers also published a reply to Mr. de Blacam by Sarah Kennedy and Louie Bennett, president and secretary of the Irish Women Workers' Union (IWWU). The union leaders began by criticising his statements as 'reckless' and then challenged his evidence. Speaking on behalf of over '5,000 women and girls', Kennedy and Bennett asserted that 'we see no symptoms of the denaturalisation of womanhood' and no evidence of the 'disruption of homes'. Very rarely were there cases of 'moral lapse'. Instead these workers played a central role in supporting their families demonstrating a 'self-sacrificing devotion to parents'. The real problem in the Irish economy, according to the letter writers, was unemployment and emigration and these should be the focus of Mr. de Blacam's anxieties. Religious leaders regularly condemned the widespread emigration of young women particularly in rural areas. Kennedy and Bennett suggested that the 'cure' for this 'evil' was employment (*Irish Press* and *Irish Independent*, 12 November 1936). The union leaders challenged de Blacam's image of women factory workers by presenting them as 'good girls' who were hard working and devoted to their parents. This suggests that the women were single, and living at home with their mothers and fathers. Louie Bennett had particularly strong views on married women working outside the home. In their letter to the press, both she and Kennedy suggested that industrial employment did not denaturalise women workers. On the contrary, once they were married these women were happy to withdraw into the domestic sphere where they made very able wives and mothers.

On 18 November, the *Irish Press* published a long letter from Aodh de Blacam defending his position and arguing that nature never intended women for industrial work. 'Their sensitive constitutions wither under it.' He went on to claim that women's 'part in life is to make a home'. However, through their pursuit of factory employment, Irish girls were losing domestic skills such as cooking, baking and managing a home. They were earning good money and thus postponed getting married, as they were reluctant to give up their new lifestyles. This was having a devastating impact on marriage rates, especially in the countryside, according to de Blacam, 'rural Ireland is dying apace under this evil'.

Also on 18 November, the *Irish Independent* published a letter from the veteran feminist campaigner Mary Kettle in which she began by citing a Bishop who had recently expressed concern about the large numbers of Irish girls leaving the country. Mr. de Blacam, she asserted, would rather have girls unemployed and emigrating in their thousands than working in factories at home. Mrs. Kettle argued that 'if we wish to effectively prevent emigration of women we must examine the root causes and remove them by giving women equitable conditions in their own country.' She referred to the fact that the League of Nations had placed the Free State at the bottom in a recent survey of women's working conditions. Kettle pointed to numerous examples of women earning less money and enjoying fewer opportunities in the workplace than their male colleagues did.

On the following day, the *Independent* published a letter by Margaret Buckley attacking Aodh de Blacam. She condemned his statement as 'an insult to women' who were 'good Irishwomen, good Catholics, good mothers, good wives'. Buckley claimed that married women who went out to work in factories did so simply out of economic necessity and that was better surely than joining their husbands who stood idle around the streets. The government needed to tackle male unemployment. Once their husbands were gainfully employment 'the women, who are now the breadwinners, will gladly exchange the factory for the home' (19 November 1936). Although Buckley defended women's right to work, the juxtaposition of women working in factories and men idling around the streets suggested the possibility of a simple substitution. It is easy to see how a similar argument could be used to justify taking women out of factories and putting their menfolk into their jobs, especially as Buckley appeared satisfied that women would gladly return to the home once their husbands found employment.

The discussions about women in industry rumbled on in the press for many weeks. On 10 December 1936, Rev. Lucey speaking at the Catholic Club in O'Connell Street, Dublin was reported at length in the *Irish Press* under the much-used headline 'Women in Industry'. He argued that 'young girls should never be allowed to go out into industry at a time when neither their minds nor their bodies were fully developed'. These girls had inadequate experience of housework and were thus ill-fitted to marriage. As they became used to earning wages and having an independent lifestyle they tended to postpone marriage. In addition, these young women were not only depriving men of marriage partners, they were also depriving men of jobs 'more women out at work meant more men out of work' (10 December 1936).

These debates on the 'woman in industry' illustrate several overlapping and competing discourses. Rev. Lucey and Aodh de Blacam vocalised a widely held concern that factories were unsuitable working environments for young women. Not only did these women lack any expertise in domestic skills but also they were in danger of being de-sexed by doing work which nature never intended for them. In addition, the lure of wages and economic independence tempted them to postpone marriage or put it off altogether. Hence, on several counts these young women were endangering their true destiny as wives and mothers. As we will see in the sections below, domestic service, especially when aided by adequate training in the skills of cooking and household management, was seen as the ideal pre-requisite for marriage and motherhood. Thus while there was little concern about the marriage prospects of young women who worked as maids (provided they did not emigrate), there was great anxiety in many quarters about the suitability or willingness of factory girls to settle down in family life. Nevertheless, there was some acknowledgement that young women preferred factory work to the drudgery and restrictions of life as a servant. In September 1937 the *Independent* carried a feature article entitled 'Girls Prefer Factories':

> In the factory the girl is finished work early. She can dress herself, have long evenings free, and go to the pictures. The factories give freedom of a kind a young girl craves for, but which a housewife will not permit. Girls in domestic service see their factory working friends finish work and go where they will, and naturally they envy them and seek similar employment. (*Irish Independent*, 21 September 1937)

However, as the letters and articles cited above indicate, the sharpest criticism was reserved for married women factory workers. Not only were these women jeopardising the welfare of their families but they were also depriving their male relatives of jobs. Women workers, particularly married women, were seen to be in direct competition with men workers. Therefore, marriage and motherhood were represented as being utterly incompatible with employment, particularly industrial work. However, as Mary Daly's research has shown, married women in the 1930s had a very low rate of economic activity (5.6% see Daly 1995). Therefore, it is likely that the potent image of the married woman worker involved a marked exaggeration of reality.

Thus young, single women were unsuitable for factory work because it hampered their femininity and marriage prospects, while older, married women were unsuitable for factory work because it hampered the welfare of their families and undermined the masculine role of their husbands. Therefore, all women were unsuited to industrial employment. While feminists and women trade union leaders criticised the many attacks on women in industry, it seems that they shared several of the key assumptions underlying these attacks. Leading trade union campaigners like Louie Bennett agreed that married women should not work in factories. Others agreed that women were being hired because they were cheaper than male workers: so while criticising unequal pay, these commentators appeared to accept that women were unfairly competing with men for industrial employment. In challenging the view that factory work 'de-naturalised' women, several female activists argued that women industrial workers remained truly feminine and would willingly exchange the factory for the home.

The discussions about women in industry were framed by the other crucial concerns of the 1930s, rising unemployment, especially among men, and rising emigration, especially among women. While critics of women's industrial employment invoked the spectre of male unemployment to challenge women's right to take jobs in factories, supporters of women's working rights repeatedly pointed to the alternative of widespread female emigration. Therefore, in my view, the 'woman in industry' came to embody not only a range of ideologies about the role of working women in the Free State, but also embodied related concerns about marriage rates, domesticity, the male breadwinner and the mounting problem of emigration. These debates came to a head with the publication of the draft constitution in 1937.

## Section 2: 'Emigrant Girls' and the Absent Body:

*Introduction:*

For much of the twentieth century the population of the 26 counties remained remarkably static. Between 1926 and 1936 the overall population of the Free State actually fell slightly. In 1926 the population stood at 2,971,992, ten years later it had fallen to 2,968,420, a decrease of 0.12% (Brown 1987: 152). Cities such as Dublin and Cork registered a slight increase in population, while rural populations declined, suggesting an internal migration from rural to urban areas (Commission on Emigration, 1955: 5). However, the main causes for such a low population density and for the failure to register any increase in population in the decades following the establishment of the Free States were the low marriage rate and the high emigration rate. By the mid-1920s, 43% of Irish born men and women were living overseas, over one million in the USA alone. This made Ireland unique; for example other European countries had, on average, approximately 5% of their population living overseas (Beale 1986):

> Emigration was closely related to social class. Few people from large farms or professional backgrounds emigrated as they were more financially secure...The majority of those on the boats to England and America were children from small farms or from unskilled and semi-skilled working class homes. (Beale 1986: 33)

Beale argues that while emigration was initially seen as a necessity, by the 1930s many young people began to view it as a preference. 'At a time when politicians were praising family life in rural Ireland, when de Valera was exalting the countryside "bright with cosy homesteads", the people of the West were streaming away, leaving the traditional way of life as fast as they could' (Beale 1986: 35). In addition to the high levels of emigration, southern Ireland also had a uniquely high proportion of female emigrants. Between 1926 and 1936 an average of 9,420 women left the Free State every year compared with 7,255 men (Travers 1995: 148). This represented a loss of approximately 1,298 women to every 1,000 men (Commission on Emigration 1955: 115). A large proportion of these women went to Britain. The 1930s marked a dramatic shift in emigration patterns from the USA to Britain as the primary destination. In fact, women were more likely than men to emigrate to Britain. During the ten-year period 1926-36 it was estimated that almost 46,000 Irish women, as compared with 30,000 men, emigrated to Britain (Commission on Emigration 1955: 116). Women going to work in Britain tended to be very young, approximately one third were aged between 15-19 years, with a further one third aged between 20-24 years (Travers 1995: 148). Half of all female emigrants, in particular those in the younger age groups, were destined for jobs in domestic service (Travers 1995). Another interesting feature about Irish emigration was that it involved a movement of people from predominantly rural areas to large urban centres. With the exception of migrant agricultural workers who worked seasonally on farms in England and Scotland, the majority of Irish emigrants in the twentieth century were to be found in large English cities such as London and Liverpool. Hence, the stereotype of the poor, young, country girl working as a maid in London does represent a reasonably accurate description of emigration in this particular period.

*The 'Girl Emigrant Problem':*

Under the heading 'An Alarming Evil', Archbishop Gilmartin of Tuam focused his lenten pastoral on the emigration of young women to England (*Irish Independent*, 8 February 1937). He was particularly critical of 'foolish girls' who set out for England without a job or friends to meet them, and who did not make contact with a Catholic agency in English cities. He said that such girls 'run terrible risks to soul and body'. Similarly, Dr. McNamee bishop of Ardagh and Clonmacnoise condemned what he described as 'the rising stream of emigration of young girls to Great Britain in circumstances of dubious advantage to their welfare, temporal or spiritual'. Girls were attracted 'by the fascination of the garish distractions of the city, and by the hectic life of the great world as displayed before their wondering eyes in the glamorous unrealities of the films'. Cinema, he argued, was breeding a discontent with 'the prosaic placidity of rural life'. Parents needed to be particularly vigilant and warn their children that the high wages on offer in England 'may well prove an illusion, being counterbalanced by the expenses attached to city life'. Emigrants may find themselves in jobs 'where modesty and virtue may be exposed to great dangers'. Dr. McNamee said that girls 'will have a better chance of happiness in the country homesteads of Ireland than anywhere else on earth' (*Irish Independent*, 8 February 1937).

Very similar views were expressed by Canon Barrett several months earlier when addressing pupils at Macroom Technical School in Co. Cork. He said that 'girls were flocking over to England' and that technical schools had been much criticised for not fully equipping these girls with the necessary skills for employment. It was known that many girls arrived in England without the prospects of securing decent employment: 'unable, in some cases, to get enough money to bring them back to the safety of their homes. Their fate was the most deplorable that could befall a girl'. However, in his opinion, girls should attend technical schools with a view to applying their learning to improving their own homes.

While he did not wish to 'set bounds to the ambition of any boy or girl attending the school', he did wish to impress upon them the need to improve their own surroundings in their own homes. (*Cork Examiner*, 9 September 1936).

These viewpoints are highly illuminating and reveal a great deal about the Catholic Church's attitude to female emigration to Britain. England was presented as urban in contrast to the rural placidity of Ireland. Thus England as a country took on all the threatening characteristics of an expensive, dangerous and immoral city. Innocent Irish girls were attracted by the promise of money, excitement and glamour. But these were illusions; unrealities fostered in large part by the cinema. Ireland was constructed as rural, safe, peaceful; its cosy homesteads were the bastion of real happiness. Only at home, in Ireland, could girls realise their true modesty and virtue, safe from the distractions and dangers of the outside world. In the lenten pastorals, and in many other commentaries which will be discussed below, there is an interesting and pervasive overlap between the imagery of 'home' meaning Ireland, and 'home' meaning the domestic setting. Thus, the sentiment that Irish girls belonged at home took on a double meaning. The theme of the body is also apparent throughout newspaper reports on female emigration. Firstly, women/girl emigrants embody the failures of the state to tackle problems of unemployment, rural deprivation and emigration. Secondly, women/girls embody the evils of emigration, the threat to morality, Irishness and Catholicism. Thirdly, women/girl emigrants represent the absent bodies of rural Ireland and hence symbolise the threat of rural depopulation, low marriage rates and falling birth rates.

By mid to late 1930s emigration was becoming a serious concern in the Irish press. Articles, editorials, letters and special features were devoted to this topic. Newspapers highlighted the phenomenon of female emigration which was generally viewed as a very particular problem that merited discussion, research, analysis and explanation. On 22 January 1937, the *Independent* carried a familiar heading that was fairly typical of the time – 'Girl Emigrant Problem'. This referred to a conference held under the auspices of the Irish Women Workers' Union (IWWU). According to Louie Bennett, the conference was inspired by the 'growing tendency for country girls to migrate to England to find jobs as domestics'. The conference agreed on the need for a training school for domestics that would also act as an employment bureau with branches in England and Ireland. Similar sentiments were expressed by the Cork Chamber of Commerce which was quoted as saying 'Young girls especially should be properly educated and trained before seeking employment...parents should be warned of the dangers that await them' (*Irish Independent*, 22 January 1937).

This article indicates one discourse which was common among educators and trade unions; an acceptance of the inevitability of emigration and a determination to provide adequate training and assistance for young female emigrants so that they would have the best chance of achieving good employment in England. This discourse was in competition with that expounded by many in the hierarchy who attempted to prevent 'girls' from emigrating. However, as will be discussed below, there were many complexities and contradictions to be found on this issue not only in the attitudes of the Catholic hierarchy but right across Irish society. An unusual article in the *Independent* on 3 February 1937 revealed some of the tensions in relation to emigration. Written by Brian T. Galway and accompanied by a disclaimer from the *Independent* editor, the article argued that emigration was necessary to maintain the delicate balance and traditions of rural Ireland. Emigration did not threaten rural depopulation, he claimed, but prevented rural overcrowding. Patterns of land ownership and farm inheritance could only be maintained if the rights of the eldest son were protected. The emigration of younger siblings enabled such patterns to continue. It is not apparent whether or not Galway had written this article with a sense of irony or sarcasm. But there is certainly a strong element of truth in his argument. As has been discussed by many commentators (Arensberg 1937, Commission on Emigration 1955, Jackson

1963, Kennedy 1973), the emigration of large numbers of young people from rural areas was not unrelated to the particular patterns of farming and land inheritance adopted in the aftermath of the great famine in the 1840s.

The attitudes of the *Irish Independent* editorial were made clear on 10 April 1937 under the heading 'Our Decaying Race'. 'Emigration is once again sapping the vitality of the Irish race'. In the early years of the Saorstat, tens of thousands of Irish people went to America where they could, at least, prosper and find fame. Figures peaked in 1925 at 30,180. In the early 1930s, however, owing to the embargo on entry to the USA, the flow of emigration was temporarily halted. By the mid-1930s, emigration had again begun to increase dramatically but the destination had shifted to England where the majority of Irish people worked as servants and labourers. An estimate based on passenger statistics from Irish ports to English and Welsh ports suggested that in 1936 28,966 people emigrated from Ireland. The editorial concluded by attacking the Fianna Fail government for its failure to deal with the emigration problem. This editorial is interesting and raises a number of points that reoccur in other newspaper commentaries. While there appears to have been a certain tacit acceptance of emigration to North America, where Irish people were perhaps at an advantage in relation to other emigrants, there was a shared uneasiness about widespread emigration to England. This may be partly explained by the feeling that Irish emigrants got the worst jobs in English cities and were denied the opportunities for fame and fortune apparently available in North America. There also appears to have been a concern about anti-Catholic sentiment in Britain and a widely expressed worry that young people, especially young girls, would be dissuaded or indeed prevented from practising their religion. There may also have been a concern that the Free State would be viewed as having failed to maintain and provide for its young people who were now pouring into English cities in an apparent rejection of the lifestyle and values of their native homeland (Miller 1990).

The editorial of the *Cork Examiner* appears to have shared the concerns of the *Irish Independent*. For example, under the heading 'Our Emigrants' published on 14 April 1936, the *Examiner* commented on the 'strong and increasing stream of emigration from the Irish Free State'. 'Many of the emigrants one sees crossing to England every Friday are young girls of not more than twenty'. Like the *Independent*, the *Examiner* pointed an accusing finger at the Fianna Fail administration: 'Four years ago the Fianna Fail government promised that emigration would cease and people would return to the Motherland instead of deserting her.' However, this promise was not realised, instead the number of people emigrating to Britain was higher than the number who left for America before the economic depression of 1929. If the reality of emigration was accepted then the country needed to ensure that its young people were educated with sufficient skills to ensure economic survival in Britain. The editor concluded by acknowledging the irony of educating people for emigration.

The editorial of the *Examiner* returned to this topic on 28 August 1936 in reaction to the publication of the census figures. The editorial attacked Fianna Fail for failing to address the unemployment problem that was directly linked to rising emigration and hence to falling population. The depopulation of rural areas was seen as directly related to poor economic conditions. The *Examiner* editorial once again returned to this theme on 6 November 1936 under the heading 'Those Emigrants'. 'It is all to the good that attention has been focused lately on the problem of female emigrants or migrants from the Free State to Great Britain.' But how, the editorial asked, was this problem to be addressed? While the Free State did have limited possibilities and resources for providing employment, politicians had not helped the situation. While politicians boasted of attracting all sorts of new factories to Ireland, they were silent on the growing dole queues. The *Examiner* was particularly critical of the government's education policy. 'If the money that has been wasted in the efforts to teach these girls Irish, and other subjects through Irish, had been applied to teaching them elementary housewifery, their position would not be so hopeless'. The editorial commented on the irony that the heaviest flow of emigration was from *Gaeltacht* areas (Irish speaking communities), where the people were strong supporters of Fianna Fail.

Although the *Examiner* editorial contained a stinging attack on the Government's policy on teaching Irish language, its main argument appears to be that girls' education should be related more directly to domesticity. If girls were properly trained in the arts of cookery, sewing and household management, then their prospects of employment and perhaps marriage would be greatly improved. Girls' lack of interest in domesticity was a theme discussed on numerous occasions in the press. In October 1936, the *Examiner* addressed the topic under the heading 'The Daily Help':

> From all the complaints heard lately it seems that the servant problem is becoming more acute. For some years past it has been increasingly difficult to locate a good maid....Special importance has been given lately to the continued emigration of young Irish girls to England, and doubtless that is one of the big reasons for the awkward state of affairs at home; but it is not the only one. (*Cork Examiner*, 16 October 1936)

Other reasons for the 'servant problem' included the fact that girls were being attracted by factory work. Factories' higher rates of pay and shorter working hours had lead many to the view that domestic work was demeaning for young women. However, the writer of this article, 'N.K.', clearly disagrees with such a mistaken impression. She argued that domestic work need not be demeaning and was often cleaner and more pleasant than factory work. If girls were properly trained and secured a good position as a domestic they would find it rewarding work.

This article raises similar themes to those addressed elsewhere; firstly, that work was available in Ireland if girls were willing to remain at home, and secondly, if girls were adequately trained in the arts of domesticity they would be able to get decent wages in Ireland. This article also reveals the class-based aspect of emigration. As discussed at the start of this section, the majority of female emigrants were from working class or poor farming backgrounds. The views expressed in the *Cork Examiner* indicate a middle class reaction to the 'servant problem'. If girls from poor families could be persuaded to work as servants in the middle class homes of Cork and Dublin then the emigration problem and the servant problem could be easily solved.

Similar arguments were made in the *Irish Press* newspaper. For example, on 1 October 1936, the *Press* carried the heading 'Advice to Girls: Priest Counsels them not to leave Ireland'. Reverend Sheil, preaching in Rathkeale, advised girls that there was no need to leave Ireland. The Catholic Registry in Dublin and Cork could find well-paid situations for all girls within a few days. The availability of work for girls in Ireland was underlined by an article in the *Press* on 16 December 1936. Hoteliers in Cork complained that they could not fill vacancies as no girls were prepared to stay and work in the city. A priest who had been informed of the situation approached several families with eligible daughters but all of them had recently emigrated to England. The emigration of all these young women was having a further impact on the local area: farmers were unable to find wives. In fact, the article was published under the rather eye-catching heading 'Will not Marry Farmers Now'. Thus the widespread emigration of Irish girls was perceived to have both short term and long term consequences. In the short term there was the difficulty of unfilled vacancies in hotels and in private service. However, in the longer term there was the more serious problem of a shortage of wives in rural areas. This was highlighted in the *Press* editorial of 28 August 1936 which pointed out that the Free State had the lowest ratio of women to men of any European country. In 1936 the figure stood at 953 women to every 1000 men. This represented a fall since the census of 1926 and was explained by the 'marked excess of females among emigrants'. In a lengthy discussion of emigration in the *Irish Independent* on 20 November 1936, Dr. Casey, the bishop of Ross argued that the disproportionate numbers of women emigrating was bound to lead to a falling birth rate, 'one may well ask where the Irish mothers of the future are to come from'.

The absence of suitable marriage partners from rural communities fuelled concerns not only about rural depopulation but also about the maintenance of traditional Irish homesteads and family values. As I have argued in earlier chapters, women represented the continuity of the Irish nation through both the biological reproduction of the national population and by passing on religious and cultural values to the next generation. The absent woman thus represented a threat not only to rural population but also to the rural way of life that lay at the heart of images of Irishness. As the embodiment of Irishness/Ireland, woman symbolised the uniqueness of cultural and religious characteristics. Emigration represented a threat to these characteristics on several levels. Not only did the women leave Ireland but there were concerns that their Irishness was under threat as soon as they boarded the boat for England.

*Untrained and Unrestrained: Gertrude Gaffney's study of Girl Emigrants*

In December 1936 the *Independent* published a much heralded series of articles on Irish girls' emigration to Britain. The articles were based on a fact-finding mission undertaken by Gertrude Gaffney:

> How many people in this country are aware that there is, and has been taking place for the past four years or so, the greatest influx of able-bodied young Irish women and men into England that has occurred since the famine years. (*Irish Independent*, 7 December 1936)

Gaffney was at pains to point out that most Irish girls did very well in Britain earning decent wages as domestic servants. However, there was a 'rapidly growing minority' who experienced poverty, loneliness and desperation in strange, unfamiliar cities, far away from family and friends. These unlucky ones could be found in 'every shelter for the destitute, in every maternity hospital, in every home for unmarried mothers, or worse still in the common lodging houses in certain parts of the great cities'.

This latter reference is presumably a hint at the prevalence of prostitution among impoverished Irish emigrants. Although the language used by Gaffney was similar to that used in the Bishops' lenten pastorals to describe the dark and threatening cities of England, her analysis was far more probing. She attempted to dig deeper and reveal the underlying causes of these problems. For example, she argued that the root cause of so many girls going 'to the bad' in England lay back home in Ireland. She wrote that an 'astounding number of girls' arrived in England with no money and no job. Many were as young as 16 years and, untrained for any occupation, they quickly drifted into trouble. Several young women who arrived in England were pregnant and had left Ireland to 'save their reputations'. This group was increasing in number, she said, and was proving a considerable burden for English charities and rescue organisations.

On 8 December 1936, Gaffney resumed her study this time focusing on rescue organisations in Liverpool. One charity told her that they had helped 40 Irish girls that week and 37 the week before. In the last 12 months they had assisted 940 Irish girls usually directing them to Catholic hostels in the city. These were mostly very young girls who arrived at Liverpool without any money. Gaffney was very critical of the parents who permitted their young daughters to set off for England alone and ill-prepared for employment. Most girls came from rural districts in Ireland and were often very ignorant about the ways of the world. They were particularly vulnerable to the undesirable men who preyed on their innocent and trusting nature.

On the following day, Gaffney focused in particular on the moral dangers which awaited these innocent young girls: 'The great danger to the younger and more flighty of these girls is...the unscrupulous loose living men they meet in the street.' The girls were friendly and chatted freely to the people they met. They were not suspicious of strangers. Gaffney then recounted a very dramatic story about a girl named 'Mary' who was attracted by a 'charming man'. He won her confidence and was on the point of luring her away from her hostel when the matron in charge of the hostel intervened and, after some argument, managed to persuade Mary of the man's evil intentions. The man eventually ran off after the matron called the police (9 December 1936). The underlying moral of the story appears to be that charming men prey on innocent Irish girls, take advantage of them and then abandon them to poverty, disease and pregnancy. But it was not just evil men who posed a threat to the decency and modesty of Irish girls.

Gaffney devoted two in her series of lengthy articles to the problem of Irish girls going into service with Jewish families. 'There are hundreds of untrained Irish girls arriving in London weekly to take up situations with Russian, Polish, German and other foreign Jews' (10 December 1936). Gaffney was careful to differentiate between these immigrant Jews who lived in the East End of London and other, more affluent Jews who ran very decent households in other parts of the city. The 'foreign Jews' represented a particular group because they were often quite poor and struggling to eke out a living. Wives and mothers worked long hours in the family business leaving the servant alone in the home to mind children, do cleaning, laundry and prepare meals. English girls were unwilling to work in such conditions so the families employed Irish girls who, being without any proper training or qualifications, were not in a position to refuse employment. They were paid 'a pittance' for working 'like machines'. Because the Jewish families had little money to spare, they frequently paid their servants in kind; for example in clothing or foodstuff. This made it very difficult for the girls to save up enough money to leave. Living in Jewish areas of East London, these

Irish maids were isolated from other Irish people and were often many miles away from the nearest Catholic church or community centre. In addition, as the Jews did not celebrate the Sabbath on Sundays, they often objected to girls having time off on Sunday mornings to make the long journey to mass. Gradually the girls lost touch with their religion and stopped going to mass completely. Thus Gaffney appears to be suggesting that living among Jews may prove to have a de-nationalising influence on Irish girls. They lose touch with their religion, their countrymen and women and their cultural roots.

Gaffney returned to the topic of Jewish employers in her next article, again she focused on the foreign, 'low class' Jews who lived in the East End of London:

> These districts are thickly populated with the foreign Jews to whom I alluded in yesterday's article; in themselves in all probability quite good people, but, because of their outlook on life and the conditions of employment they offer, not desirable employers for a Catholic girl brought up in the simplicity of the countryside. (11 December 1936)

This quote is very illuminating and reveals several dichotomies. The Jews embody otherness through their nationality, outlook, lifestyles, culture, food and religion. Interestingly, it is not the Irish emigrants who symbolise foreignness but the Polish, German and Russian Jews. Thus the 'foreign Jew' is juxtaposed to the 'Catholic girl', both groups defined by their religion, which is apparently synonymous with their nationality: Central European versus Irish. Britishness or Englishness remains absent from the discussion although these encounters occur in East London. The second dichotomy is the familiar one of city versus countryside. It is noteworthy that Gaffney used the metaphor of the low-class Jew to represent the dark side of life in the big city. As George L. Mosse has argued, in Nazi Germany in the 1930s Jews were frequently represented as dark, mysterious characters who occupied the sinister quarters of the city, while German Aryans were shown amidst the healthy, open spaces of the countryside (Mosse 1985). Gaffney described the Catholic girl who was brought up in the simplicity of the rural setting. In this way, the innocence, goodness and naturalness of the Irish girl was emphasised in contrast to the Jewish embodiment of the squalid, unhealthy, frightening city.

Gaffney then related a very detailed and dramatic story about a 19-year-old Irish servant girl who was accused of theft by her Jewish employers (11 December 1936). She was arrested and remanded in prison awaiting trial. Fortunately, a nun came to hear of her plight and hired a solicitor to defend her. The girl was acquitted and then offered a bed in the convent until she found a new job. Here the convent, so often a symbol for the incarceration of young women (see chapter on infanticide) represents a sanctuary from the dangers of life in the lonely city. Once again it was Jews who represented the threatening evil which awaited to ensnare unsuspecting Irish innocents.

On 15 December, Gaffney explored the other dangers that face Irish emigrants. She examined two categories of girls: those who got 'into trouble' (i.e. became pregnant) in Ireland and those who got 'into trouble' in England. In the case of the former, she argued, it was particularly unfair that charities in England should be 'saddled' with their upkeep. Some charities attempted to send girls back to Ireland but they were either unwilling or unable to return to their families. Gaffney cited several nuns, priests and social workers who spoke out against the uncharitable attitude towards unmarried mothers in Ireland. Parents back in Ireland rarely agreed to take their daughters home after they became pregnant. In fact, some parents had forced the girls to emigrate to England once their condition was known. One priest told the story of a young girl who arrived in an English city pregnant and alone. Her mother had given her barely enough money for the boat fare and now she was destitute. The priest personally contacted the mother asking for the girl to be taken home but she refused. The priest wrote to the girl's local parish priest in Ireland but he agreed with the family that the girl should not return home. An elderly nun told Gaffney that she had encountered many similar incidents, unmarried mothers were treated like 'outlaws' in Ireland.

Charities in England encouraged the young mothers to find employment and place their babies in foster care. The mothers visited the babies and paid for their upkeep. This was important for both mothers and babies. Young women who simply abandoned their babies were more likely to 'get into trouble' again in the future. The charities faced the added problem of trying to find Catholic homes to adopt abandoned babies. Sometimes the families in Ireland exacerbated the problem by agreeing to take the young women back home but refusing to take the babies, thus encouraging the abandonment of babies. Gaffney quoted one Catholic social worker as saying: 'These girls are the scapegoats of a tradition of puritanism that will not admit that things are as they are.' The general opinion of charity workers in England was that these women and girls 'are more sinned against than sinning' (15 December 1936).

Gaffney's series of articles was unusually frank and open in its discussion of the darker side of life in England and the particular problems faced by young, untrained Irish emigrants. Away from the guiding influence of family and friends, in a strange city, they were vulnerable to temptations. In addition, without proper qualifications they faced an uncertain economic future. Gaffney made it clear that the majority of female emigrants did well in England, they got good jobs and made a decent living for themselves. However, by focusing on the minority who experienced serious difficulties, she was hoping to reveal the many things that could go very badly wrong. She believed there was a need to publicise these problems because people back home in Ireland either did not know or simply did not care what happened to these young women once they boarded the boat for England. She was also determined to halt the worrying trend of very young, very poor girls travelling to England and arriving in cities like Liverpool completely destitute where they either fell on the mercy of charities or were lured into lives of immorality.

Gaffney's series received the full backing and support of the *Irish Independent* editorial. Her articles also sparked off many discussions, letters and articles. For example, on 21 December 1936, Elizabeth O'Connor of the IWWU wrote to the paper pointing out that young, country girls arriving in Dublin City experienced many similar problems to those witnessed by Gaffney in Liverpool and London. Girls from rural areas who had no domestic training frequently lost their jobs after a short time. They found themselves out on the streets with no money, no accommodation and no friends in the city. O'Connor was among many commentators who proposed that a residential technical college and employment bureau be set up in Dublin so that girls could be both properly trained for domestic service and placed in decent employment. O'Connor's letter is interesting in challenging the dichotomy of England/city, Ireland/countryside. By presenting Dublin as a city with all the associated problems and disadvantages of other cities, she located issues of unemployment, poverty and the vulnerability of young women and girls right at the centre of Irish political and commercial life.

On 23 December 1936, Archbishop Gilmartin of Tuam speaking at a prize giving ceremony for students in Galway referred to Gaffney's series of articles in the *Independent*. He praised the series for highlighting 'the awful dangers of emigration'. Quoting selectively from Gaffney's research, he said that although wages in England seemed very attractive, once expenses such as food, travel and accommodation were deducted, there was little difference between the wages there and the wages available here at home. He concluded that young people would be 'happier and safer' working at home.

*Conclusion:*

As mentioned at the start of this section on emigration, there were several competing discourses at work in the discussions of female emigration to Britain, particularly English cities, in the 1930s. The issue of education and training was widely debated. However, there were some contradictions apparent in these discussions. While there appears to have been general consensus that girls needed more practical domestic training, some commentators believed that this would improve the prospects of Irish young women emigrating to England, for others, however, this training was aimed at encouraging these women to work in Ireland and eventually to settle down, marry and start a family. Thus the crux of the matter seemed to be whether young women and girls should be prepared more adequately for emigration or whether they should be strongly dissuaded from emigrating. But, as several commentators realised, women and girls had a number of reasons for emigrating. In some cases employment was not the sole or even the primary reason. According to members of the Catholic hierarchy, women and girls were rejecting employment in Ireland and were being lured abroad by the unrealities of cinema and the promise of excitement and glamour. Gaffney offered a different and more radical explanation which highlighted some of the comfortable realities in Irish society. She suggested that a growing minority of young women and girls who had deviated from the sexual norms were being forced into emigration to protect the reputations of their families and the illusion of moral probity.

However, despite their different explanations, Gaffney and the hierarchy share a concern for the moral wellbeing of Irish young women emigrating to England. There does not appear to have been a similar concern about the moral wellbeing of Irish young men. This may be explained by the fact that Irish women were expected to embody a particularly stringent code of morality and virtue. There were few who expected Irish men to do likewise. The newspaper discussions on emigration begin to reveal some of the underlying problems with the moral expectations being placed upon Irish women and girls. On the one hand, it was feared that once they were away from the guiding influence of the Catholic Church these moral sanctions completely broke down as soon as the girls stepped off the boat at Liverpool. On the other hand, as Gaffney suggested, girls were being forced to emigrate in order to maintain the illusion of morality and respectability. Thus emigrant girls simultaneously embodied both the fragility and hypocrisy of that moral code.

## Section 3: Woman, Citizen and Worker – the Constitution of 1937

*Introduction:*

> It has been a sorry year for women in the Saorstat. We have been placed among the lowest on the black list issued at Geneva showing the status of women in various countries. We have seen the Government...not only recognise but impose a lower wage standard for women than for men. We have seen the same political parties give impetus to the antifeminine ramp in the Conditions of Employment Bill, and we have witnessed the disedifying beginnings of a campaign to exclude women altogether from the industrial employment in which they have worked for centuries. (Gertrude Gaffney, Leaves from a Woman's Diary, *Irish Independent*, 1 January 1937)

Although this statement was written several months before the publication of the draft constitution of 1937, it indicates the extent to which feminists were already growing resentful of government policy on the employment of women outside the home. For most of the 1930s the press had reported many vocal attacks on the woman worker from a number of quarters. The rising level of unemployment among men was being linked to the employment of women in a range of jobs:

> During the last couple of months there has been a move to start a sex war, with officialdom looking on approvingly at this red herring being so conveniently drawn across the trail of an unemployment problem which it is unable to control. (Gaffney, 1 January 1937)

In her column, Gaffney challenged the view that women were responsible for male unemployment. She argued that women were actually underrepresented in many sectors of the economy, particularly in the professions. Although there was 'a fairish' number of women doctors, they comprised a very small percentage of the total number of doctors in the country. 'We have so few women solicitors and barristers that one cannot begin to reckon them in percentages'. Gaffney then turned to her own profession of journalism, where 'we have fewer than a dozen qualified women to thousands of qualified men'. Finally, in the political sphere, she wrote, 'the story is even more depressing'. The majority of women worked in sectors such as domestic service, clerical work and particular industries like weaving and spinning, where men either did not wish to work or where they did not have the appropriate skills to be employed. Thus, Gaffney concluded, women could hardly be said to be keeping men out of work (1 January 1937).

Gaffney's argument was a fairly common one among feminists of the period. They argued that men and women did not compete directly for jobs but were actually located in different sectors of the workforce. Thus legislation and employment practices aimed at excluding women from the work place would not be directly beneficial to men's employment prospects. They argued that female employment was a 'red herring', a government ploy to explain unemployment among men by making a scapegoat of the woman worker. As mentioned earlier, certain types of women workers in particular sectors were especially vulnerable to scapegoating. The woman industrial worker was more likely to be targeted than the domestic servant, while the married woman worker was far more likely to be criticised than the single young girl. These debates and arguments that had been bubbling under the surface for many years suddenly burst out into the open when the draft constitution was published in May 1937. For the first time, the role of woman was specifically addressed in the constitution in ways that threatened to undermine equality and construct a separate, unequal position for women in Irish society. The remainder of this section will focus not only on newspaper reports of the constitutional debates but will examine the role played by two rival national dailies in framing and defining those debates. In particular, I will analyse the ways in which the *Irish Press* and *Irish Independent* represented the feminists who led a vocal campaign against the draft constitution.

*De Valera and the Sex War:*

> Women had no part in framing Bunreacht na hEireann [Irish Constitution]. Not one woman took part in drafting it. Of the 152 TDs [members of parliament] who had an opportunity to comment on the draft, only three were women....Outside the Dail, a number of women's organisations protested in vain against certain articles – so much so that de Valera admitted knowing that he had a 'bad reputation with women'. (Scannell, 1988: 123)

The Irish Constitution of 1937 has been described by Lentin as 'a definite product of its time' (1998: 9 ). In framing definitions of the nation, national identity and national collectivity, it narrowly defined Irishness within ethnic, religious and gender boundaries (Lentin 1998). In keeping with the focus of this book, I will focus here on the gender ideology underpinning this important document. On 1 May 1937, the full text of the draft constitution was published in the *Irish Independent*, meanwhile the *Irish Press* devoted almost the entire newspaper to publishing the full text in both Irish and English. While many of the articles were simply reproduced from the existing Free State constitution, including the restoration of the Seanad (upper house) which de Valera had temporarily abolished, there were several new developments and it was these which formed the main focus of debate over the next two months. The *Irish Press* praised the draft document saying that 'it confers the widest political rights on the citizen' and 'it provides for equality for all and privileges for none' (1 May).

The *Independent* unsurprisingly adopted a rather different perspective, paying particular attention to the proposed office of President who was to be elected by the people every seven years. Under the heading 'On the Peacock Throne', the *Independent* editorial of 5 May reported that 'Even Mr. De Valera's own tied organ [the *Irish Press*] has not denied that the post of president under the new constitution is being created by Mr. De Valera for himself.' Up to this point de Valera, as Prime Minster of the government, was President of the Dail and hence was usually called President de Valera. The newly proposed office of President would be largely ceremonial and quite separate from the Dail. Henceforth, to avoid any confusion of titles, the head of the government would be more commonly known as the *taoiseach*.

The *Independent* showed its usual condemnation of de Valera and looked for aspects of the constitution which could be criticised and attacked. Therefore, one must question whether the strong focus on women's rights under the new constitution, which was to occupy the paper for many weeks, was motivated by a genuine concern for equality or by a desire to attack de Valera:

> No clauses in the constitution attracted more attention at the time than those which related to women. Indeed such was the intensity of the reaction against his initial proposals that de Valera was forced to drop some of the contentious provisions. (Travers, 1995: 159)

Certainly in the newspaper debates the three articles of the draft constitution relating to women drew the most heated exchanges. Article 40, in particular, seemed to represent a very real threat to women's rights as citizens:

> All citizens shall, as human persons, be held equal before the law. This shall not be held to mean that the State shall not in its enactments have due regard to differences of capacity, physical and moral, and of social function.

While Article 41 recognised the value of women's work within the home, it also suggested that mothers should not engage in labour outside the home.

> In particular the State recognises that by her life within the home, woman gives to the State a support without which the common good cannot be achieved. The State shall, therefore, endeavour to ensure that mothers shall not be obliged by economic necessity to engage in labour to the neglect of their duties in the home.

This Article can be viewed as a form of 'romantic paternalism', an attempt to honour the contribution to the nation-state made by mothers and housewives. However, as Scannell argues, it can equally be viewed as 'grossly offensive to the dignity and freedoms of womanhood' (1988: 125). It concentrated on the danger of mothers neglecting their duties in the home but made no mention of fathers' duties (Scannell 1988). By speaking of *woman's life within the home*, it implied that the natural and proper vocation of all women was within the domestic sphere. This assumption about woman's proper sphere was reinforced in Article 45 which referred to women's 'inadequate strength' and endeavoured to ensure that women would not be forced to enter avocations unsuited to their sex or strength.

On 6 May, a feature article by a well-known lawyer, John A. Costello, was published in the *Independent* under the banner headline 'New Constitution Curtails Women's Rights'. He argued that it:

> comes as a surprise to find the status of women affected, if not expressly, certainly by implication. We read the somewhat grandiose statement that all citizens shall be held equal before the law, but we then discover that the substance of that declaration is taken away by the provision that the state may, if it likes, in its legislation declare them to be unequal. (*Irish Independent*, 6 May 1937)

Costello went on to argue that the specific reference to the 'inadequate strength of women' opened the door to all sorts of prohibitions being placed upon women's employment rights. He criticised the removal of the guarantees of equal citizenship, which existed under the old constitution of 1922 by the omission of the phrase 'without distinction of sex'. The fact that the new constitution proposed to distinguish between the sexes would lessen women's claim on equal rights. Costello concluded that the draft was 'a burnt offering to feminists and feminist associations'.

On the following day, 7 May, Gertrude Gaffney devoted her weekly feature, 'Leaves from a Women's Diary' to the constitution. She claimed that the new constitution sounded the 'death knell of the working woman'. She related this directly to the personal motives of President Eamon de Valera who 'has always been a reactionary where women are concerned'. His aim had always been to keep women 'in their proper place'. He was planning to extinguish women's rights piece by piece, beginning with employment rights. 'We are to be no longer citizens entitled to enjoy equal rights under a democratic constitution, but laws are to be enacted which will take into consideration our "differences of capacity, physical and moral, and of social function"'. But if the president's aim was to abolish male unemployment, then he was 'making the mistake of his life'. As Gaffney had argued in her previous articles, men and women did not compete directly for employment. De Valera, she argued, was out of touch with the real world and was living 'in a remote and distant political world of his own'. Gaffney argued that de Valera's attitude to women workers was influenced by Herr Hitler. However, in attempting to ban women from the work place, government legislation was primarily aimed at 'factory girls' and if they were thrown out of work what would become of them? Many would simply leave Ireland and emigrate to England. This, according to Gaffney, would further reduce marriage rates and family prospects in Ireland.

This is an important point which related back to Gaffney's series of articles on emigration which were published in the *Independent* in 1936 and re-issued as a booklet in early 1937. As has been discussed at length in the previous section, the dilemma for policy makers was how to balance training and employment practises in Ireland with the steady stream of emigration to Britain. Young women had made it clear that if they could not find suitable, well paid jobs at home they would leave the country in very large numbers. Thus while de Valera was determined to construct cosy homesteads with 'stay at home' domesticated wives and mothers, the reality was that thousands of young women were voting with their feet and rejecting this model lifestyle. While Hitler may have been able to promote a German ideal of domesticated motherhood, Ireland's long tradition of female emigration provided women with an alternative to the 'hearth and home'. Gaffney was at pains to remind de Valera that he owed Irish women a debt of gratitude and that his draft constitution was an insult to women who had made great personal sacrifices during the military campaign for independence:

> But for the women of Ireland Mr. de Valera would not be in the position he holds today. He was glad enough to make use of them to transport guns and munitions, to carry secret despatches, and to harbour himself and his colleagues, when it was risking life and liberty to do any of these things. (Gaffney, *Irish Independent*, 7 May 1937)

Now de Valera wanted women to return to the Middle Ages, denying them their 'God-given right' to work for a living, to be 'little more than a chattel'. This would make Ireland an international 'laughing stock'. Gaffney concluded this long article by reminding women that they still had the vote, until de Valera saw fit to take it away from them, and they should use that vote to defeat the constitution.

Meanwhile the *Irish Press* continued to offer a very different interpretation of the constitution. As the two papers took up very distinct positions in relation to the constitutional debates, the animosity between them appeared to increase. The *Independent* dismissed the *Press* as de Valera's 'tied organ' (5 May 1937), while the *Press* retaliated by calling the *Independent* the mouthpiece of the opposition party Fine Gael (19 June 1937). On 10 May, both the front page and page two of the *Irish Press* were given over to de Valera's detailed response to his critics. As well as addressing the many other criticisms of the draft document, he devoted several paragraphs to the question of women's rights. In relation to the claim that the constitution undermined women's right to enfranchisement, he said 'there isn't a single shred of foundation for that statement. Women and men, as far as the franchise is concerned, are exactly equal in this constitution'. However, he admitted that the new document was different in several key ways from the existing constitution:

> It is true there was a phrase in the old constitution which is not in this constitution – 'without distinction of sex' – and I deliberately left that out because it was a phrase applicable to a time when women were only just emerging from the position of political inferiority and it was a badge of their previous inferiority. (*Irish Press*, 10 May 1937)

Obviously, de Valera was keenly aware of the many criticisms that had been made against him personally. However, his intention was to firmly refute those criticisms rather than taking on board the suggestions that his opponents were making. While he acknowledged that 'women are mentioned in other parts of this constitution' he denied that this was intended to 'deprive them of rights'. 'No it is for the purpose of protecting them where they need protection, in my opinion'. He then went on to quote the articles relating to women's life within the home and women's inadequate strength (Articles 41 and 45). 'I want the critics to tell us what is wrong about that, and not simply to get off by saying that I have a prejudice against women', an allegation which he dismissed as 'nonsense'. He urged women to read the draft document for themselves and not to be misled by those with a vested interest. He was confident that if they read it they would vote for it. He asked what his opponents wanted; did they wish to see women 'forced into vocations unsuited to their age, sex or strength?':

> There is nothing to stop any woman from entering any vocation, but we want to ensure that the social system will be such that they cannot be forced into work which they would not undertake were it not that they were compelled by the social system to do it. (*Irish Press*, 10 May 1937)

This long statement by Mr. de Valera revealed a great deal about his attitude to women and his very personal relationship to a constitution that he had drafted. His use of phrases like 'I deliberately left that out' and 'where they need protection, in my opinion' indicates his role in framing a constitution around his own personal beliefs. This attitude was to become even more apparent in the Dail debates where he passionately defended every article of the constitution as his own personal project.

It was the personal nature of de Valera's relationship to the constitution that worried many critics, especially feminists who had a deep mistrust of his attitude to women's role in public life. As Scannell has argued, history has shown that de Valera's critics were correct to fear that the State would give Article 41 'the most restrictive interpretation' of women's rights (1988: 126).

*Poisoning the Minds of Women:*

Not only did the *Irish Press* provide detailed coverage of de Valera's viewpoints but it also used its editorials to defend his position and to attack his critics. The *Press* saved its sharpest attacks for feminists. On 11 May, that paper published a letter from Mrs. Mary S. Kettle written on behalf of the Joint Committee of Women's Societies. While the letter consisting of two paragraphs was located towards the back of the paper on page 14, the *Press*'s attack on the letter took up the entire editorial column. The editorial was headed 'A Gratuitous Libel':

> We do not think we are wronging Mrs. Kettle when we say that she showed herself only too eager to follow the lead of Mr. Costello, K.C. and to accept his assurance that in Bunreacht na hEireann there was some cryptic clause or ambiguous language which would have the effect of placing women in an inferior position from that which they now occupy. (*Irish Press*, 11 May 1937)

According to the editor, Mrs. Kettle and other members of the Joint Committee of Women's Societies had taken up a position of hostility towards the constitution for which there was not 'a shred of reason or justification'. Her letter was dismissed as 'wire reasoning and fallacious arguments'. The editorial quoted her letter almost line by line, refuting all of her arguments. For example, she claimed that articles 40, 41 and 45 posed a serious challenge to the rights of working women. Quoting the draft constitution and de Valera's statements, the editor argued that women's rights were in no way undermined and there was no necessity to change a word of the new document. The editorial concluded by demanding that Mrs. Kettle 'apologise to the men whom she has grossly and wantonly libelled'.

On the same day, the *Irish Independent* also published several letters on women's status in the constitution including an identical copy of Mary Kettle's letter. But unlike the *Irish Press*, there was no criticism of these letters, on the contrary the *Independent* appeared to give full backing to the attack on de Valera being so ably vocalised by its own journalist, Gertrude Gaffney. In a letter full of praise for Gaffney, the veteran suffragist campaigner Hanna Sheehy Skeffington argued that she knew Mr. de Valera very well and that his 'ideal is the strictly domestic type of woman who eschews "politics" as male concerns, the fascist ideal now working under Mussolini and Hitler and other dictators'. The women of Ireland, she concluded, must demand restoration of their previously honoured rights (*Irish Independent*, 11 May 1937).

On 12 May 1937, the *Independent* published several more letters on this topic. One letter in particular was given prominent position on the top of page 5 and printed under the large headline 'Worse than the Middle Ages: Women and Draft Constitution'. This was written by Professor Mary Hayden, another veteran of the suffrage movement. Using her knowledge of history, she argued that women had more rights to work, own property and hold public office in the Middle Ages than they would have under de Valera's constitution. She said that the draft constitution offered women false promises of 'needless safeguards' and 'vague declarations' about women's value in the home. In reality, however, it proposed to limit 'opportunities of earning' as well as limiting woman's civil status and 'her whole position as a citizen'.

On the same day, both the *Irish Press* and the *Independent* published a long letter from the IWWU which argued that Article 40 'gives the state power to restrict the rights and liberties of certain citizens in view of differences of capacity, physical and moral, and of social function'. This was dangerous not only to women but also to certain types of men particularly in the climate of fascism. This was presumably a reference to the working rights of disabled, old and infirm men. The letter was also highly critical of Article 41 which focused on women's role within the home. Instead of such narrow restrictions, the IWWU proposed that there be full recognition that:

> the part played by women for the common good outside the home, in education, in social service, in culture, in workshop, on the farm, had now become indispensable to a civilised state...It is surely invidious to introduce a clause which makes it appear that only the woman **within** the home can contribute to the common good. (*Irish Independent* and *Irish Press*, 12 May 1937, emphasis in the original)

On the following day, 13 May, the *Press* devoted a two-column editorial to attacking the letter from the IWWU and another letter by Mary Kettle. The former letter was criticised for being 'based on misconceptions'. Article 40 did not specifically mention women and, according to the editor, was not intended to remove women's right to work. Instead this article merely pledged to protect the weak from being abused and exploited. The women's trades union was accused of reading 'into the section something which never entered the head of its framers and which, by no principle of interpretion could it be made to mean'. However, while the IWWU were merely accused of misunderstanding the constitution, Mary Kettle was accused of attempting 'to poison the minds of the women of the country against the government, to make them believe that the head and other members of that government were their enemies' (*Irish Press*, 13 May 1937).

In the continuing war of words between women's groups and the editor of the *Irish Press*, Mary Kettle wrote yet another letter to the paper on 14 May. She pointed out that 'Jousting with the Editor in his own paper makes for an unequal contest.' She added that while very able women had gone through the constitution article by article in a detailed and systematic way, the editor of the *Press* had merely repeated his assertions over and over without offering any real evidence to support his claims. The editor and Mr. de Valera, she argued, merely tried to reassure women that their fears were groundless yet they firmly resisted any attempt to insert a clause on equal rights.

As will be discussed in the Chapter five on Republican women, the use of the editorial to launch personal attacks on particular individuals was fairly common practice in the *Irish Press*. In 1936 Mary MacSwiney was ridiculed in a very personal way in the editorial columns of the paper. In 1937, the editor turned his attention to Mary Kettle. While these two were very different women from different political perspectives, they shared a deep mistrust of de Valera and his Fianna

Fail party. The fact that they wrote regular letters to the press, including the *Irish Press*, gave the editor an excuse to reply to their charges using the strongest possible language. As Mary Kettle put it, a 'jousting' match with the editor of a paper is a very unequal contest in which the editor will always have the last word. In many cases the editor's responses were far longer than the original letter (see 11, 12, 13 and 18 May 1937). Located in a prominent position in the paper and written in the authoritative voice of the editor, the editorial held many advantages over the letters' page.

Everyday the *Independent* and the *Press* devoted pages of coverage to the Dail debates on the constitution. While the issue of women's rights was repeatedly raised by opposition politicians, other issues of concern included the powers of the president, the censorship of the press and the relationship between the Free State and the northern six counties. De Valera was accused of merely confusing the relationship between the two parts of the island in an attempt to conceal the lack of any real progress in overcoming the divisions between north and south. Articles 2 and 3 which famously laid claim to the whole island of Ireland (until amended in 1999 as part of the Good Friday agreement) were criticised by many opposition politicians in the 1937 debates for claiming to deliver something which was completely beyond the power of the Free State government (*Irish Independent* and *Irish Press* 14-15 May).

On 15 May both of the papers reported that a delegation of women's groups went to see de Valera. The president was quoted as saying that he did not share their apprehensions about the impact of the constitution on women's rights. However, he did promise that he would insert two clauses in the constitution, firstly, guaranteeing that women would not be excluded from the franchise and secondly, preventing any law being passed which would disqualify women from the rights of citizenship.

On 22 May the *Independent* reprinted a letter which had been sent to the president by the Irish Women Citizens and Local Government Association, a group originally founded in the late 1800s and a key player in the suffrage campaigns of the early 1900s. The letter demanded the restoration of Article 3 of the original 1922 constitution. This article expressly stated that there should be equal rights for all citizens 'without distinction of sex'. The letter also called for the amendment of Articles 41 and 45. The letter concluded that 'the position of women in the Saorstat (Free State) has deteriorated in recent years from the ideal implicit in the Proclamation of 1916 and the Constitution of 1922'. The fact that suffrage groups and individual suffrage activists mobilised against the draft constitution suggests the extent to which women's hard won rights of citizenship were seen to be under threat. The various victories which Irish women had achieved, including universal suffrage in 1922, appeared to be safeguarded in the first constitution of the newly established Free State. The fact that these rights were coming under attack 15 years later clearly led some feminists to believe that de Valera was influenced by the fascist policies of Germany, Spain and Italy.

A long letter by Professor Mary Macken was published in the *Independent* on 26 May and in the *Irish Press* on the following day, 27 May. In her letter she made the connection between the policy of excluding women from industrial jobs and rising emigration among young women. She said that female emigration, which was directly linked to wage levels and job opportunities in the Free State, would do little to improve marriage rates or enhance future cosy Irish homes. Any government policy that was likely to increase female emigration was very short sighted indeed. Macken also replied to those who argued that the constitution was merely following Catholic teaching on family life. As a Catholic she could not see any justification for the constitutional attack on women's rights as citizens. This issue of Catholicism and women's citizenship was taken up again by Professor Mary Hayden in a letter published in the *Independent* on 3 June 1937.

Hayden cited a recent document written by the International Union of Catholic Women's Leagues in which they demanded equal citizenship rights for women. While demanding an adequate family wage for married men, the International Union argued that women should not be restricted from working outside the home if they so desired. Hayden concluded that it was gratifying to find that such an enormous body of Catholic women should share the opinion of Irish Catholic women who were demanding equal rights in the constitution. Thus Hayden, like her fellow professor Mary Macken, argued that there was no contradiction between Catholicism and equal rights for women. It is highly significant and very indicative of the climate at the time, that two such prominent and well-known female academics felt it necessary to justify their demands for equality not merely in terms of feminism but in terms of Catholicism as well.

On the same day, the *Independent* reported a heated exchange in the Dail between two opposition T.D.s and Mr. de Valera. Professor O'Sullivan (Fine Gael representative for Kerry) and Dr. Rowlette (Independent, Dublin University) argued at length that women's organisations had very real concerns about political and economic discrimination under the provisions of the draft constitution. Dr. Rowlette, supported by Professor O'Sullivan, proposed an amendment to delete the qualification of 'differences in capacity, physical and moral, and of social function'. De Valera, who appeared to be very defensive, rejected the claim that such an amendment was necessary. On 5 June, the *Independent* returned to the Dail debates on women and the constitution under the headline 'President's Attitude on Rights of Women'. In an apparently heated debate that was reported at great length, de Valera challenged the statements of his critics. He said that 'he resented very strongly suggestions that he had some reactionary views about women. That was not true; and he had never shown it in public or private. He believed that the culture and progress of communities would be very well estimated by the standard and position that women occupied'. But he then added that he overwhelmingly rejected all the proposed amendments to articles relating to women. 'I have made up my mind, and I will not accept these amendments'. With these words, de Valera once again revealed his close personal relationship to the constitution and his reluctance to accept any suggestions for its improvement.

Nevertheless, he was obviously under growing pressure and becoming increasingly defensive about his constitution. It was probably in this context that he agreed to make some small efforts to placate the very vocal feminist lobby groups. For example, on 29 May the *Irish Press* reported 'Women's Position to be Met'. In response to persistent lobbying by a number of T.D.s including Mrs. Bridget Redmond (Fine Gael) one of only three women in the Dail, de Valera agreed to insert an amendment to Article 16, adding the phrase 'without distinction of sex' to the right of every citizen, aged 21 and over, to vote and be eligible for membership of the Dail. He also inserted an amendment to Article 9 guaranteeing that no person could be excluded from citizenship by reason of their sex. On the 10 June, the *Press* reported another successful amendment this time in relation to Article 45. 'The inadequate strength of women', a phrase which had proved so controversial was to be omitted, instead the paragraph was to read as follows:

> The State shall endeavour to ensure that the strength and health of workers, men and women, and the tender age of children shall not be abused, and that citizens shall not be forced by economic necessity to enter avocations unsuited to their sex, age or strength. (The *Irish Press*, 10 June 1937)

While this amendment was to win the approval of the IWWU, it did little to reassure other women's groups. If women had any doubts about the roles there were expected to play in the Saorstat of the 1930s then they would have found the words of Bishop Kinane illuminating. Addressing the Irish Technical Education Association conference in Waterford he said that there was insufficient attention paid to teaching domestic science. 'Undue attention is paid to subjects that are of very little practical value to most of our girls':

> The home is woman's sphere. Most of our girls are destined ultimately as mothers and wives. Much of the comfort and happiness of the household will depend upon their capacity to discharge efficiently the obligations that thus fall to them. (*Irish Independent*, 9 June 1937)

These views were remarkably similar to those expressed by Canon Barrett in the *Cork Examiner* on 9 September 1936 when he advised pupils and teachers at Macroom Technical School that girls should learn the domestic sciences with a view to improving conditions in their own homes. The view was apparently shared by many priests and bishops that girls' education should be aimed not at long-term employment but at a future of domesticity and motherhood. In such a climate it is little wonder feminists feared that the constitution of 1937 represented a legal basis for their gradual exclusion from public life.

Meanwhile, in the Dail the constitution was passed by 62 votes to 48 and was then presented to the people at a general election in July 1937. Opposition politicians criticised the Fianna Fail government for turning the constitution into a party issue, using it as an election ploy to distract attention from the serious economic issues that should have formed the basis of election campaigning.

On 18 June 1937, Gertrude Gaffney once again devoted her regular column to the campaign against the constitution under the headline 'Last Minute Fight to Save their Rights'. This referred to an open meeting to be held at the Mansion House, Dublin on 21 June, organised by the Women Graduates Association. Gaffney gave her wholehearted support to the meeting saying: 'if we go down this time we are down for good. Not only will we find ourselves shut out of the labour market, excluded from all the good jobs in the civil service' but things may go the way of Germany where women were pushed back into the home and denied any public voice. Like other feminist commentators, Gaffney did not directly challenge the authority of the Catholic Church but rather sought to find some support from among the clergy. She cited a friendly priest who had assured her that the State had no moral right to determine whether or not a married woman should take up a job outside the home.

The day after the women's meeting, the *Independent* carried a lengthy report. 'Over 1,500 women from all parts of the Free State attended in the Mansion House, Dublin, last night a meeting held under the auspices of the Women Graduates Association' (22 June 1937). The meeting strongly urged all women to vote against the constitution. Speakers included Professor Mary Macken and Professor Mary Hayden, the latter was quoted as saying: 'Is woman's sphere to be limited to the home? I say no (applause). We do not want flattery – what we want is liberty to work.' Mary Kettle was quoted as saying that 'the only protection women asked and needed was the clear, unequivocal statement of equality of rights and opportunities in the constitution'. Hanna Sheehy Skeffington and Dr. Kathleen Lynn, the veteran Republican activist who had participated in the 1916 Rising, were also among the speakers.

The *Irish Press* also carried a report of the meeting and quoted many of the same speakers. However, beside this report, in an interesting juxtaposition, the *Press* printed a letter from Louie Bennett on behalf of the IWWU under the heading 'Really Serious Menace Removed'. Bennett pointed out that although no members of the union appeared on the platform at the Mansion House meeting, they still supported women's fight for full rights as citizens. However, the committee of the IWWU considered that de Valera's amendments to Articles 9, 16 and 45 removed the worst menaces to women's rights. Thus they could not share the view of other women's groups in wholeheartedly opposing the constitution. It is difficult to say if de Valera deliberately introduced minor amendments to these articles in an attempt to split the feminist opposition to his constitution. Certainly, the decision of the IWWU to withdraw from the campaign against the constitution was 'a bitter blow' to the other women's groups (Ward 1997: 327).

It is noteworthy that all of the leading women in the anti-constitutional campaign were of advanced years and had been active in public life for several decades. One is struck by the absence of younger women. While newspaper accounts of militant Republicanism in the 1930s refer to scores of young women playing an active role in organisations such as Cumann na mBan, there does not appear to have been the same influx of younger women to take up the mantle of feminism in the Irish Free State. The absence of young blood perhaps reinforced the stereotype that these feminists were bitter, elderly spinsters or lonely widows who understood little about the reality of family life.

Negative, stereotypical representations of these feminist activists were invoked by the editor of the *Irish Press* on 23 June under the heading 'Feminine Alarms'. 'We do not think the public will be inclined to attach too much importance to the meeting organised by the National University Women Graduates Association'. The editorial asserted that there was no foundation to their arguments. Far from exercising discrimination against women, the constitution had, according to the editor, 'improved women's status'. While pointing out that 'no restrictions' were placed on women's activities, the editorial claimed that the constitution 'rightly' acknowledged woman's role in the home as 'the sphere in which she can perform the most useful functions, in which she can display the qualities that best adorn womanhood'. Once again the editor condemned 'the prime movers in this agitation' who had been uttering 'shrill cries of alarm at a non-existent danger'. 'On the strength of their own imaginings', these women had come out in open hostility to the government and set themselves up as 'saviours of their sex'. The language and imagery of this editorial are very interesting and reveal the ways in which feminists were represented. Words like 'shrill', 'alarm', 'imaginings' conjure up an image of hysterical women who are deluding themselves and others about the real dangers of the constitution. In setting themselves up as the 'saviours of their sex' they are presented as elitist, snobbish and out of touch with reality.

These negative stereotypes of feminists were also employed by government ministers. For example, minister Sean MacEntee, speaking at a Fianna Fail election rally in Dublin, said that the constitution held no threat to women's rights as citizens. 'The truth of the matter is that a lot of the women who are talking now about women's rights have not men of their own to let off steam against' (quoted in the *Independent* on 24 June 1937). This view was challenged in the *Independent* on the following day, 25 June, by Gertrude Gaffney who said that the majority of the women who addressed the Mansion House meeting were mothers who were well aware of the financial and other responsibilities involved in bringing up children. These women spoke from real life experiences not from some image or ideal of what Irish family life ought to be.

On 26 June, the *Independent* carried a short report under the heading 'Cumann na mBan Condemn Constitution'. Interestingly, this women's group condemned the constitution not on the basis of its impact on women's rights but on the matter of political sovereignty and independence. They argued that de Valera was using the term 'Eire' to describe an independent country that in effect excluded the six counties and thus accepted *de facto* partition. Eire, no matter how much sovereignty it attained, could never be an Irish Republic. It is not entirely surprising that one of the oldest and most organised groups of women in the country did not take a more active role in the campaign for women's rights. Since its inception in 1914, Cumann na mBan had never claimed to be a feminist organisation and had always prioritised Republican concerns over women's interests.

On the day of the election, 1 July, the *Independent* published a letter from 'a woman voter' in which she pointed out that the Free State had the lowest marriage rate in Europe and, therefore, many women had neither children nor husbands to care for, neither had they homes of their own to look after 'except the corners they make for themselves by the work of their heads and hands. There are many of them supporting widowed mothers. It is a bitter irony to lecture such women on their place in the home!'.

The election results proved to be very close but it is impossible to say whether or not this was connected to the large numbers of women who turned out to vote (see *Independent* 2 July 1937). When the results were announced Fianna Fail had 69 seats, while the combined opposition parties had 67 seats (*Irish Independent* 7 July 1937). On the following day, 8 July, the *Independent* editorial was devoted to the subject matter of the constitution. 'From whatever angle it may be viewed, few can regard the history of the draft constitution as satisfactory'. It should have been prepared by a 'body specifically selected for the purpose', such a body should have represented all political interests not merely those of Mr. de Valera. Although some amendments were won by the opposition it remained a 'party document' and contained several 'serious blemishes':

> It lowered the status of women citizens, it vested in the future president powers which are capable of being abused, it empowers the state to interfere with freedom of opinion, freedom of the press and freedom of association; it makes provision for vesting unlimited powers in military tribunals. (*Irish Independent*, 8 July 1937)

The public was given the opportunity of voting simply 'yes' or 'no' to the entire document a fact which, according to the editor of the *Independent*, may have explained why over 100,000 votes were spoiled by voters who simply could not make up their mind on all aspects of the detailed document. The editorial concluded by arguing that just over 51% of voters were in favour of the constitution.

*Conclusion:*

The debates on the Constitution of 1937 reveal many conflicting discourses in Irish society. De Valera's document was drafted under the advisement of the Catholic Church and thus was framed by Catholic social teaching (Beaumont 1997). The influence of Catholic beliefs and values was clearly visible in those sections dealing with women's rights and duties. Although it entitled women to vote, to be elected to parliament and to become citizens on the same basis as men, Article 41, 'an unparalleled construction, conceived women, in the spirit of patriarchal Catholicism, primarily as mothers' (Lentin 1998: 11). The dominant image of women throughout the constitution was as wives and mothers who fulfilled their duty to the State through their roles within the home. This was challenged by opponents of the constitution who proposed alternative images of women as workers and as active citizens. Although there are obvious overlaps between the woman as worker, citizen and mother, the constitutional debates tended to represent these aspects of womanhood as separate and competing.

Although de Valera did give in to pressure and introduced amendments to three of the Articles relating to women, he refused to amend any of the sections relating to woman as wife and mother. The amendments to articles 9 and 16 protected the rights to political citizenship which women already enjoyed, therefore, it could be argued, that these amendments were largely symbolic, giving the impression that de Valera was willing to compromise, and that he was not the reactionary he seemed to be. By guaranteeing enfranchisement and the right to sit in Dail Eireann 'without distinction of sex', de Valera was not offering anything new. He was merely acknowledging the most basic rights of the woman citizen to cast her vote every 4 years. The fact that there were only three women members of the Dail in 1937, half the number there had been in 1922, suggests that women's political citizenship was not a serious threat to the status quo.

Although Article 45 related more directly to the woman as worker, the amendment introduced by de Valera was ambiguous and still allowed for the exclusion of women from particular sectors of the workforce. But it was his absolute refusal to amend Articles 40 and 41 that revealed de Valera's true vision of women in Irish society. Article 40 enabled the State to treat women differently from men and to emphasise women's particular 'social functions' as wives and mothers. Article 41 underlined women's duties 'within the home' and endeavoured to ensure that women would not be obliged to work outside the home. Thus women's place within the privacy of the domestic sphere was written into the constitution. According to this discourse, Irishwomen's primary duty and responsibility to the State were enacted through their maternity and domesticity.

However, feminist groups and other opponents of de Valera challenged this discourse. They proposed the alternative view that women embodied citizenship in similar ways to men, i.e. through active participation in politics, the economic sphere and civil society generally. Far from seeing the private sphere as a self-contained domestic haven, cocooned from the outside world of politics and economics, feminists argued that women's experiences within the home were largely determined by economic and political factors. Thus the woman as citizen was presented as an active agent who could make choices about her life, marriage, career, etc. While de Valera's constitution promised to protect women from the necessity of participating in public life, feminist groups sought to protect women from what they saw as their virtual exclusion from public life.

The role of the press in the constitutional debates is particularly interesting. This section of the chapter has focused on two diametrically opposed newspapers. While both of these papers devoted considerable coverage to the issue of women's rights and the constitution, they approached the topic from contrasting perspectives. The *Irish Press* staunchly defended the constitution and criticised all of those who opposed Mr. de Valera. In challenging both the constitution and de Valera's very personal relationship to it, the *Irish Independent* provided a space where critics and opponents of the government could freely express their points of view. This may explain why women's groups were given such different coverage in these two national dailies. Not only did the *Independent* allow feminists generous access to its letters' pages, but it gave support to feminist views in its editorials and feature articles. However, it is difficult to say whether this attitude was motivated by a genuine support for feminism or by a deeply held dislike of Mr. de Valera and his party. The *Irish Press* also printed numerous letters from women's groups and individual feminist campaigners but for a very different purpose. The *Press* used the excuse of printing letters to then launch bitter attacks on the authors. Entire editorials were given over to personal attacks on particular feminists. These women were singled out for special treatment by the *Press*. Stereotypes of hysterical, elitist, alarmists were used to portray the women as irrational and dangerous. Feminists were used to represent all that was wrong, misleading and ill informed in the opposition to the constitution. Thus the newspapers did not merely report the many acrimonious debates on the constitution but actively participated in them and in so doing continued to play a key role in helping to frame and define representations of women's role and proper sphere within the nation.

'The Spinning Wheel Symbol of Creative Work', *Irish Press*, 12 March 1936, shelfmark 234. Reproduced by permission of the British Library.

IN A DUBLIN TENEMENT:—This Dublin family, eight including father, has to live in this typically overcrowded one-room tenement in the City's slums.

permission of the British Library.

'Yes – This is Dublin' *Irish Press,* 3 October 1936, shelfmark 237. Reproduced by permission of the British Library.

'Landed at Golf Links' photograph of Lady Heath, *Irish Independent*, 24 August 1928, shelfmark 141. Reproduced by permission of the British Library.

# CHAPTER FOUR:

## MATERNAL BODIES: FAMILY, HOME, MOTHERHOOD AND THE NATION

*Introduction:*

The family is a key site not only for the biological reproduction of the nation but also for the transmission of cultural traditions; thus ensuring the continuity of heritage, language, religion and identity. The trope of family permeates national rhetoric and symbolism. 'Nations are frequently figured through the iconography of familial and domestic space. The term nation derives from 'natio': to be born' (McClintock 1993: 63). The trope of family also frames women's relationship to the nation. If the family is a microcosm of the nation and the home is the foundation stone of the nation, then 'woman' is not simply the mother of the family and the keeper of the home but the mother of the entire nation. Women's political, economic and legal status within the nation-state can be submerged within their primary roles of maternity and domesticity. Thus, as we have seen in Chapter three and the discussion of the Irish Constitution of 1937, women's position as citizens can be circumscribed within the ideology of home and family.

On 22 November 1922, the *Cork Examiner* published a lengthy article by Rev. J.S. Sheehy based on his address to the influential conservative campaign group, the Catholic Truth Society. Entitled 'The Influence of Women in Catholic Ireland', this paper clearly outlined the perceived perimeters of women's roles in the new Irish Free State. Drawing upon the long-established imagery of a feminine, motherly Ireland, he argued that Ireland was woman and woman was Ireland. Thus, in his view, the nation and the woman became convertible terms. Women were the inspiration and pride of all that was good within the country. 'A nation is what its women make it'. This was especially true in the case of mothers who 'reigned within the homestead'. 'Mothers should realise that for them, at least, the home is the sphere of their best activities'.

To this equation of mother and nation, he added the Virgin Mary as the mother of the Catholic Church. Catholicism ensured that the influence of women remained 'sweet and salutary'. Mary, the mother of God, was the inspiration of all Irish mothers and mothers, in their turn, were the inspiration of the nation: 'This high ideal of womanhood has always kept the nation faithful and strong'. Hence, in their role as mothers of the nation, women represented not only the moral integrity and continuity of the nation but also its distinctiveness from all things foreign and alien. 'Be Irish and Catholic in your heart and soul, and your outward conduct will be irreproachable' (*Cork Examiner*, 22 November 1922).

But this is not to imply that women only represented the moral strengths of the nation. National weaknesses and corruptibility were also represented through gendered symbols. In fact, the biblical dichotomy of the virgin Mary versus the sinful Eve, underpinned Church images of the good Irishwoman/Irish mother and the bad Irishwoman/Irish mother. For example, on 12 May 1926, the *Irish Independent* published a sermon by Archbishop Gilmartin in which he outlined the two types of Irishwoman: 'The first is the daughter of Eve who ate the forbidden fruit', this woman read bad books, watched indecent, foreign films and indulged in sensual dances. She personified the moral corruption of modern life. However, the second type of woman was 'the sister of Mary Immaculate who brought life and hope and comfort'. She was good, homely and dutiful. The stability and respectability of the nation rested upon her. The Archbishop concluded by reminding his congregation that 'the future of the country is bound up with the dignity and purity of the women of Ireland'. Thus while women were represented as the guarantors of moral integrity, their low resistance to moral corruption necessitated constant monitoring and regulation. Women needed to be protected from their own base instincts and desires, all temptations needed to be removed (Ryan 1998a). This was not only the ideology underpinning campaigns for censorship of films, books and information, but also informed the regulation of the private sphere of family life.

This chapter will examine various representations of home and family in the Irish Free State through an analysis of different images of Irish motherhood. Firstly, I will focus upon images of the idealised 'mother of many children' in her cosy country cottage. Secondly, I will assess the image of the poor, urban mother in the tenement slums. Although both of these representations depict humble, simple womanfolk, they are located within competing and contradictory images of Irish society; the rural idyll versus the city slum. These images are underpinned by a dichotomy of rural health and vitality versus urban decay and sickness. But it would be simplistic to assume that the Irish countryside was always portrayed as good, pure and innocent. My third case study will focus upon disorderly, criminal and deviant behaviour. The inadequate or absent mother represented the potential weakness and immorality of family life and hence of the entire nation. The fact that this mother was frequently represented in rural society, especially in the 'wild west', not only complicates representations of the 'Irish mother' but also challenges the simple dichotomy of urban decadence versus rural idyll.

In the final section of this chapter I will look at representations of the idealised mother of the nation drawing in particular on the newspaper obituaries of Mrs. Margaret Pearse who died in 1932. By comparing her eulogies with those of other notable women who died in the same year, I will theorise about the processes through which particular women may be included or excluded in nationalist iconography.

## Section 1: Spinning Wheels and Country Cottages

Between March and April 1936 the *Irish Press* newspaper featured no less than four separate photographs and articles about the role of the spinning wheel in the Irish home. However, even by the feature writers' own admission, the spinning wheel had become quite outmoded by the mid-1930s and was consigned in many cases to the attic or the cowshed. Thus the images of the spinning wheel as a central feature of the Irish cottage was probably more of an aspiration than a reality. Nevertheless, it is clear that this image, and its associated gender stereotypes, were still powerful signifiers of national identity.

On the 12 March 1936, the *Irish Press* 'women's page' carried the headline 'The Spinning Wheel – symbol of creative work'. It was accompanied by a photograph of a young woman, dressed in modern fashions, sitting at a spinning wheel in front of a large open fireplace. The furniture of the room suggested a simple, rural cottage. However, the fact that the photograph was printed courtesy of the Country Shop, a Dublin city based enterprise devoted to the sale of all things rural, suggests a more complex picture. It is likely that this is a specially posed photo and that the young woman sitting at the wheel is a model and that the cottage, furniture and even the wheel itself form part of a carefully constructed set, aimed at representing a particular ideal of Irish life and Irish womanhood. The lengthy feature article claims that the spinning wheel is now enjoying a welcome renaissance in Irish homes. Irish 'homespun' material is now being valued more and it can be bought in the leading stores of Paris, London and New York. This claim is not supported by any sales figures. By locating Irish homespun in modern, cosmopolitan contexts, the article is perhaps attempting to make the traditional material seem more attractive to fashion-minded young Irish women. The importance of home spinning to young women is outlined in the rest of the article:

> Proudly the woman of the house draws up her little stool and begins to spin. Watch how deftly she handles the wool...Looking in over the open half door the passer by will greet her with a cheery 'God bless the work'....Not only the mother but the daughters as well will be taking their turn at it. They hope thus to be spared the necessity of going away to Scotland or England. (*Irish Press*, 12 March 1936)

Hence the drain of emigration, which was becoming such a serious concern in the 1930s, in particular the very high numbers of young women emigrating from rural areas, could be stemmed if daughters could participate in cottage industries and stay at home 'where they belong'. This feature paints a very romantic picture of family life. Women were proud to sit and work in their homes, seeing the world over the top of their half-doors. Home also takes on two meanings in this context. Home stands for the cottage, the family home, it is represented as safe, secure and loving. Home also stands for Ireland. Thus young women will not simply remain at home, in Ireland, but also will be contained within the domestic sphere of the cottage. The article goes on to say that:

> It doesn't take much to make the average country woman happy and contented. All she wants is enough to keep things going and she is ready to work hard for that. (*Irish Press*, 12 March 1936)

The rhetoric underpinning this article needs to be located not only in the context of fears about the increasing emigration of young women but also the fears about women going into factories and taking the jobs that were once performed by men. Thus while it was clear that young women needed an occupation to prevent them from catching the boat to England, there was concern that giving them factory jobs might result in even higher male unemployment. Therefore, the spinning wheel represented the ideal solution; keep young women at home (in Ireland) by keeping them gainfully employed at home (in the cottage). The feature concludes with a poetic view of life in the rural family home:

their cottages soft, warm-roofed, with love inside them. No wonder that the sweet scented smoke from the turf fire hovers like a halo overhead before it fades away to join the gently moving clouds. (*Irish Press*, 12 March 1936)

The image of the spinning wheel appeared again, one month later, in a feature article by Aodh de Blacam on the necessity of saving money (*Irish Press*, 24 April 1936). Entitled 'Use your wages well: An Appeal to Rural Workers to Become Savers', the article was again accompanied by a photograph of a spinning wheel. In this photo the woman sitting at the wheel appeared more traditional, she was not dressed in modern clothes but instead wore a long skirt and shawl. The caption accompanying the picture read 'The spinning wheel emblem of old Irish thrift'. However, it was clear, on closer examination, that this photograph was also posed and carefully staged. The woman who occupied the foreground of the picture sat out of doors in a grassy enclosure. Behind her, almost out of the shot, was a small crowd of curious on-lookers all dressed in modern clothing. Thus rather than being a rural woman carrying on her everyday work of spinning, she appeared to form part of an exhibition of arts and crafts.

A few days later on 29 April 1936, the *Irish Press* again featured a photograph of a woman and her spinning wheel. She was described as a 'Connemara woman', a label which conjures up images of the rural Western seaboard of Ireland, the Gaeltacht region, a place which represented the essence of traditional Irishness (see Nash 1993). The woman embodied these qualities through her clothing. She wore a long, full skirt, thick, dark stockings, heavy, flat shoes and a small shawl around her head. However, this woman with her spinning wheel was also posing, representing an image, conscious of her audience. She was, in fact, exhibiting her work at the Spring Show in Dublin.

In all three of the incidents described above, women and their spinning wheels were used to represent a particular, idealised image of traditional Irish society; thrift, industriousness, rural regeneration, a happy, cosy cottage life. Yet even in the process of representing these images it is apparent that the spinning wheel and the woman at her stool were being carefully constructed, even staged. Behind the images lay quite complex and contradictory realities of life in the Irish Free State. For example, behind the image of the cosy cottage lay a complex web of political policies and programmes that attempted to keep rural labourers 'rooted in the land'. As Walsh (1999) has argued, while the Fianna Fail government of Eamon de Valera built tens of thousands of cottages in rural Ireland, this could not stem the flow of migration to towns and cities and emigration to England. The idyllic image of happy homesteads dotted around the countryside was very far removed from the very real problem of urban overcrowding and inner city slums. For the most part the newspapers, especially the pro-Fianna Fail *Irish Press*, supported government policy and lauded the programme of building even more rural cottages. In the 1930s in particular the rural cottage came to represent the very essence of Irishness.

On 22 February 1936, the 'women's page' of the *Irish Press* carried a photograph of a white-washed, thatched cottage in a rural setting surrounded by trees. A woman can be seen standing in the doorway, in front of her two small children are standing in the tidy, well kept yard. The topic of the article is 'Splendid new housing'. However, it is noteworthy that the cottage featured in the picture is not representative of the more functional style of new housing being constructed (see Walsh 1999), instead this picture seems to harp back to the more traditional rather than the modern cottage:

> So far as housing goes the state is doing good work. Thousands of people each year are moving from cabins and hovels to fine new houses with their plots of land. New possibilities of life and comfort are opened to many of these tenants...In the new houses as in the old the kitchen remains of course the principal living room where the mother and children under school age pass their day, after the father has gone to his work. (*Irish Press*, 22 February 1936)

The article goes on to offer useful advice about the potential dangers to children in the kitchen and suggests that mothers erect a fireguard whenever they leave the room and that small children should be placed in a play pen to protect them from the hazards of burns, etc. The women's page as usual presents itself as knowledgeable, useful and helpful. It gives expert advice in an authoritative voice. The relationship between the women's page and its target readership will be discussed in more detail below. The image presented in this lengthy article is one of busy, domestic mothers and happy, playful children. The father is out at work and is thus completely absent from the picture. The kitchen is the heart of the home and the centre of women's lives. But the woman is not simply located in the home, she embodies the home. Just as the inadequate or absent mother embodies the negative aspects of disorderly homes, the idealised, good mother represents the homely qualities of warmth, sustenance, cosiness and cleanliness.

But it was not just the *Irish Press* that presented an idealised image of the simple, rural housewife and her family. On 2 January 1936, the *Irish Independent* carried a special feature on a county Galway family. This family was deemed worthy of attention because 11 children had been born in a period of 10 years. A large photograph showed the family gathered around the kitchen table for dinner. While some of the younger children stared quizzically into the camera, the father and mother smiled proudly. The caption beneath the picture read 'Happy Mother of 11 Children'. Interestingly, the article focuses almost entirely on the mother, Mrs. Ryan. While she is quoted at length, there is no comment from the father. In all, Mrs. Ryan gave birth to 12 children but one died. She had three sets of twins, two sets of twins were born within a twelve month period; thus she had four babies in just one year. All the information on the birthdays, ages and names of the children is covered in considerable detail by the unnamed *Independent* reporter who also gives some personal impressions of the family.

As the reporter arrived at the 'little farmhouse' situated in 'a backward part of the country' he/she was greeted with the 'sound of happy boyish laughter'. Mrs. Ryan is described in considerable detail also:

> She is a typical Galway woman, dark haired and erect. Only 39 years of age, she is so alert and youthful looking that she might easily be taken for the elder sister of her large family...her outlook on life is refreshing in its cheerfulness...The children are the picture of health and like the house itself everyone of them is absolutely spick and span. (*Irish Independent*, 2 January 1936)

Mrs. Ryan is quoted throughout the article and she is presented as an articulate, sensible and highly organised woman. Although she may be 'cheerful' and 'happy', she does not underestimate the work involved in rearing her family. 'It has not always been easy for there are a lot of mouths to feed, and they take some feeding, we consume all the foodstuffs grown on the farm'. The report of Mrs. Ryan's experiences is punctuated with comments from the journalist, for example, 'with little reference to herself this good woman talked on about her children.' The youngest would soon go to school and then 'she would have more time about the house to knit, wash, sew and cook for them along with feeding the fowl, milking the cows, feeding the pigs and the other numerous duties of a farmer's wife'. There is no direct mention of the farmer himself and what his duties involve. He is simply the man who as a farmer and a father does not need to justify his time, work, cleanliness or efficiency. The article casually mentions that the family live in a three room cottage. However, it is apparent that this is something which worries Mrs. Ryan: 'as the children grow up we will be terribly cramped for space, and it won't be healthy for so many of us to be living is such a confined space'.

Athough such large families were becoming increasingly rare in Ireland at that time (see Commission on Emigration and Population 1955), Mrs. Ryan is presented in fairly conventional narratives. She is the 'good woman', a conscientious mother who neither expected nor received much help from her husband in feeding and caring for their large family. The reader can rest assured that the family are clean, happy and well fed, though Mrs. Ryan does raise the one jarring note about being over-crowded, yet she is not presented as complaining and dissatisfied. Although her circumstances are extreme, Mrs. Ryan is represented as the ideal, simple, rural peasant woman who copes with whatever life throws at her. She is proud of her many children and does not see it as unfortunate to have had so many pregnancies in her short married life. Nevertheless, there is something in the nature of the report which constructs Mrs. Ryan and her family as 'other'. They live in a 'backward' part of the country. This is not the usual family represented in the women's pages of the newspapers. The Ryans are far removed from the urban, middle classes to whom the paper is usually addressed.

Although Mrs. Ryan may be seen as exceptional, she was certainly not unique. On 16 July 1936, the *Independent* quoted another 'mother of many children'. Mrs. Katie Kerry advised Irish women 'don't wait, marry young'. She had married at 16 years of age and had eighteen children, seven of whom were now married giving her a total of 23 grandchildren. Mrs. Kerry is described as 'an active, robust woman, with more than the usual fund of characteristic humour'. Despite her many children and grandchildren, she proudly boasted that she had 'not a grey hair in her head'. 'She lives in a bright little cottage, whose only fault is that it becomes flooded in the winter. In spite of this everything in her home looks cheerful and happy'. This article needs to be located in the context of the Free State's peculiarly low marriage rate, late marriages and fears of a falling birthrate especially in rural areas (Commission on Emigration and Population 1955). Both Mrs. Kerry and Mrs. Ryan married young and had lots of children, in that respect they were not typical of rural women of their generation. They embody an aspiration, an ideal of motherhood, not only in having many children, but also in being happy and cheerful, contented with their lot in life. They are both represented in cosy rural cottages despite the fact that the Ryans' cottage is too small and the Kerrys' cottage floods in winter.

This ideal of a contented rural peasantry was propagated not only in the press and pulpit but also in political circles. On 3 April 1936, the *Independent* published a feature article entitled 'Woman T.D. Shows the way to an Irish Utopia'. This referred to a rather passionate speech in the Dail by one of the three women T.D.s, Mrs. Concannon (Fianna Fail). In responding to a Fine Gael T.D. who had commented upon the gloomy plight of Irish farmers, she introduced 'the feminine viewpoint' and 'an entirely new note' into the discussion. She argued that life in the Irish countryside could be vastly improved if more domestic science were taught in schools. This would enable farmers' wives to keep their families well fed and happy. The newspaper article described her speech in rather sceptical terms:

> She painted a glowing picture of the Arcadian delights she had in mind – the big kitchen with its big turf fire, presided over by a wife who was a first class cook, and who in addition was an expert bee-keeper and an authority on poultry rearing and dairying. (*Irish Independent*, 3 April 1936)

Clearly the author of this report was not entirely convinced by such an image. He echoed the scepticism expressed by a Labour T.D. who, pointing to the rising costs of tea, sugar, jam, candles, soap and butter, argued that domestic skills were of little use when food prices were so high. The T.D. said that Mrs. Concannon's 'idyll' could only be achieved if housekeeping allowances were greatly improved.

In this article, the *Independent* newspaper is playing an interesting role. Firstly, it is reporting a political speech which drew upon the kind of rural idyll which the paper had also evoked in its articles on Mrs. Ryan and later on Mrs. Kerry: the contented rural housewife in her cosy cottage, surrounded by her well-fed family. Secondly however, by citing an opposition politician and by describing Mrs. Concannon's image as a 'utopia', the report suggests that her idyll is unrealistic and unattainable. This critique of Mrs. Concannon may be explained by the fact that she was a member of a Fianna Fail government that the *Independent* blamed for the economic failures in the country. Thirdly, this article indicates the complexity of newspaper reporting. Newspapers did not speak with monolithic voices. As I have previously mentioned in relation to representations of the flapper or modern girl, newspapers were made up of different, competing narratives. While an image like the flapper or the idealised rural housewife may have been lauded on specific occasions, the same image could be mocked and criticised on other occasions. This may have varied depending upon the opinion of a particular journalist, the context of the discussion or the perceived target audience.

It is clear that newspapers did not just aim at one specific target audience but often aimed at several audiences simultaneously. For example, while the *Press* and the *Independent* aimed at different ends of the political spectrum, their readership was mediated by age, sex, class and geographical location. Each paper aimed to include professionals, the lower middle classes and the skilled working class. As national dailies, they also targeted urban and rural readers. However, despite attempting to reach the widest possible audience, the papers were often influenced by an assumption of their 'average' reader. All of the newspapers carried dozens of advertisements for a vast array of products ranging from clothes and cosmetics to household goods and medicines. The majority of advertisements were aimed at the female consumer, especially the housewife and mother. Hence, the target reader was someone with sufficient disposable income to afford at least some of these products. While this 'average reader' was usually more implicit than explicit, on rare occasions some journalists described their notion of 'the reader'. For example, on 21 March 1936, Anne Kelly, editor of the *Irish Press* women's page, claimed that its average reader was married, her husband out at work all day, with most of her children at school. This busy woman had many things to occupy her time 'the dinner, clothes for herself and the children...new curtains, fresh paint, the gas or electricity bill'. The role of the women's page, according to Kelly, was to give advice and provide economical, useful tips.

It is apparent that the women's pages of the national and provincial papers directed themselves to women from middle class and professional backgrounds who could afford to indulge in the lifestyle discussed in the various fashion and recipe features. Articles were usually underpinned by a differentiation between the modest means of the rural cottage dweller and the more sophisticated and affluent urban housewife or the career oriented bachelor girl. 'Country folk' and the urban poor were frequently depicted as 'other', i.e. different, exceptional, curiosities. They were not the 'average reader', the target audience, the subject of articles, but were more likely to feature as the object of discussions, analyses and reports. This became particularly apparent when the *Irish Press* published a series of articles on inner city slums in 1936.

*The Festering Evil of Slums*

On 1 October 1936, the *Press* launched a series of articles on the 'festering evil' and 'deadly menace' of slums. According to the editorial, the slums were 'a legacy of alien rule' which the Fianna Fail government was now endeavouring to remedy. The extent of the problem was made very clear by the various statistics on overcrowding, disease and infant morality cited in the editorial. For example, while the average infant mortality in the Free State was 63 per 1,000, in the tenements of Dublin it was 119 per 1,000. The report was accompanied by a photograph of a woman and five very dirty, shabby young children sitting in a chaotic little room which was clearly in a bad state of repair. The entire family of six children and two parents lived in that one room.

In subsequent reports the *Press* claimed that 90,000 people lived in one-room dwellings in the tenements of Dublin. In all, approximately 20% of the city's population were located in the slums. Various doctors and other experts quoted in the reports gave eye-witness accounts of the rats, insects and other health risks that were to be found throughout the tenements (2 October 1936). On 3 October, the unnamed reporter argued that, in the extremely overcrowded conditions, it was the bigger families who suffered the most and they should be 'entitled to the utmost consideration from the city authorities'. On 5 October, an unnamed source at Dublin Corporation was quoted as saying that he would prefer to move families out of city centres into the countryside: 'Healthier children will be reared and more contented citizens will be produced'. He added that free transport could be provided to enable people to commute to work in the city.

These two quotations are very revealing and suggest the yawning gap between myth and reality in the Free State. While the 'mother of many children' was an ideal image much praised in the pulpit, press and in political circles, the reality of urban overcrowding and high infant mortality presented a very different story. However, a simple solution that reinforced rather than challenged the mythical image of the rural idyll, was to relocate the problem families of the city slums out to the countryside where they could become happier, healthier and more contented citizens. Presumably this would also help to reverse trends of rural depopulation. This 'solution' draws upon the city/countryside dichotomy and underlines the image of the city as dirty, unhealthy, evil and immoral. By contrast, the countryside, the essence of Irish society, is represented as clean, healthy, innocent and good. This dichotomy was visually represented by two contrasting photographs that appeared in the *Irish Press*.

Photographs usually accompanied the reports on the slums. With very few exceptions, these photos featured women and children, men were not present. On 5 October 1936, the *Press* juxtaposed two interesting pictures. The first showed a group of women and children standing in the cluttered backyard of 'a labyrinth of tenements'. One woman standing in a doorway watches over a group of young children dressed in dark, drab, dirty clothes. The other picture featured a new housing scheme on the outskirts of Dublin. A woman and her four young children pose in the doorway of their new house. With lace curtains on the window and lots of flowers in the garden, this picture presents a complete contrast to the dark and dirty backyard of the slums.

The women and children embody these contrasts. The woman in the new house is holding a healthy baby in her arms. The little girls are wearing ribbons in their hair, their clothes are clean and bright, they are smiling and look the picture of health and contentment. Despite the different locations, these pictures are remarkably similar. In these carefully posed photographs similar techniques are used to represent very different versions of motherhood and domesticity. Both feature women and children standing in a doorway, half inside the home, half outside. Their facial expressions, their clothes and general demeanour, visibly represent their particular circumstances. While the smiling woman in the suburbs is holding a healthy baby, the hope for a future generation, the women in the slums look despairingly at their miserable little children. It is apparent that these photographs speak for themselves as no additional information is provided about the women and their families.

All the reports on the slums focused on women and children. Each day, the report concentrated on the story of one particular mother and her children usually including a photograph and an interview with the woman. The photographs typically depicted the mothers and children either standing in the doorway of their tenement or crowded inside the tiny one-room dwellings (see for example *Irish Press*, 13 and 17 October):

> Look at that poor child will you! cried one of Dublin's young mothers, as she uncovered the thin, white body of her little one. See the way the bugs have bitten him. Bites everywhere all over his body. Always the same we just can't get rid of them. (*Irish Press,* 8 October 1936)

This quote is from a mother of three young children who, along with her husband, live in 'the garret of a rickety, old three storey building' which had been officially declared unfit for human habitation. The couple are described as being 'devoted to their children'. This tenement, in common with others, has one lavatory and one tap in the yard. Mothers have to carry buckets of water up several flights of stairs many times each day. Even though concerns about the slums were usually framed in terms of the risks to health, it is possible to analyse representations of the slum problem on a number of levels. In the context of nation-building the slums posed many dangers. Although these women were performing their duty as mothers and giving birth to many babies, these children were unlikely to grow up healthy and productive citizens. Detailed descriptions, like the insect bites on the baby's body above, were common and underlined the threat to an entire generation of Dublin City children. But the slums also represented a threat to standards of morality and decency. Reports on overcrowding frequently referred to large numbers of people sharing one bed. For example, on 17 October, the *Press* carried the headline 'Nine Sleep in One Bed', referring to a mother, father and seven children, including a girl of 12 years and new born baby, who all shared one bed.

The concern for modesty and decency was clearly stated by Reverend Irwin, Church of Ireland Bishop of Limerick. 'How can we expect morals when the sexes are so closely associated as they are in these slums'. He added that overcrowded living conditions provided people with 'no chance to maintain their self-respect' (24 October 1936). Although the *Irish Press* reports had begun by highlighting the slum problem in Dublin City, it soon became apparent that other cities such as Limerick, Cork and Waterford also had slums where thousands of poor people were living in unsanitary and overcrowded conditions. On 2 November, the *Press* reported the case of a family in Waterford City. Fourteen people lived in just one room. When the reporter arrived, he was unable to gain admittance because the mother of the family was giving birth to her thirteenth child. In a later interview she was quoted as saying that it was a terrible situation when a girl of 15 had to share a bed with her brothers of 16 and 17 years of age. Although it was never addressed explicitly, the circumstances in which mothers continued to become pregnant and have a baby on almost a yearly basis, despite sharing a bed with their teenage children, posed a serious challenge to notions of privacy and morality.

As will be discussed at length in the following section, the health and stability of family life, and hence of the nation, was frequently gauged by the maintenance of moral standards. Families were expected to cope with the problems of poverty, illness and deprivation, while adhering to a strict code of Catholic morality and decency. Thus no matter how poor a family was, any use of birth control was not only sinful but illegal. While the Church and State were slow to respond to the urgent needs of families in the tenement slums of Dublin and other cities, they were quick to condemn and punish families who deviated from the norms and rules of social behaviour.

## Section 2: Disorderly Bodies: Representations and explanations of domestic and family deviance.

*Moral Policing:*

> The Cult of the Blessed Virgin Mary, with all its overtones of sexual abstinence, was actively promoted. The Church took to policing the most intimate details of people's lives, embarking on one of the most remarkable campaigns of moral engineering ever attempted. The family

was the central institution through which this policy was enforced.
(M.Ryan, 1994: 90-91)

Despite notions of 'family privacy' and 'the sanctity of the home', the 'moral policing' of family life was carried on extensively by the apparatuses of Church and State throughout the 1920s-1930s (Fahey 1995). Although the Irish Catholic family was frequently idealised and glorified as the bastion of morality and decency, strenuous efforts were made to ensure that family life did not deviate from the narrow dictates of Catholic doctrine. The extent to which this was successfully achieved may be gauged by the conflicting newspaper reports throughout the period. Thus, constructions of a passive, pious, priest-ridden people need to be counter-posed against competing representations of life in the new state. Throughout the 1920s-1930s newspapers, in particular provincial newspapers, were full of accounts of violence, abuse and crime. The fact that these were often related to family conflicts and centred upon the home could be interpreted as a direct challenge to the usual idealised image of the Irish Catholic family-home. However, as Mark Ryan (1994) and F.S.L. Lyons (1989) have both suggested, the prevalence of violence and lawlessness within the private sphere may well have been used to justify the intensive 'moral policing' which was such a core aspect of government and Church policy at that time.

This section examines a range of newspaper reports that highlight the ways in which private individuals were policed and punished. Drawing on a spread of examples, including allegations of child abuse, possession of illegal substances, domestic violence and sexual assault, I explore representations of the victims and perpetrators of offences. In addition, I examine the various ways in which disorderly behaviour was interpreted and explained. Firstly, gendered representations tended to contain images of disorderly men and women within notions of evil, brutality, savagery, victimhood, vulnerability and immorality. In this way deviance could be explained away as abnormal individual behaviour. The Catholic clergy and hierarchy frequently blamed such behaviour on the corrupting influences coming into Ireland through foreign newspapers, films and books. In reporting and reiterating these Church explanations of disorderly conduct, the newspapers reinforced the view that such behaviour was, in fact, largely the result of foreign influences. Offences such as rape, child abuse and other sexual assaults could, therefore, be safely dismissed as something new, recent and inherently 'unIrish'. Secondly, there was a subtler, less explicit, discourse that located disorderly behaviour in the context of ignorance and backwardness. This discourse was underpinned by a class bias that emphasised the civilising influence of the respectable middle classes. Both the slum dwellers of urban centres and the rural peasants of the west of Ireland were frequently represented as uncivilised and uncouth as well as dishonest and immoral. Thus while the first explanation rooted disorderly behaviour in alien, outside influences, the second explanation pointed to more localised, endemic factors. While it is possible to see these two discourses as utterly incompatible and diametrically opposed to each other, I believe that they are both informed by the nation building project.

The prevalence and frequency of deviant behaviour could be seen as undermining attempts to foster a shared sense of Irishness, an 'imagined community' with common values and beliefs. Thus, both the discourse of foreign corruption and the civilising discourse emphasised the need for conformity to a shared national code of values and morality enshrined in Church doctrine and State legislation. Both discourses represented deviance from the norm, as not only dangerous, but as threatening to national unity. The national norm was circumscribed by class, gender and location, as well as by religion and nationalism. As a microcosm of the nation, the family became the locus for concerns about the problems underpinning Irish society. As Fahey (1995) has argued, the family was alternatively glorified as the bastion of Catholic decency and morality or vilified as disorganised, undisciplined and dysfunctional. Such representations were frequently focused on women as good mothers or inadequate mothers and as good daughters or wayward daughters. Therefore, whether disorderly behaviour was blamed on foreign corruption or local backwardness, it was represented as a problem urgently in need of official intervention and regulation.

*Female Victims:*

Although women figured largely as victims of deviant and threatening behaviour, they were also represented as disorderly characters and as absent or inadequate mothers. In representing both vulnerability and culpability, women embodied the potential dangers, threats and chaos of a disorderly, unrestrained society. Thus women's innocence as well as their maliciousness were frequently used to underline the need for the regulation and supervision of private lives.

In 1928, the *Sligo Champion* reported two unrelated stories which, nevertheless, shared a number of significant features and which raise questions about representations of violence and cruelty against women and children in the early years of the Free State. On 28 January, the *Champion* carried a story under the headline 'Shocking Case of Cruelty'. This focused on a case brought against a local Sligo farmer by the NSPCC. In some ways there was nothing unusual about this story. All the papers in my study printed regular reports, usually based on the cases of the National Society for the Prevention of Cruelty to Children (NSPCC), in which parents, usually fathers, were prosecuted for cruelty and neglect. The case reported in the *Sligo Champion* exemplified these other cases. When the NSPCC inspector visited the house he found a falling down shack. There was no front door, the roof was leaking and the floor was covered in pools of water. The inspector discovered a 15-year-old 'imbecile' girl locked into a room. Her mother was dead and so her father locked her into the room every day while he went out. There was no fire or food for the girl. The court sent the girl to the county home and fined the father 40 shillings plus costs.

On 16 June, the *Champion* carried the heading, 'Two Years Hard Labour'. The Sligo Circuit Court had recently heard a case against three men aged between 17 and 21 years. The men were charged with 'indecently assaulting an imbecile girl'. The accused and the victim were all named. The girl had since been committed to Sligo mental hospital. The men were found guilty and sentenced to two years hard labour. As was usual in reporting sexual assaults details were limited, the words 'sex' and 'sexual' were not even mentioned. In common with other such cases, the newspaper article simply stated that 'The evidence given is not fit for publication'.

Both of these cases focused on female victims of male cruelty. The fact that the young girl in each case was an 'imbecile' added to the sense of her as a helpless victim. She bore no responsibility for her fate. The men in each case were found guilty and punished, according to the gravity of their crime. The girls were removed to institutions for their own safety. It could be argued that in both cases it is the women who experienced the most serious form of incarceration. It is almost as if the solution to such crimes was to remove helpless women and girls from sight and thus from temptation. Wives and daughters regularly featured as victims of violence within families. In a country which constructed the family as the model of Catholic and Irish morality, the repeated emphasis on disorderly families could be seen as threatening to the stability of that idealised image. Hence it is necessary to analyse the processes through which family violence, cruelty and neglect were explained and contained.

On two separate occasions in 1928, the *Limerick Leader* used the same dramatic headline 'Brutal Assault'. In the first case on 2 May, the full headline ran 'Brutal Assault on Child'. 'A brute' was sentenced to two months imprisonment after a passer-by discovered the man in a field pinning his little daughter to the ground while he repeatedly beat her with his fists. The child was semi-conscious when rescued. In this brief report little or no background information was given about the man or his family. The label 'brute' represented him in a very particular way and also offered a partial explanation for his actions. The term 'brute' conjures up the image of an animal, a stupid creature, something from a lower order, not quite like normal people. It distances him from other men and so sets him apart from decent society.

A similar image was constructed on 4 August when the headline 'Brutal Assault' was again used in the *Leader*. A Limerick man was sentenced to 6 months hard labour for beating his wife with two sticks while in a drunken rage. The woman sustained very serious injuries. This story relies not just on the image of the 'brute' but also on the fact that he was drunk to offer some explanation as to why a man would inflict such serious injuries on his wife. This story was not entirely unusual. Cases of domestic violence were frequently reported in the national press but more especially in the provincial press where court cases involving local people were regularly presented as interesting and even entertaining. In such cases, drink was regularly used not so much as an excuse but as an explanation.

For example, on 20 March 1928, the *Connacht Sentinel* reported a court case from Co. Clare, under the headline 'Mother's Appeal'. The NSPCC inspector visited the home and found no food at all in the house. The children were without adequate clothing. The NSPCC applied for the three children to be taken away from their parents and sent to an industrial school. In court, the mother pleaded to be allowed to keep her children. She explained that the family was experiencing hard times as several livestock had recently died. She added that her 'big lazy husband' spent the family income on drink. The judge described her 69-year-old husband as 'a disreputable scoundrel...addicted to drink'. While the court viewed this woman as a 'good' woman, she was deemed to be unable to look after the three children. All three were removed from the family home and sent to a special residential institution for children (commonly called an industrial school). However, the mother was allowed to keep an older girl aged 13, as the judge stated that she might be of help to her mother. The father was sent to prison for three months.

In this case, as in those highlighted above, the victims of cruelty appear to be punished more severely than the perpetrators of the crimes. In each case the children and young 'imbecile' girls were committed indefinitely to institutions. The men did not get away without punishment, but their sentences were of a fixed term, usually 3 to 6 months for child neglect and 2 years for indecent assault. Although it could be argued that these children were taken away for their own protection, it is also apparent that the wishes of both parents and the children themselves were not taken into account. Only on very rare occasions did the judge decide to allow children to remain in the family home.

One such case was reported in the *Connacht Tribune* on 11 February 1928. The headline – 'Poor Parents'- immediately suggests a more sympathetic tone in this court case. The headline also suggests an explanation for child neglect. An NSPCC inspector applied to the court at Oughterard to have a family of children committed to an industrial school. When the inspector visited the farm, which was described as 'remote', she found the children 'running wild on the mountain'. They did not attend school. In 1926 primary education was made compulsory and this appears to have been rigorously imposed (Fahey 1995). The provincial papers repeatedly reported cases of parents being fined for failure to send their children to school on a regular basis. In the particular case at Oughterard, there was no accusation of any physical cruelty; the charge was neglect and failure to send their children to school. The mother of the family testified in Irish, although the father could speak English as well as Irish. At a time when the government was making Irish compulsory in schools and for all civil servants (Lyons 1989, Kelly 1999), this family represented an ideal bilingual, rural farming family. The image of children freely romping around the open countryside could be read as a happy, positive picture. But instead it is presented as 'wild', untamed, unregulated, outside of official institutions. The children did not attend school and it is implied that they were not properly supervised. This much freedom was not good for children or for families who were expected to conform to the appropriate norms. The competing images of this family reflect the competing images of the West of Ireland. While the west was frequently presented as native, authentic, traditional, Irish speaking, untainted by corrupting foreign influences (Nash 1993), it was simultaneously viewed as wild, sensual, unrestrained, unorthodox, and even uncivilised. The 'wild west' was in need of urgent regulation by the church and the state. However, in this particular court case it is apparent that the judge shared some of these ambiguities about the lifestyle embodied by the family. He refused to take the children away from their parents. Instead he argued that the family, as farmers on bad, mountainous land, was entitled to assistance under the terms of the Land Commission, this would enable them to substantially improve their living conditions. Although we have no way of knowing what became of this family, it seems that they were given a second chance despite the case brought against them by the NSPCC. Perhaps the judge was influenced by the fact that no physical cruelty was reported, neither was there any mention of the parents indulging in alcohol. As the headline suggests, the problem was identified as one of poverty. But it is probable that poverty was a common theme running through the vast majority of court cases instigated by the NSPCC.

The NSPCC's annual general meeting was reported in the *Connacht Sentinel* on 19 June 1928. The organisation investigated between 180-200 cases in the Galway region every year. But only about 5% of those involved actual physical cruelty, most cases related to 'hunger and neglect'. This report did not explicitly state that there was a correlation between poverty and 'hunger and neglect' but it is clearly evident in the instances discussed above that an overwhelming majority of the cases which reached the courts involved poor, working class or small farming families.

Similar reports appeared in the press throughout the 1920s-1930s. For example, on 12 March 1936, the *Cork Examiner* reported NSPCC statistics for the year ending June 1935. In Cork city and county 474 cases involving a total of 1,269 children were investigated. In all 2,026 visits of inspection were made. The editorial of the *Examiner* praised the valuable work of the society and encouraged people to make generous donations to enable their continued good work. Like the other provincial papers, the *Examiner* carried regular reports of court cases involving the NSPCC. On 13 May 1936, under the heading 'Child Neglect', it was reported that a Fermoy man was charged with unlawfully neglecting his two young children aged three and two years old. On receiving information from an unidentified source, an NSPCC inspector visited the house. In its lengthy account of the court case, the newspaper carried a very detailed, and quite graphic, description of the condition of the house and the children. In one room the inspector found a dog, lying on a bed, tearing a cow's head. There were other dogs in the house and discarded bones and dogs' mess were found in several of the rooms. The children were dirty and poorly clad, and they had vermin on their bodies. In his defence, the father said that his wife had been in hospital for several weeks and he had been unable to provide the children with clean clothing. He also told the court that out of his 12 shillings unemployment assistance, he paid 5 shillings per week in rent. He had got rid of the dogs and was now making an effort to clean the house, this point was verified by the inspector. However, the children were removed to an industrial school and the judge said that he would review the situation in three months, by which time the man should have improved his circumstances.

In this case, as in several others reported in the press, the absence of a mother, whether temporarily or permanently, was linked to the father's inability to cope. The dirty condition of the children and their clothing was directly related to the fact that the mother had been absent, in hospital, for several weeks. This may explain why no action was taken against the father. In fact, the court appeared to be sympathetic and gave him three months in which to improve his situation. This seems to suggest that the children may well have been returned to their parents. A very similar case was reported in the *Examiner* on 18 June 1936, under the heading 'Slept on Floor: Alleged Neglect of Four Children'. An NSPCC inspector who visited the family home in Co. Waterford reported that it was 'very badly kept'. 'There was no furniture and the father and children slept on the floor on a litter of rags and sacks'. The children's clothes were inadequate and they 'showed signs of vermin'. The youngest child, aged 7 years, showed signs of malnutrition. The mother was dead and while the father had previously promised to get adequate bedding, to date he had not done so. He was described as a labourer and it was noted that he did not drink. He made no objection to the two younger children being placed in an industrial school. Again this case illustrates the absent mother and the father unable to cope with young children. Although it is apparent that the man had been given previous warnings about the condition of his children, he seemed unable or unwilling to do anything about it. However, he was not punished and he appeared quite willing to allow his youngest children to be removed to an institution. The cases shown here begin to suggest the intersection of class, poverty, parenthood and the legal apparatus.

*Drunk and Disorderly Women:*

In the cases discussed so far women have been constructed in passive or victim roles, while men have been constructed as perpetrators of violence. But it would be simplistic to argue that women were only ever represented as victims. On several occasions women were singled out for special attention as inadequate mothers who exerted a bad influence on their children. These cases frequently involved alcohol. On 9 June 1928, the *Connacht Tribune* carried a story under the headline 'Women in a Snug: Carrying Children in Arms'. A woman publican was fined 10 shillings 'for allowing two women of the tinker class to consume liquor on her premises while they had children in their arms'. The judge was reported as saying 'I do not want to make this court a court of public morals, but it should not be necessary for the Civic Guards to compel publicans to cease giving drink to women'. He promised to inflict maximum penalties on such publicans. 'People of the description of the two women found in this public house are no addition to the clientele of any public house'. The women were reported to be well known for begging and annoying 'respectable people in the town'. From this report it is not entirely clear if the main objection to these women was the fact that they were drinking in a pub while carrying their small children in their arms or the fact that they were simply drinking in a public house in the first place. It is likely, however, that the chief objection to their presence was the fact of their being 'of the tinker class', i.e. members of Ireland's traveller community. These women could not enter a reputable establishment because they were likely to annoy the respectable clientele. However, there is no evidence that they were annoying anyone and, by being secluded in the snug, they were unlikely to encounter any of the other clientele. Although it is apparent that the publican, ironically also a woman, had no objection to their being in her pub, the police and the judiciary labelled it an offence. As Ronit Lentin (1998) has argued, it is a classical stigma strategy to deny people access to public services and public places of entertainment. She adds that traveller women are doubly discriminated against both as women and as members of the traveller community (Lentin 1998: 17). This is clearly evident in the case of the 'women in the snug'. By their very presence in the pub, these traveller women and their children represented a transgression of social norms and the rules of social interaction. By bringing their children into the pub they failed to conform to appropriate norms of motherhood. Good mothers remained at home in the private sphere.

The pub was not the only public space where respectable women, especially mothers, were not welcome. In September 1928, the *Irish Independent* carried a report calling for a government investigation into the growing numbers of women indulging in gambling:

> The most flagrant evil is the widespread betting among children and women. The craze for betting affected women to an alarming extent. They are frequently to be seen in the betting houses in the poorer quarters with children in their arms. (*Irish Independent*, 10 September 1928)

Like the story of the traveller women drinking in a pub with children in their arms, this paragraph conjures up an image of irresponsible and disorderly mothers carrying their innocent babies into disreputable places and, presumably, leading them into a wasted life of debauchery and excess. In the same month a similar story was also reported in the *Connacht Tribune*. Under the heading, 'Women and Betting Craze', the *Tribune* carried an account of a speech by Mr. Shanley to the Galway Regional Saving Committee (a nation-wide organisation which attempted to get people to buy savings certificates). Mr. Shanley was reported as saying that 'betting as a craze' was developing 'among women and even children...Men were able to control themselves more or less, but it seems the women never knew the time to stop, and every day they spent large sums backing horses.' Women also appear to be scapegoated for the fact that children were becoming caught up in the 'betting craze' (*Connacht Tribune*, 15 September 1928).

In these stories women are represented as disorderly and as inadequate mothers showing a bad influence to their children. They have transgressed gender roles by entering public arenas and revelling in the pleasures usually enjoyed only by men: drinking and gambling. Such bad habits amongst women had to be stamped out if Irish society were to remain stable and healthy. Hence, it is apparent that women have a moral responsibility for their children, which takes precedence over their own enjoyment and pleasure.

While the police and judiciary pursued the regulation of licensed premises, it was the unlicensed liquor trade, which occupied increasing amounts of police time and newspaper copy. Throughout the 1920s-1930s, the Free State authorities waged a relentless war against the illegal and unregulated trade in poteen, a highly potent alcoholic drink made from potatoes. Civic guards raided and searched farms, private homes, dances, even entire villages in their pursuit of this spirit. According to press reports, these raids appear to have been carried out with a heavy hand and allegations of assaults were common. Raids were most intense in Connacht where the distilling, sale and consumption of poteen were at a peak, but raids were also frequent in Kerry and Cork. Entire families often ended up in court where penalties, even for possession of the smallest amount of poteen, were extremely severe.

On 17 January 1928, the *Connacht Sentinel* carried the headline 'Alleged Shebeening'. This referred to a widow who was convicted of operating an unlicensed pub selling poteen and other liquor. She was fined £10 for having poteen, £2 for running a shebeen and was bound over to the peace for three years. It is noteworthy that the penalty for being in possession of poteen was five times higher than the penalty for running an illegal pub. A similar case was reported on 15 May 1928, under the amusing headline 'Poteen in Bed'. A widow was charged with possession of poteen. She was holding a dance in her house where 'a large crowd of country people had gathered'. The guards searched the house very thoroughly and eventually found a bottle of poteen in a bed, hidden between her two sleeping children. In court, the woman said that she was very poor and had been given the poteen as a gift when her children were sick (poteen was widely believed to have medicinal properties and was often given to adults and children suffering from colds and flu). The court clearly did not accept her story as she was fined £6 and given three months in which to pay.

But such reports were not confined to the pages of provincial newspapers. The prosecution of 'poteen' cases was frequently reported in the national press. On 20 January 1932, the *Irish Independent* carried the story 'Mothers in Poteen Charges'. According to the report, two mothers were among a group of people charged at Carndonagh district court. While one woman's husband received a sentence of six months, she was not imprisoned because of her large family of thirteen dependent children. However, the other woman, whose husband was not implicated, received a sentence of one month's hard labour for selling poteen. The judge was reported as saying that the moral aspect of this case was of more significance than the lost revenue to the state.

On 9 September 1932, the *Irish Press* carried the heading 'Woman Sent to Jail: Justice on Evils of Poteen Traffic'. This report related the story of a woman from Co. Donegal who was sentenced to three months imprisonment. A 17-year-old girl who was also charged with possession of poteen with intent to sell, was given a suspended sentence. District Justice Walsh was quoted as saying that in that region of Donegal 'the women were worse than the men. Many of them ran shebeens and carried poteen about'. Similar consternation and frustration were expressed by a judge at a case in west Cork reported in the *Irish Press* on 9 May 1936. A woman aged 68 years old was fined the maximum penalty of £200 for distilling poteen. A second woman, a widow aged 61 years, appealed against her fine of £50 but the judge ruled against her. The judge congratulated the civic guards on their efforts to stamp out the 'poteen evil'. He added that 'he did not think there could be found in any part of the country women approaching 70 years of age who could come into that court so brazenly, having no regard for the oath. He did not believe one word of what they said' (*Irish Press*, 9 May 1936).

On 18 April 1936, the *Independent* carried the heading 'Leitrim Poteen Cases'. 'An imposing array of appliances and materials for the manufacture of poteen were exhibited and a strong aroma of the product pervaded the district court at Rooskey'. A woman was charged not only with harbouring illicit spirits but also with 'assaulting and obstructing' the police sergeant who went to her house. Her daughter was additionally charged with damaging the sergeant's overcoat. It is clear from the report that the civic guards were pressing for a severe penalty to be imposed on these women. They claimed that the fines, which had been previously imposed, were merely regarded as 'overheads' within the 'poteen industry'. The woman was fined £6 and her daughter was fined £1 and five shillings.

In several of the cases cited above, women were not merely distilling and transporting poteen but they were also running illegal pubs – shebeens – and hosting unlicenced dances. These 'criminal' activities raise interesting questions about the boundaries between the public and private spheres. Clearly, the domestic sphere could be used not only to manufacture and conceal illegal substances but also as an unregulated place of business. An interesting example of the alternative uses which one could make of a large cottage kitchen were suggested by a report in the *Irish Press* on 10 March 1936. The headline clearly summarised the story 'Unauthorised Dance: Sixty People Found in Kitchen by Gardai'. A woman from Co. Galway was fined £1 for holding an unauthorised dance in her kitchen. The gardai (civic guards) testified that they found 60 people in a space measuring 18 feet by 12 feet. In her defence the woman pleaded that she was very poor and had only held the dance to raise money for her daughter who was emigrating to England. The judge complained that current legislation on dance halls (the Dance Halls Act of 1935) was ineffective in controlling these kinds of private, unlicenced dances. Taken in tandem with the earlier newspaper accounts of mothers and daughters proudly sitting at their spinning wheels in their clean, cosy kitchens (*Irish Press*, 12 March 1936), this story reveals very different and complex aspects of life in rural Ireland. Firstly, the harsh reality of female emigration is underlined by the mother's desire to raise money to aid her daughter's departure. Secondly, the fact that up to 60 people were willing to crowd into the kitchen and pay money for the privilege of doing so reveals not only the great need for entertainment in rural areas but also the extent to which people were willing to flout the law in the pursuit of pleasure. Thirdly, this story indicates the complex intersections between the public and private spheres as the police raided the woman's home and summoned her to appear in court.

All of the newspaper stories discussed above raise very similar issues about the regulation of private lives in the Free State. The civic guards, like the NSPCC inspectors, appear to have had extensive powers to enter and search private properties. The courts imposed severe punishments on those people who appeared before them. It is noteworthy that all the cases discussed so far involved poor people, particularly poor women from remote rural areas of the west, north west and south west of the country. These widows, elderly women and mothers of large families were obviously attempting to make some money in any way they could. It was not entirely uncommon at the time, especially in rural areas, for women to run illegal public houses, shebeens, and even small dancehalls from their homes. In all the cases cited above, which are typical of the many reported during the 1920s-1930s, the women were singled out for especially severe punishments. These women were represented as serious offenders, disorderly women who flouted the law and resisted any regulation by the State authorities. In addition, as one judge pointed out, there was the moral aspect of the issue. As mothers from rural, western regions, these women should have embodied the essence of Irishness, the continuity of traditional, religious values and the Gaelic way of life (Nash 1993). Instead they embodied all the negative features of the 'wild west'; disorderly, unrestrained, dishonest, abusive, dangerous and immoral. This dichotomous construction of poor, rural women as wild and disorderly and simultaneously as good, traditional and religious, embodied the complex and contradictory representations of rural Ireland, particularly the west. While the rural Irish idyll of cosy, frugal homesteads was glorified in nationalist rhetoric, there was the contrasting image of rural Ireland as uncivilised, backward and in need of regulation.

These contrasting images mirrored the blurred boundaries between the public and private spheres as private homes were regulated and scrutinised by a range of public bodies and officials. As has been argued elsewhere (McDevitt 1997), there were attempts by the State, Church and cultural groups to impose a civilising process on Irish society. In the 1920s-1930s this manifested itself in an intense regulation of the lives and lifestyles of private individuals and resulted in a raft of very intrusive legislation which attempted to determine what people could and could not do (Fahey 1995). As Mark Ryan (1994) has argued this amounted to a moral straitjacketing of the Irish people. Thus it is apparent that despite their claims to celebrate Irish traditions and the idyllic rural way of life, the Catholic Church, cultural nationalists and the State, were deeply suspicious of what went on inside many Irish villages and private homes. But while many of the problems associated with Irish society could be blamed on ignorance, poverty, drunkenness, especially the consumption of unregulated alcohol, and the lack of respect for law and order especially in remote rural areas, it was also common to look for blame elsewhere. As was mentioned at the start of this chapter, the Catholic Church often blamed moral degradation on the evil influences that were coming into Ireland from abroad.

*Evil Influences: Jazz, Dancehalls and the foreign press.*

On St. Patrick's Day, 17 March 1928, the *Kerryman* reported a recent lecture given at the Dublin Literary Society which pointed out that the 'jazz life' and the 'craze for pleasure' were having an adverse effect on the health and well being of Irish youth. 'The jazz spirit – in everything as well as in dancing – is responsible for whatever decadence there is in the country'. The condemnation of jazz and modern dancing was widely reported in the Irish provincial press in the 1920s-1930s. Jazz and the so-called jazz life style came to epitomise everything that was inherently alien and morally corrupting. On 9 January 1928, the editorial of the *Limerick Leader*, a paper very sympathetic to cultural nationalism, referred to 'so-called modern dances' as 'imported monstrosities', 'apish and heathenish inventions'. The origins of such dances were made even clearer in a report of the Limerick branch of the Gaelic Athletic Association [GAA]: 'African dances that have come to this country of late'. The GAA was adamant that such dances should not be held at any of its venues or functions. 'Leave those savage dances to the uncivilised peoples and for God's sake get away from the jazz bands' (*Limerick Leader*, 4 February 1928).

These dances were deemed to be particularly threatening and dangerous to the virtue and morality of young women and thus, by association, threatened Irish Catholic values. In a special Christmas day edition in 1926, the *Connacht Tribune* printed an article entitled 'Culture in Catholic Ireland – The Flower of Motherhood'. As the mothers of future generations, Irish girls represented the continuity of the nation and its religious tradition. But this could not be taken for granted. Girls and young women needed to be prepared for their future roles. 'Look on the young girl as a tender plant, one to be guided, guarded and protected'. Interestingly, while it was usually mothers who were burdened with sole responsibility for rearing their daughters (Valiulis 1995b), this article addressed fathers:

> Do you think man, if you had a daughter...you would prepare her for it [motherhood] by sending her half-naked into a dance hall at Christmas to dance savage, sensual dances with any man....One dance with one evil, bad minded man, taking advantage of his lurid opportunity may ruin that girl totally. (*Connacht Tribune* 25 December 1926)

Although this article places the blame for the girl's 'ruin' on a bad man, like other articles there was a focus on women's bodies – 'half-naked' – as a probable cause of leading men astray. Modern girls needed to be 'protected' or restricted for their own good. As discussed in Chapter two, the link between modern fashions, modern dances and sin was repeatedly made in the papers. The dance hall was particularly threatening because it provided an opportunity for young people to mix unsupervised, to indulge in sensual dancing and to consume large quantities of alcohol. The growth of entertainments in the 1920s not only created an increasing number of public spaces for women but also led to fears about women's uncontrolled and unchaperoned freedom (Nava 1995, Valiulis 1995b).

Young people, especially young women, were criticised for leaving the safety of their homes and travelling about the countryside unsupervised. In April 1928, the *Irish Independent* reprinted a lenten lecture of Father Doyle entitled 'the Empty Home':

> For many a boy and girl home was not a home at all. Rather it was a hotel or a lodging house where meals were swallowed and beds were slept in – at least when that all-night dance did not keep them out of it. (*Irish Independent*, 2 April 1928)

Father Doyle said that modern young people were always looking for a 'good time'. Girls whose lives used to be 'bounded by the narrow circle of family friends and domestic duties', 'were today scouring the country on bicycles or motors or aeroplanes, or straddle-legged horseback alone, or preferably with some lonely male'. Father Doyle's imagery is underpinned by an interesting use of the public/private dichotomy. He praises the past era when a girl's life was 'bounded' by family and domesticity. The restrictions of the home are constructed as safe, secure and protected. The modern freedoms of the public world are, by contrast, constructed as unladylike and potentially dangerous.

The physical as well as moral dangers posed by modern lifestyles and entertainments were frequently outlined in the press. For example, on 19 June 1926, the *Connacht Tribune* carried the headline 'After the Dance'. This refers to an incident that took place in the most westerly and remote parts of the State – the Aran Islands. A young local woman was assaulted after a dance. In reporting on the court case, the paper gave only a brief outline of the actual details of the assault but did mention that she sustained injuries to her breast when a young man forced her over a wall into a field. The woman won the case and was awarded compensation. This type of case was not uncommon and drew attention to the risks posed by late night dances and the long journeys home afterwards, especially on dark country roads. It should be pointed out that all-night dances were very common, particularly in rural areas.

A similar case of violence after a dance was reported at length in the *Wicklow People* in January, February and March 1926. Unfortunately, in that case the woman was unable to escape her attacker and was murdered. On 13 February 1926, 'Catholic Notes' used the murder to make a point about the dangers of all-night dances. Referring to the 'tragedy that befell the young country girl on the lonely mountain side', the article claimed that:

> Her horrible fate is the almost certain doom of many girls now living in our towns and cities. For the road she took is now followed by many other girls ...let them halt and think and pray before it is too late. Night walking, country roads, dances, drinking led to her fall and to her death. (*Wicklow People*, 13 February 1926)

It is note worthy that 'her fall' is deemed to be separate from 'her death'; this probably refers to her fall from virginity and seems to imply that she was raped. Emphasising that the young woman had been drinking, the article argued that drinking in dance halls had become a serious problem, especially among women. This point was reiterated at a meeting of the temperance society in Bray, Co. Wicklow. Again using the example of the girl's murder, the report claimed: 'She began her career of ruin and shame by drinking at a dance'. Several other murders and 'disgraceful things' had recently taken place which all involved alcohol. The point was emphasised that these crimes had occurred not in England, but here in Ireland (*Wicklow People*, 13 March 1926). While it may have been expected that such incidents would occur in England, it is presented as deeply disturbing that they should take place in Ireland. Such behaviour is thus constructed as alien, not part of Irish society but a product of the foreign jazz lifestyle invading and corrupting the country.

Cases of this nature were reported in the provincial press on a regular basis, however, they also appeared on occasion in the national dailies. On the 13 July 1928, the *Irish Independent* carried the story of a court case under the dramatic headline 'Ugly Head of Evil'. A man found guilty of committing 'serious offences against a girl under 16' was sentenced to the maximum prison term of two years. Judge Doyle referred to the offences as 'desperate and deplorable misconduct which is beginning to show its head amongst the boys and girls of some parts of Ireland'. The judge went on to say: 'Misconduct which was once unknown in Ireland, and which is still, thank God, so uncommon as to cause a thrill of horror and to be properly described as unIrish' (*Irish Independent*, 13 July 1928).

He agreed with the wisdom of the Bishops in endeavouring to preserve 'the chivalry of the Irish boys and the maidenly reserve that was the boast at all times of Irish girls'. By citing the judge's words in such detail, this report appears to be endorsing the opinion that these types of offences were alien to Irish society until recent time. They were 'unIrish', the implication being that they are coming into Ireland from abroad, part of the degrading and demoralising foreign corruption that the Bishops were campaigning to censor. This attitude was clearly illustrated in a sermon by Dr. O'Doherty, Bishop of Galway. A report of the sermon was printed in the *Independent* on 16 May 1928 under the bold headline 'Bishop's Call To Nation'. In a stirring rallying cry to the nation, the Bishop vehemently condemned English newspapers that were flooding into Ireland: 'There were, in a great many of the papers, articles of the most shocking kind, subversive of family life, subversive of the very simplistic ideals of Catholic morality.'

Such papers were 'not fit to enter any decent Catholic household'. Thus the 'decent home' was defined in accordance with strict Catholic doctrine. The ideal Catholic home was a bastion of morality and virtue where decent families were protected from the threats posed by outside corruption. However, it was clear that decent Catholic families could not be relied upon to protect themselves from such threats. The Church and State were required as the enforcers of moral safeguards and standards. Hence, as well as lobbying for restrictions on dance halls, the Catholic Church was putting mounting pressure on the government to introduce stringent censorship controls on publications. Because this was aimed largely at curbing English papers coming into the country, it had the backing of most Irish newspapers, which, in any case, probably resented English competitors. The Church's objection to these publications was usually couched in terms of their demoralising and denationalising influences on young people. As Bishop O'Doherty concluded:

> These are the things that are bought by young people and read by them, and is it any wonder their young minds are corrupted and polluted, and their bodies brought to shame? (*Irish Independent*, 16 May 1928)

The Bishop of Ferns made similar points in his lenten pastoral reprinted in the *Wicklow People* on 25 February 1928. Focusing on the pernicious effects of 'evil literature' which 'comes to us almost entirely from abroad', he warned parents to be vigilant. Young people needed to be protected so that they were 'not contaminated by reading dangerous and unsuitable material'. He added that 'the perusal of undesirable literature tends to produce or had already produced idle and dissolute and worthless people who become a burden upon the industrious section of the community'.

Thus evil literature was the cause not only of idle, wasted lives but also of a wide array of sinful behaviour. It threatened to weaken the control which parents and the Church exerted over young people. It contaminated young Irish men and women corrupting their minds and bringing their bodies to shame. All of these themes were brought together in a lengthy article published in the *Limerick Leader* on 23 July 1928. Reporting on the celebrations of the 60th anniversary of Limerick Arch-Confraternity of the Holy Family – a Catholic lay organisation –, the *Leader* printed the full text of Father Morgan's sermon to the organisation. His sermon focused on the agents of Satan: 'foremost amongst these is the press...the filthy novel...the foul newspaper...pictures in the cinema that night after night are working havoc on the souls of Catholic boys and girls'. 'Allied to the press is another powerful weapon in the hands of the agents of Lucifer...the love of amusement'. All of these agents of Satan/Lucifer worked together to undermine the Church but the Church was fighting back: 'The Church is the great antagonist of Lucifer. Under her and aided by her, who is herself indeed divine, the true children of God fight the battles of the Lord.'

Thus the Church was established as the only hope against the intrusive and all-pervasive powers of the foreign press and entertainment industry. By taking this position, the Church was not only reinforcing its position as the saviour and protector of Irish-Catholic culture but also justified its role as the moral police force of the nation.

## *Conclusion:*

Amidst the numerous press stories of violence, neglect and lawlessness, it seems difficult to sustain the myth of the pious, law abiding, God-fearing Irish family living contentedly in their frugal homestead. In attempting to explain the frequency and persistence of disorderly behaviour in Irish society, two apparently contradictory arguments were widely employed. The first explanation blamed criminal and immoral behaviour on the evil influences that were coming into the country from abroad. Imported newspapers, films and books polluted the mind and brought the body to shame. Serious offences, particularly those of a sexual nature, could therefore be dismissed as 'unIrish'. This explanation was closely related to the growing campaigns for censorship. The second explanation was related to the 'civilising process' and constructed deviant and disorderly behaviour in terms of backwardness and ignorance. Drunken, violent and abusive behaviour, whether in remote rural areas or in poor urban areas, could be contained and controlled by the civilising influence of authority. This is particularly apparent in relation to the policing of the poteen trade in the west of the country. Both of these explanations were used by Church and State to legitimise the close scrutiny of the domestic sphere.

Although the Catholic Church and the State frequently invoked the idealised image of good Catholic homes filled with disciplined, obedient children and authoritative, responsible parents, I have suggested that negative family images were also widely employed and highly useful. Wayward children, inadequate or absent mothers and neglectful fathers played a key role in the discourses of Catholic Church and State. Images of the Irish home were underpinned by complex and shifting constructions of the public/private dichotomy. On the one hand, the safety of the domestic sphere was associated with images of 'decent homes', while, by contrast, public spaces such as dancehalls and other forms of entertainment represented evil and threats to morality. On the other hand, the existence of disorderly and deviant behaviour inside Irish homes, and the repeated allusions to this in the press, pulpit and courtroom, justified processes of inspection and regulation by public institutions. Women were central to this process in several ways and represented the blurring of boundaries between the public and private. As mothers of the nation, women were held responsible not only for the biological continuity of the Irish population but also for the continuity of Irish culture, values and traditions. But women could not be trusted to carry out these important tasks unsupervised. Through their maternity and sexuality women embodied the potential deviance which pervaded the private spaces of domesticity as well as the public spaces of dancehalls, cinemas, pubs and betting establishments. As both victims and villains women symbolised the need for official intervention and regulation in upholding moral values as well as law and order.

As this chapter has demonstrated women had a complex and multifaceted relationship to the overlapping constructs of family, home and nation. In the next section of the chapter I will look in more detail at the ways in which women's role as mother of the nation was used in nationalist rhetoric and iconography.

## Section 3: Mothering the Nation

In three consecutive months in 1932 three elderly women died, each one of whom had made a particular contribution to the nation and each was eulogised in the national press. However, these three women, all of whom were mothers, were each represented in different ways. Although each could potentially be seen as a national heroine only one was elevated to the status of national icon, only she appeared to have the appropriate characteristics to make her a symbol of national motherhood, indeed, the mother of the nation. This section examines the press reports of the deaths of these three women and analyses the processes through which women may become incorporated into nationalist iconography and national biography. In addition, I will raise questions about the requisite qualities necessary to achieve the dubious honour of emblematic status. Although this section does not focus entirely on obituaries, they do form a large part of the sources for my analysis. It is important, therefore, to begin by raising some points about obituaries.

According to Wendy Webster, when newspaper obituaries 'move beyond a simple notice it is usually into the conventions of biography, but a biography which is moulded by the timing of the account....obituaries often serve as acts of memoralising, honouring their subjects' (Webster forthcoming). In her analysis of the *Times* newspaper, Webster argues that obituaries are presented as 'dispassionate and objective records' and narratives of 'exemplary lives'. They are usually written anonymously in an authoritative voice that presents 'facts' about the life of the deceased person. While death notices provide us with details about the lives of particular individuals, they also serve a greater purpose in defining the overall identity of a nation and its noteworthy citizens. Newspaper obituaries build a story of a national past but with an eye to defining the national story for future record. Obituaries are often structured with reference to significant national events, for example, Webster points to World War I and World War II as key events that shape the national story of Britain. In Ireland, particularly in the 1920s-1930s, events such as the Easter Rising of 1916, helped not only to frame national history but also to select those important individuals who had taken some role in that fateful rebellion. In addition, people are selected for inclusion in a national biography that frequently resembles a family story. Anne McClintock (1993) has argued that nationalisms draw upon family narratives and images to represent the nation. This is particularly significant for the ways in which women become represented as wives and mothers of great men and as mothers of the nation. Webster's historical research on the *Times* obituaries suggests that women have usually been contained within family stories so that a 'woman's obituary could ...become just one more notice of a famous man' (Webster forthcoming).

In April 1932, almost exactly 16 years after the fateful uprising of 1916, an elderly woman died at her home in Dublin. That home was a shrine to her two dead sons who had both been executed by British firing squad for their part in the uprising. Through the heroism of her sons this mother was elevated to the status of martyr, her silent, selfless sacrifice placing her within the inner circle of nationalist rhetoric and symbolism.

On the 23 April 1932, the *Irish Press* carried the front page banner headline 'Mrs. Margaret Pearse Dies at St. Endas: Mother of the Easter Week Leaders'. The sub-headings say that she was 75 years old and as a T.D. (member of the Irish parliament) had voted against the Anglo-Irish Treaty. The biographical details describe how she married Mr. James Pearse 'a Devonshire man' (note not an English man) who worked as a sculptor in Dublin. She was a Poor Law Guardian, a T.D. and later was on the executive of the Fianna Fail party. She had been a manager at St. Enda's school (founded by Padraic Pearse) since 1908. Two photos accompany this front page article; the first is a small portrait of Margaret Pearse, the other is a group photo of a school reunion at St. Enda's where she is shown seated in the front row. On the inside of the paper there is both a lengthy editorial and a detailed feature entitled 'In Memoriam: Mrs. Pearse'.

The editorial claims that while the famous Pearse sons inherited their daring and sense of purpose from their father, 'she it was who gave to Padraic and William Pearse the knowledge and love of Ireland'. In Easter 1916 when the two young men embarked upon their fight for Ireland 'they went out that morning with their mother's blessing. In her heart she knew what was to befall them':

> In her the womanhood of Ireland was enshrined – that great womanhood which has preserved for the Irish nation its heritage of nationality and its heritage of faith. For it was the women of this nation, who like the great women of Galilee, stood closest to the cross and saw their sons die for truth. (*Irish Press*, 23 April 1932)

This short paragraph reveals a great deal about the construction of women within Catholic nationalist rhetoric. Through their role as mothers, women not only biologically reproduce the nation, they also preserve the heritage, traditions and faith of the nation. In the context of militant nationalism, women's primary role is to sacrifice their husbands and especially their sons to the cause. Through the death of their heroic sons, women, as mothers, bear the grief and loss of the nation with a stoic silence. Mrs. Pearse embodies Irish womanhood but in so doing she also embodies the Irish nation. The references to Galilee and 'the cross' also locate her in the context of religion as the mother of Christ. This metaphor is repeatedly used in the press to describe Margaret Pearse. But it is important to analyse where this imagery originated.

The title of the feature article, 'In Memoriam: 'She represented nationhood itself', clearly demonstrates the female embodiment of the nation and quotes at length the poem that Padraic Pearse wrote to his mother shortly before his death. It is simply but tellingly entitled 'The Mother':

> I do not grudge them: Lord, I do not grudge
> My two strong sons that I have seen go out...
> The generations shall remember them and call them blessed,
> But I will speak their names to my own heart
> In the long nights, (*Irish Press*, 23 April 1932)

This poem is remarkable for several reasons and tells us a great deal more about the mentality of Padraic Pearse than it does about his mother. Although the poem is written in her voice, it offers Pearse's version of events. It clearly and, as it happens, accurately foretells the 'blessed' place that he would be ascribed in Irish history. However, he also ascribes the place that his mother will occupy in Irish history. She is 'the mother'; selfless, silent, passive and accepting rather than actively involved in the struggle. Thus, although subsequent leaders, especially Eamon de Valera, used Mrs. Pearse as an iconic figure of Irish motherhood, I suggest that it was in fact Padraic Pearse himself who first defined this role for her. She was to be the keeper of his flame, she was to enshrine national motherhood, she was, through giving birth to him, the mother of the nation.

These themes were picked up and reinforced in the *Irish Press*'s 'In Memoriam': She represented nationhood itself'. The article concludes by quoting another poem by Padraic Pearse, again spoken in the voice of his mother 'Mary: thou didst see thy first born son going to death amid the mockery of men for whom he died. Receive my first born son and keep him by thee till I come to him' (*Irish Press*, 23 April 1932). In this extraordinary quote Pearse appears to be comparing himself to Christ and in so doing is comparing his mother to the Virgin Mary. Pearse like Christ nobly sacrificed himself for the greater good, while Mary, like Margaret Pearse, willingly sacrificed her first born son. Thus Padraic Pearse appears to have deliberately and consciously bequeathed his mother to the nation as a link with the heroic dead, she was the living symbol of his sacrifice. Although she may well have willingly adopted this role, it is apparent from his poems that her son clearly intended her to play this part.

But it is possible to offer alternative readings of Mrs. Pearse. Through her many years of work at St. Enda's school, her endeavours as a publicly elected figure, Poor Law Guardian and T.D., and her public speeches, she seems to have been far from the silent, passive figure represented above. Although the *Irish Press* described her as 'white-haired, gentle, motherly, homely', she was, arguably, also a very strong, determined and hard working woman who remained very active in public life despite her advancing years. The *Irish Press* reveals that her last public speech was given only one month before her death. However, it is increasingly apparent that Mrs. Pearse as a real woman was often considered less important than Mrs. Pearse as an icon; two pieces of information in the *Irish Press* suggest this conclusion. Firstly, it is briefly mentioned that despite her own wishes for a private ceremony, her funeral would in fact be a very public occasion. Secondly, it is also briefly mentioned that before her death she asked on several occasions to see President de Valera but as her illness was not seen to be too serious he was not summoned. It is not clear who took the decision not to summon the President, was it her own family or his officials? However, once she was dead the President played a key role in her funeral and gave what has now become a very famous graveside eulogy.

Thus Margaret Pearse occupied important public and private roles and in so doing represented the complex interconnections between these two spheres. She was a private woman who, because of her sons' activities, was catapulted into public life. However, she appears to have taken her public role very seriously and worked tirelessly well into her later years. Thus Mrs. Pearse, this national icon of idealised motherhood, transcended the usual domestic roles ascribed to women in Irish nationalist rhetoric. But Margaret Pearse was denied a public life in her own right as an individual woman. Instead, her place in the public life of the nation appears to have been circumscribed by her primary role as the mother of martyrs, the keeper of the flame. In this way any possible transgression of gender boundaries was carefully avoided. This is particularly apparent in the graveside eulogy of Eamon de Valera.

Mrs. Pearse's funeral was an occasion of massive public outpouring of grief. One could speculate that this was partly a way of compensating for the fact that her dead sons had never had the honour of such public funerals. However, it is equally possible to speculate that the newly elected Fianna Fail government was anxious to derive as much nationalist sentiment as possible from this event. For three days, the *Irish Press* devoted pages of coverage to her lying in state and the thousands of people queuing to pay their respects (25 April); to the thronged streets as her body was brought to Rathfarnham church (26 April); to the impressive funeral cortege which stopped for one minute outside the General Post Office on O'Connell's Street – the headquarters of the Easter Rising (27 April). The headline 'Moving Scenes at Yesterday's National Tribute – 100,000 Gather to Watch Funeral', suggests the scale of this event (*Irish Press*, 27 April 1932).

President de Valera's funeral oration was carried in several national newspapers including both the *Irish Press* and the *Irish Independent*:

> But for the fame of her two sons the noble woman at whose grave we are gathered would, perhaps, never have been heard of outside the narrow circle of her personal friends. Her modesty would have kept her out of the public eye. (*Irish Independent*, 27 April 1932)

De Valera went on to say that although Mrs. Pearse knew in advance that her sons were planning to die in the Easter uprising 'this loving and tender woman resisted the promptings of her mother's heart; she did not seek to hold back her sons; she bade them go'. He concluded his eulogy by drawing upon the image of Mrs. Pearse to support the future efforts of his own political agenda:

> The memory of her life remains with us, as a source of strength in the work that lies ahead, the work of realising the ideal for which she suffered and her sons gave their lives. (*Irish Press*, 27 April 1932)

In analysing this graveside oration, Maryann Valiulis (1995a) claims that de Valera was actually outlining his ideal of Irish womanhood, the type of womanhood he would aim to institutionalise during his many years in office. She argues that de Valera's ideal woman was passive, had no work of her own to do and lived only to fulfil the wishes and needs of her husband, sons and brothers (1995a: 118). I agree with Valiulis and would further add that political leaders and the press were less interested in the real and more complex qualities of Margaret Pearse than in her usefulness as a shared national symbol of idealised womanhood. As Eavan Boland (1989) has argued, once women are raised to the level of national icon they become inevitably simplified, contained, reduced to stereotypes, and the reality and complexities of their lives are rendered invisible.

Mrs. Pearse's allegorical status is made clear in a feature article published in the *Kerryman* newspaper under the heading 'Stabat Mater':

> Roisin Dubh had sent forth her pitiful appeal and Mrs. Pearse was the first to answer....All down the ages the glorious sacrifices of Irish mothers have sanctified the beautiful traditions of this land of ours. And Mrs. Pearse was the symbol of Irish motherhood. (*Kerryman*, 30 April 1932)

In being raised to emblematic status Margaret Pearse is contained within the gendered iconography of the nation. Roisin Dubh, the female embodiment of Ireland, appeals for sacrifices and Mrs. Pearse, the embodiment of Irish motherhood, is the first to respond. In its concluding paragraph, this feature article closely echoed Pearse's own poem by saying that with her death Mrs. Pearse would not only be reunited with her sons but would 'be welcomed by another Mother, who also gave the Son of her heart to a glorious ideal'. Thus the imagery once evoked by Padraic Pearse to compare his mother with the Virgin Mary had become indelibly linked to the image of Mrs. Pearse. She is forever inscribed in the symbolic repertoire of Irish motherhood, mother Ireland and mother church.

However, as mentioned at the start of this section, the process by which women become incorporated into the iconography of a nation is by no means straightforward or guaranteed. In illustrating this process I will draw upon two other women who died within a short time of Mrs. Pearse. In May 1932 another elderly woman died; a woman who had played an active part in the cultural nationalist movement and who had helped to revive many of the ancient symbols, legends and myths which Terence Brown (1987) has argued were so important to the newly emerging Irish state. On 24 May 1932, the *Irish Independent* announced the death of Lady Augusta Gregory. She was described as a 'great dramatist' with a 'remarkable career' and also as a 'great writer'. 'Much that emanated from her pen is destined to live in the literary history of Ireland'. She was 73 years old. On the 28 May 1932, the *Kerryman* devoted four short paragraphs to the death of Lady Gregory, recounting several of her main achievements. She joined the Irish language revival group, the Gaelic League, when it was first established and developed a keen interest and working knowledge of the Irish language. She translated many works from Irish into English. She was a director of the Abbey Theatre and wrote over 25 plays. Both of these newspaper accounts are very straightforward and matter of fact, they review the many accomplishments of Augusta Gregory but avoid any sentimentalism.

The *Irish Press* offered similar coverage of the death and funeral of this great woman. Under the front page headline 'Death of Lady Gregory: Loss to Drama and Irish Theatre', the *Press* carried a reproduction of a portrait of Lady Gregory. In addition to her work in translating Irish stories especially those relating to

*Cuchulainn* and *Finn Mac Coull*, she was also an outspoken campaigner for Irish independence. During the war of independence she wrote several articles in British newspapers exposing conditions in Ireland. She was assured a place in 'the annals of the nation' because of her work for Irish drama and literature. W.B. Yeats is quoted as saying that she was 'passionately patriotic' and 'worked her whole life for Ireland' (*Irish Press,* 24 May 1932).

The *Irish Press* editorial of the same day described her as 'one of the few writers who thought with the thought of the Irish people and felt with their feelings....She dies respected by a nation which has had many writers and among them not so many friends'. This was a thinly veiled attack on the Anglo-Irish writers and dramatists who were seen by many in the Irish Ireland movement as less than nationalistic in their outlook and writings. On the 25 May, the *Press* announced that Lady Gregory would be buried in a private ceremony in Galway. President de Valera sent a message of sympathy and would be represented by local T.D. Mr. Little. On the following day the paper carried a short account of her funeral:

> When Lady Gregory was laid to rest today in a tree shaded corner of the Protestant plot at Prospect Hill Cemetery Galway, her request for simplicity was fulfilled, and there was nothing in the funeral or graveside service to indicate the passing of a great personage. (*Irish Press*, 26 May 1932)

In my view, this short paragraph is very telling. Firstly, it clearly underlines the Protestantism of Lady Gregory, a point to which I will return later. Secondly, it contrasts markedly with the funeral ceremony of Mrs. Pearse. Although both elderly women had requested simple, private funerals only one woman had that wish honoured. How can this marked difference be explained? In many ways Lady Gregory would seem to have been a more interesting and formidable character than Mrs. Pearse, she was certainly more affluent, more travelled and more famous: as an influential and celebrated writer and theatre director, as a member of the aristocracy, as a linguist, as the colleague of such famous writers as Synge and Yeats. Lady Gregory had other qualities too, she was a mother whose son had died (but not fighting for Ireland), she was a nationalist, she was dedicated to the preservation of the Irish language and culture. However, it is very clear from the press reports outlined above that she was not about to be incorporated into nationalist iconography.

Lady Gregory was a rich Protestant aristocrat, and although she supported cultural nationalism, her association with Yeats and other writers clearly placed her in the Anglo-Irish literary set. In addition, she was an active, outspoken woman who achieved international recognition in her own right for her own work. She confidently and successfully occupied the public sphere of the theatre and the arts. In that sense she was very far removed from the idealised mother described above by Maryann Valiulis (1995a). Clearly de Valera and other influential nationalists saw little to be gained from eulogising the life and work of Lady Gregory or attempting to raise her to emblematic status. She was too much of a real, complex, dynamic woman to be contained within simple iconic stereotypes.

But one does not have to be a Protestant and an aristocrat to be excluded from national iconography repertoires. On 16 June 1932, the *Irish Press* announced in very simple and matter-of-fact manner that Mrs. Wheelwright had died in New York. Formerly Miss Catherine Coll, she had emigrated to the United States as a young woman. She was married twice and had had two sons. Her first husband was Mr. Vivian Juan de Valera. The death of President Eamon de Valera's mother was greeted with little fanfare and no official outpouring of public sentiment. This was a reflection of the fact that the funeral took place far away in the United States and perhaps more significantly that de Valera himself did not attend. Even the press reports were surprisingly muted. The *Kerryman* newspaper gave a short biography of Mrs. Wheelwright on the 18 June 1932. This reveals the nature of the relationship between the President and his mother.

He had last seen her during a visit to the States in 1930. Born Catherine Coll in Bruree, Co. Limerick in 1856 she had emigrated to the USA at the age of 23. Two years later she married Vivian de Valera in September 1881 and just over one year later in October 1882 their only child Eamon de Valera was born. Her husband died in 1884. Mrs. de Valera then decided to send her three-year-old son back to live in Ireland with his grandmother and uncles. Three years later she married Charles Wheelwright and had two children, a girl who died and a boy who later became a priest. 'Up to the last, Mrs. Wheelwright took the liveliest interest in the Irish movement for independence'. Her home in Rochester, New York remained a very Irish household:

> To meet in her Rochester home was to forget the United States and live again in an Irish country homestead, with its motherly friendliness. (*Kerryman*, 18 June 1932)

She gave her son many of her characteristics: 'her honesty, her shrewdness and her delightful sense of humour'.

This short biography offers a particular representation of Mrs. Wheelwright but it is also very restrained and avoids all the nationalist symbolism and religious sentimentalism heaped upon Mrs. Pearse. It is quite clear from the press coverage, or lack of it, that Catherine Wheelwright was not about to join Margaret Pearse in the repertoire of national iconography. Unlike the latter, Mrs. Wheelwright did not 'represent nationhood itself'. There are many reasons for this and several of them flow from de Valera himself. While he praised the motherly qualities of Mrs. Pearse, he did not praise his own mother, perhaps because he hardly knew her. She had sent him away when he was just three years old, to be raised by his elderly relatives. During the remaining years he had rarely seen his mother. She had remarried, changed her name, and had had a new family. She had not sent for Eamon to rejoin her. The impact of his childhood on de Valera has been discussed by many commentators (see T.P. Coogan 1993). It is possible to speculate that part of his romanticism around the traditional Irish family and the devoted Irish mother stemmed from the absence of these in his own young life. Of course, it is also possible to dig deeper and to speculate that Mrs. Wheelwright was not all that she seemed. Her husband, the mysterious Spanish gentleman, Vivian Juan de Valera, about whom very little is known, has never been fully explained and the rumours that she was in fact unmarried when Eamon was born have gathered pace in recent studies (see Coogan 1993). In any case, the fact remains that for whatever reason, Catherine Coll Wheelwright did not fit the role of idealised national mother that her own son helped to define in the 1930s. While Mrs. Pearse could be comfortably accommodated within notions of Catholic Irish motherhood and raised to the level of a near sainthood, other women proved more complex and unacceptable.

Thus in terms of analysing the processes through which women become incorporated into nationalism as cultural symbols and icons, it is important to note that some women are more easily incorporated than others. This may not be a true and accurate reflection of these women's qualities and characteristics or indeed of their actual contribution to the nation. In fact, it may be far more a question of whether or not they can be made to fit with nationalist and religious ideals of femininity. Thus a woman who could be simplified and contained within the image of 'mother of martyrs' may be a more acceptable national icon than a woman who was an activist, an artist, a worker, a politician. This may be particularly the case for those whose traditional motherly or womanly qualities are tarnished or questionable.

*Conclusion*

The three sections of this chapter have used a number of case studies to examine the related themes of motherhood, home, family and the nation. In so doing I have indicated the need to interrogate simple dichotomous constructions such as urban versus rural, public versus private and ideal versus real. Disorderly families, absent or inadequate mothers, immorality and lawlessness transcended both urban and rural settings and blurred the boundaries of domestic privacy and public scrutiny. Concerns about family life, morality, law and order were mapped onto the gendered constructions of domestic and public spaces. Rural Ireland was represented both by the idealised, cosy cottage and by images of the lawless 'wild west'. Slums and tenement dwellings represented both the hardships of family life but also the dangers of disease and immorality in overcrowded urban spaces.

Home and family were crucial parts of a national iconography that framed women in particular and limited ways. This is evident in the many newspaper stories about disorderly women just as much as in the obituaries of national heroines. Women's role was in the home and that home should be a microcosm of the Catholic nation. Any deviation from the norm was presented as suspicious and potentially threatening to national stability.

# CHAPTER FIVE:

## REBELLIOUS BODIES

*Introduction:*

Women are still largely neglected in histories of the Irish Republican movement. Accounts of military campaigns tend to celebrate masculinity, either ignoring women or representing them as victims or mourners. Sarah Benton (1995) highlights the 'cult of manliness' associated with the militarisation of Irish politics. She argues that the armed Republican movement was overwhelmingly male dominated. While her assessment is largely correct, I suggest that a concentration on male leaders overlooks the diverse roles which women did play. While many Republicans may have officially presented themselves in exclusively masculine terms, the reality was often more complex and even contradictory. In recent years sources are being uncovered which suggest that women actively participated in militant Republicanism in the early decades of the twentieth century (Ward 1995, Taillon 1996, McCoole 1997, Ryan 1999, Ryan 2000). For feminists the image of women carrying arms and participating in warfare raises many uncomfortable questions. But, as Nira Yuval-Davis (1997) has argued, women have taken active parts in nationalist conflict in many countries world-wide.

While they may have been excluded from histories of the War of Independence and the Civil War, Republican women were regularly depicted in the mainstream press of the period. Newspapers offer a complex array of images of Republican women. While simplifying women's involvement in the War of Independence, the press vilified women activists in the Civil War. Focusing on the mainstream southern Irish newspapers of the period, this section analyses the gendered representations of militant women. Variously labelled as 'furies', 'die-hards' and 'neurotic girls', Republican women were singled out for special, negative attention by the Press. In particular during the Civil War (1922-23), Republican women were constructed as evil and disorderly, even more deadly than their male comrades-in-arms. Drawing on content analyses of a range of newspapers, I examine not only the ways in which these images and representations were constructed but also explore reasons why Republican women were deemed so threatening to public order and private morals. I further suggest that the dissemination of negative images of these women may well have informed how they have been represented in historical accounts; either excluded as insignificant or ridiculed as mad.

## Section 1: Representations of Republican Women in the Campaign for Irish Independence.

In the early twentieth century campaigns for Irish independence, with the exception of the Easter Rising of 1916, the period of most intense military engagement can be broken down into two, closely related phases; The War of Independence and the Civil War. The War of Independence, also known as the 'Tan War' or the Anglo-Irish War, officially began in 1919 and culminated in the truce of July 1921. This period witnessed the militarisation of Ireland on a grand scale; tens of thousands of British troops occupied towns and villages, imposing martial law and strict press censorship. With limited weaponry and vastly outnumbered by the British, the Irish Republican Army [IRA] used local knowledge and local support to carry out one of the first guerrilla wars. In their attempts to locate and defeat their hidden adversaries, the British were accused of widespread official and unofficial reprisals on civilian populations. Homes and businesses were raided and destroyed, families were made homeless and thousands of people were taken into custody (Barry 1997, Conlon 1969, Ward 1995). In this context battle lines were blurred, the domestic arena becoming as militarised and dangerous as the hillsides and city streets. While a gendered division of labour underpinned this militarisation, as in all armed conflicts women's roles expanded to include many of the activities of war:

> From the onset of the 1916 Easter Rising through the struggle for independence and the civil war, women assumed a prominent role in putting Ireland's case for freedom before the world. (Valiulis 1995a: 119)

During the War of Independence, the IRA relied very heavily on female involvement at two key levels. In the domestic sphere women provided a network of 'safe houses' across the country where they nursed, fed and concealed men 'on the run'. Outside the home women were increasingly used as intelligence agents, couriers and despatch riders. However, this may be a misleading dichotomy of activities, in many cases these tasks were closely related and interchangeable. As the boundaries between home and battlefront were increasingly blurred, domestic labour could be redefined to include information gathering, concealing and transporting weapons. Thus women's roles and activities transcended the public and private divide. Many of these women were from Republican families; their husbands, brothers, sons and boyfriends were active in the IRA (Brennan 1980, Clarke 1991, Keyes McDonnell 1972, MacEoin 1980). However, that is not to imply that they were merely female sympathisers and supporters of the movement, several hundreds, perhaps thousands of women were actively involved in the armed conflict as members of Cumann na mBan (Conlon 1969, Ward 1989, Fitzpatrick 1990). Tom Barry's autobiography provides some insight into the work of the Republican women's group Cumann na mBan:

> Cumann na mBan was now well organised. No work was too dangerous or too strenuous for those fine women, numbering in West Cork about

> five hundred. Without the aid of this organisation the Army [IRA] would have found it very difficult to carry on. (1997: 63)

Founded in 1914, by 1921 Cumann na mBan had reached its largest membership, at the annual convention 400 delegates represented 800 branches (Conlon 1969). By now it had been placed on a military footing and was, according to Ward (1989), an army of women. Training camps were set up where officers spent six hours per day on first aid, drilling, signalling, map reading and care of weapons.

However, between 1919-1921 only about 50 women were arrested and imprisoned (McCoole 1997). Most received short sentences, though some were imprisoned for periods of up to one year, the longest sentence was handed down to Nurse Linda Kearns for transporting weapons and wanted men in her car. She was sentenced to 10 years but dramatically escaped from prison along with three other Republican women (Buckley 1938, MacEoin 1980). The autobiographical accounts of Republican women demonstrate the level of their involvement in the conflict (Clarke 1991, Conlon 1969, Comerford, Coyle and Humphreys in MacEoin 1980, Keyes McDonnell 1972). Accounts by Republican men also highlight the active parts played by women (Barry 1997, Brennan 1980, O'Donoghue 1954, O'Malley 1992, 1994). In his biography of IRA commander Liam Lynch, fellow Republican Florence O'Donoghue wrote that 'the women rendered heroic service'. He praised 'the young and active girls organised in Cumann na mBan, who carried despatches, nursed the sick and wounded, providing clothes, first-aid equipment, funds and risked their lives as freely as the men' (1954: 107).

But if so many women were actively involved in the War of Independence why were so few arrested and imprisoned? Women's roles within the guerrilla warfare were secret and hidden, using a range of disguises and deceptions to avoid detection. In addition, the British military authorities tended to view women as sympathisers of the movement rather than active participants. This is demonstrated by the ways in which women were treated by the troops. Women were attacked, intimidated, beaten, insulted, driven from their homes. The particular 'punishment' for Republican women was to have their hair crudely cut off by gangs of soldiers. However, only occasionally were these women arrested. As will be discussed below, this contrasts markedly with the treatment of Republican women during the Civil War only one year later when hundreds were arrested and incarcerated. Such discrepancies are also reflected in the newspaper coverage of Republican women.

My study of mainstream newspapers during the War of Independence suggests that the predominant representation of women in the armed conflict was as victims rather than perpetrators of violence (Ryan 2000). However, as fighting intensified between late 1920 and early 1921, press reports made increasing references to the arrest and court-martialling of women. These include Dr. Ada English charged with possessing Cumann na mBan literature (*Irish Independent*, 25 February 1921), Eithne (Annie) Coyle charged with possessing a map of Roscommon military barracks (*Cork Examiner*, 2 March 1921), and Lillian Hawes charged with being in possession of confidential evidence relating to forthcoming courtmartials (*Cork Examiner*, 23 March 1921). There were also brief reports relating to women concealing or conveying arms and ammunition – Eileen Kehoe (*Cork Examiner*, 9 February 1921) and Mary Rigney (*Irish Independent* 14 Feb. 1921) – but such concise accounts gave little information about women's varied roles within the Republican movement. Women were not yet seen as significant players in militarism.

The one 'sensational' exception during this period was Mary Bowles. Accounts of her arrest and courtmartial were carried by the main daily newspapers throughout January and February 1921. When arrested in county Cork she was found in possession of a Lewis machine gun plus a service revolver and an automatic pistol, 'loaded in every chamber' (*Cork Examiner*, 17 January 1921).

The fact that she was also wearing body armour, beneath her blouse, signified her preparedness for using her weapons. The *Irish Independent* and the *Freeman's Journal* carried a photograph of her body armour (19 January 1921). Newspaper reports presented Bowles as very knowledgeable about weaponry; she had copies of several military manuals. The *Cork Examiner* reported that while in her cell, she chipped some plaster from the wall and 'drew a perfect pattern of a machine gun, and all its working parts' (5 February 1921). This report also mentioned the age of the 'sensational' prisoner, she was just 16 years old. Her sentence was widely publicised on the 25 February 1921, 'To be detained in a Catholic Reformatory until she attains the age of 19'. In my view, by being sentenced to a reformatory rather than a prison Mary Bowles was regarded as a junvenile delinquent not a political prisoner. Perhaps the fact that so few women were caught in possession of weapons prevented the authorities from fully appreciating the complex and diverse roles that even very young women were playing in the militant Republican movement. By the time of the Civil War perceptions of women's involvement had changed markedly and school girls as young as 15 were being sent to adult prisons (McCoole 1997).

Newspaper coverage of the War of Independence and in particular representations of Republican women need to be located not only within the context of strict press censorship but also in relation to perceptions of the conflict itself. While none of the mainstream newspapers could be considered pro-Republican, as the fighting intensified and the death toll rose, the press became increasingly critical of British policies in Ireland. Between 1920-1921 newspapers published photographs of burned out shops and homes, the deaths of civilians were repeatedly highlighted and allegations of British army torture and intimidation were reported. Despite the constraints of press censorship, newspapers like the *Cork Examiner*, *Irish Independent* and the *Freeman's Journal*, managed to convey the growing international concerns about what was going on in Ireland. Within this context the predominant portrayal of Republican women, apart from brief reports of arrests and imprisonment, was of mourning relatives and victims of violence.

Graphic but carefully worded accounts of attacks on women were reported in the press without explicitly accusing the British military of an official policy of reprisals. Such press reports suggest that women were attacked as Republican supporters and sympathisers rather than being suspected of direct complicity in the war. For example, on the 27 October 1920, the *Examiner* reported that a young woman, Miss O'Grady, was dragged from her bed in the middle of the night, thrown into a pond of freezing water and had her hair cut off. On the 28 October 1920, the paper reported that the O'Sullivan family home was raided by the military and while her father was locked into the house, Miss O'Sullivan was forced outside where 'the girl's hair was crudely cut off or almost dragged from her head'. The *Examiner* does not explain why these particular women were abused in this way. One can only speculate about the extent of the women's Republican sympathies and their active involvement in the armed struggle.

Thus the mainstream press offered very scant information about Republican women during the War of Independence. When featured at all they were either depicted as helpless victims or as shadowy characters who helped conceal arms and documents. We know from other sources that as many as three thousand women were members of Cumann na mBan and each branch of Cumann na mBan was closely affiliated to local brigades of the IRA (Ward 1989, Sheehan 1990). Of course, it is unlikely that all these women were active participants in the conflict, though it is probable that many were involved to varying degrees. It is a testimony to their success as secret undercover agents that so few were arrested. Ironically it is partly due to their secrecy and near invisibility that Republican women have been largely omitted from historical accounts of the War of Independence. This approach contrasts markedly with the press coverage of women in the Civil War. Nevertheless, while newspapers are useful in providing images and representations of women, they are deeply flawed in providing accurate historical information on the extent and level of women's involvement in the warfare.

## The 'furies'; women and the Civil War

In July 1921 a truce was declared between the British government and the Republican forces. Later that year a treaty was negotiated which set out the partition of Ireland and the semi-independence of the southern Free State. However, the terms of the treaty proved divisive splitting the Republican movement in two. As the political leaders argued about the finer points of the treaty, the IRA fractured into the official army of the Free State and the hard-line Republicans who continued to be known as the IRA or by the more disparaging term 'irregulars'. With the British authorities pressing the new Free State government to quell IRA opposition, civil war seemed inevitable (Litton 1997). Cumann na mBan was the first national organisation to officially reject the treaty (Conlon 1969). In addition, all six women members of the Dail voted against the treaty and sided with the Republican aspiration for a united Ireland independent of British control. Thus, from the outset, women were very visibly and publicly associated with the anti-treaty movement (Clarke 1991).

In the ten months of bitter civil war that followed the Republicans were outnumbered by the Free State Army that, supported by Britain's military might, inflicted severe casualties among their former comrades (Litton 1997). To judge from Ernie O'Malley's autobiography, it would appear that Cumann na mBan women were even more actively involved in the Civil War. 'Now they were our comrades, loyal, willing and incorruptible. Indefatigable, they put the men to shame by their individual zeal and initiative' (1992: 148). However, unlike the War of Independence when the IRA was fighting a foreign foe, now the adversary was largely made up of former comrades who 'were well aware of their hiding places and personnel' (Litton 1997: 88). The impact on Republican women was equally apparent, the invisibility and secrecy which had protected them throughout the previous conflict was now seriously undermined.

Images and representations of Republican women now changed considerably, the official acknowledgement of their involvement fuelled the increasing criticisms being levelled against them by the Catholic Church, Free State politicians and the press. In an attempt to belittle the role of Republican women, President Cosgrave declared that they 'should have rosaries in their hands or be at home with knitting needles' (Fallon 1986: 102). In October 1922, the Catholic Church excommunicated all Republicans who were carrying on a 'system of murder' (Ward 1989: 109). Cardinal Logue particularly 'deplored that a number of women and girls have become involved in this wild orgy of violence' (Fallon 1986: 98).

Between 1922-23 the press repeatedly highlighted women's active participation in the armed conflict (Ryan 1999). Questions need to be raised not only about how these women were represented but also about why the press paid them so much attention. In some ways, of course, the mainstream press was merely echoing the views of the Free State government and the Catholic hierarchy. As before, newspaper images of Republicans must be understood within the context of strict press censorship, but now that censorship was imposed by Irish not British authorities. In any case, as Frances Blake (1986) has argued, most newspaper editors were deeply opposed to the Republicans whom they blamed for starting the Civil War and plunging the country back into destruction and chaos. Many believed that winning the semi-independent 'Free State' had been a considerable achievement. There was a general desire for peace and stability; public support for the Republicans was in decline. 'The Irregular forces, in most areas of the country, found that they were fighting without local support' (Litton 1997: 88).

Press reports reflect much of this exasperation with the Republicans. Thus it is impossible to use newspapers as accurate records of what actually went on during the violent Civil War. Nevertheless, the press does suggest something of the extent of women's involvement in the fighting and the range of activities they undertook. In particular, the images and representations are extremely valuable in providing an insight into the construction of these women as dangerous and disorderly subversives whose participation on the Republican side was seen to demonstrate the depravity, cowardliness, violence and evil of that campaign.

Under the heading 'Young Girls Throw Bombs' the *Cork Examiner* reported that:

> Throughout last night, as well as during the early hours of this morning, a number of attacks were made on National troops in different parts of the city...An attack was made on a Crossley tender ....The principal attackers were some young girls, who threw bombs at the vehicle – a new feature in street attacks. (*Cork Examiner,* 16 October 1922)

The report stressed that casualties were mainly civilian.

At a time when most of the men were either in prison or on the run, official demonstrations of Republicanism were frequently undertaken by women. An article in the *Examiner* entitled 'Procession to Glasnevin' (4 December 1922) reported that: 'This evening at 3.30, a memorial procession in honour of the eight men recently executed in Dublin took place from the Mansion House to Glasnevin Cemetery. The procession was headed by a pipers' band and a contingent of Cumann na mBan in uniform'. The spectacle of women in Republican military uniform was an important demonstration not only of women's commitment to the Republican movement but also of their organised militarism. But while parading in military uniform was important for Republican women, the use of disguise to avoid attention was of equal importance.

'Girls with Machine Guns' (*Cork Examiner*, 23 September 1922) relates to the arrest of three 'irregulars' in Kerry. An eyewitness reported that two young women had escaped from the scene, concealing machine guns under their shawls:

> The soldiers had no suspicion of the innocent-looking peasant girls, who were apparently on their way home from market. (*Cork Examiner*, 23 September 1922)

This article evokes an image of humble, rural, 'peasant girls' wearing the traditional shawl. The apparent innocence and naturalness of this image sharply contrasts with the brutal reality of women 'irregulars', enemies of the state, concealing dangerous weapons beneath their clothes. But the article also suggests some of the complexities around the roles of women Republicans who played with their femininity and donned traditional female attire when engaged in activity which was very far removed from acceptable feminine behaviour. The *Irish Times* reported that a 'young woman named Flynn was arrested by National troops at Youghal' (13 January 1923). No explanation is given for the initial suspicion of this young woman, but it is reported that on being searched she was found to have 'fifty rounds of ammunition inside her corset'. These examples illustrate the blurring of boundaries between privacy and publicity, between feminine and masculine roles. While wearing the most traditional feminine attire, these women were engaging in dangerous activities within a masculine, militarised arena. But these examples also suggest how Republican women negotiated through and used their femaleness while participating in warfare.

Such was the growing concern about women carrying arms and ammunition that the Cograve government issued a report highlighting this apparently increasing phenomenon. The *Irish Independent* carried the report under the headline 'Neurotic Girls':

> The irregular propagandist makes much of the arrest of a few of the female supporters of their party. Neurotic girls are amongst the most active adherents to the irregular cause, because hitherto it has been safe to be so. They disfigure the walls of Dublin with lying propaganda, and they are active carriers of documents, arms and ammunition. Many of them have been known to accompany men on expeditions of murder, concealing arms in their clothes until required, and taking them back when used, relying for safety on the chivalry of those whose deaths they were out to encompass. (*Irish Independent*, 1 January 1923)

On the same day the *Irish Times* published 'Mr. Cosgrave's Review'. Reflecting on the first year of the new state President Cosgrave acknowledged that every society had its share of troublemakers or 'Die-hards':

> In England, fortunately for her, the 'Die-hards' are men with whom the pen dipped in gall is mightier than the sword; but unhappily in Ireland the 'Die-hards' are women, whose ecstasies at their extremest can find no outlet so satisfying as destruction – sheer destruction. Weak men in their atmosphere seek peace in concurrence with their frenzy, and even children are exalted by having revolvers thrust into their little hands. (The *Irish Times*, 1 January 1923)

As Sarah Benton (1995) has argued, militant Republican men sought to emphasise such manly values as courage, loyalty and strength. However, from both of these newspaper reports it is apparent that the obvious presence of women among the Republican ranks was used by their political opponents to undermine those manly virtues. The participation of women was used to present male Republicans as the very opposite of manly, for example, weak, cowardly, shielding behind women's underskirts. In Cosgrave's statement Republican men are presented as weak creatures who cannot control their frenzied women. There is something quite sexual about the description of women experiencing ecstasy through violence and destruction. The mention of little children having revolvers thrust into their hands helps to construct the image of irresponsible mothers rearing the next generation of violent Republicans.

The Cumann na nGaedheal government certainly appears to have acted on its promise to arrest female suspects. While the British army may have underestimated the involvement of women in the War of Independence, the Free State government made no such mistake. By 1923 over 300 women were being held in Kilmainham jail, in addition, women were also imprisoned in Mountjoy and Cork jails as well as in several smaller prisons and barracks around the country. In total, Ward (1989) estimates that there were over 400 women prisoners during the Civil War.

The press carried regular reports of women being arrested and imprisoned. The following extracts all appeared within a four-week period. Under the headline 'County Kerry several Women Arrested' the *Irish Times* reported the arrests of: 'Ethel and Sheila Harnett, Ralina Ryan, Hannah Lyons (National Teacher), Hannah O'Connell, Norah Healy and Miss Randall, active ladies in the irregular movement in Kenmare' (*Irish Times*, 6 January 1923). In the weeks that followed the *Irish Independent* reported that: 'A number of ladies were arrested in Sligo on Saturday. They include Miss Glynn, Chapel St., the Misses Mullen, Charles St. And Miss Malone.' (*Irish Independent*, 15 January 1923). The *Irish Times* reported that in County Louth two young women, Bridget Kelly and Mary ffrench were arrested and removed to Mountjoy Prison (*Irish Times*, 18 January 1923). The danger posed by these women was suggested by a brief report carried by the *Cork Examiner* – 'Lady's Abortive Attempt to Escape'. This referred to Maire Comerford who was arrested while driving out of Dublin. 'Miss Comerford had a revolver in her possession. While being taken to Dublin she made a daring but unsuccessful attempt to escape by jumping out of the car. Miss Comerford has been for a long time one of the most notorious women Republicans in the city' (The *Cork Examiner*, 9 January 1923). This article is unusual in using the term Republican rather than the more common 'irregular'. It also emphasises that these women were not simply carriers of dangerous weapons but they themselves were also dangerous. Reports of armed women actually threatening violence were common.

'Girls with Webleys' (*Cork Examiner* 22 January 1923) refers to the practice of women painting Republican slogans and propaganda on city walls and buildings. Under the strict censorships laws it was one of the only means of communication available to the Republicans. On the Sunday evening a constable of the Dublin Metropolitan Police observed a young woman who was defacing a wall of Trinity College in the centre of Dublin city. 'He proceeded to take her into custody when two other young women brandishing Webley revolvers, approached him, and ordered him to clear away and cease interference with the young lady he was about to take into custody. The policeman had no alternative but to comply with the demands the two armed young ladies'.

During the War of Independence, Mary Bowles was constructed as a 'sensation', a curious aberration from normality, a juvenile delinquent. However, during the Civil War, Republican women were constructed as organised, armed, dangerous and highly subversive. On 1 February 1923 the *Cork Examiner* carried a report: 'Armed woman holds up Dublin policeman'. 'The walls of public buildings in Dublin were defaced during the night by parties, who painted on them such messages as "fifty-five executions and the Republic still lives", "Marie Comerford and Sheila Humphreys now on eighth day of hunger strike". 'The manner in which this work is executed is an illustration of the part which women are taking in the present disturbances'. The article recounted that 'a policeman on duty near Trinity college suddenly found himself surrounded by a half a dozen determined young women. One of them whipped out a revolver and covered the officer, while her companions carried out their mural operations'.

*Conclusion:*

While the mainstream Irish press tended to ignore or underestimate women's active involvement in the War of Independence, by the time of the Civil War things had changed. Mainstream newspapers regularly referred to women's involvement in the conflict. Reiterating the language of Free State politicians, the press represented Republican women in entirely negative terms as 'die-hards' and 'neurotic girls'. The mainstream press was bound by strict censorship rules but that alone is insufficient to explain the very particular representations of women Republicans. As Frances Blake (1986) has suggested many in the press deeply opposed the Republicans and blamed them for starting the civil war. But why was women's active involvement now being so explicitly highlighted? And why were these women depicted as evil, unnatural and unwomanly?

It has been suggested by Litton (1997) that women were more actively involved in the Civil War than they had been in the War of Independence. However, it is difficult to be certain about the exact numbers of women participating in either conflict. Although the numbers of women arrested and imprisoned varied dramatically between the two wars, that alone is not an accurate indication of the overall extent of women's involvement. It is true to say that the number of Republican men fighting in the Civil War was considerably less than in the War of Independence and, therefore, it can be argued that the ratio of women to men did, in fact, increase. As Margaret Ward suggests, during the Civil War women's support became even more valuable to 'the small, roving guerrilla bands struggling against the remorseless advance of the Free State' (1989: 187).

In the context of a bitter Civil War which was opposed by the majority of the civilian population, the active and visible involvement of so many women was not only very remarkable but also presented a major propaganda opportunity to their opponents. While the ideal Irish woman was the self-sacrificing mother, the giver of life, women who actively participated in the taking of life were deemed abnormal, inhuman. Republican women, in particular, the women of Cumann na mBan, transgressed acceptable gendered boundaries (Gray and Ryan 1997). They wore military uniform and carried weapons; they were political, confident and outspoken. They challenged the authority of the Catholic hierarchy and were undeterred by excommunication (Buckley 1938, Fallon 1986). The Free State, supported by the mainstream press, used these women in attempting to undermine Republican men, questioning their manliness, courage and strength. The presence of so many women among the Republican forces represented the irregularity and the illegitimacy of the Republican cause. Hence these women were not only constructed as disorderly but they were also seen to represent the disorderliness of the entire Republican movement.

In my view, the construction of these women as organised, assertive and dangerous subversives, shaped not only reactions to them during their lifetimes but, as will be discussed in the next section, also influenced how they were represented throughout the remainder of the 1920s-1930s. The end of the Civil War marked a turning point for women's role in Irish political life. With the defeat of the Republicans, the women found themselves on the losing side and in somewhat of a political wilderness for most of the 1920s. In a state beset with economic and political problems, Republicans became the bogeymen and women, blamed for causing political instability, fear and unease (Gray and Ryan 1998). Both Ward (1997) and McCoole (1997) argue that women activists were specifically targeted by the Cumann na nGaedheal government; they were represented as threats to public order and national stability. Government minister Kevin O'Higgins claimed that Republicans included 'men and women, particularly women, whose driving force was hate' (Fallon 1986: 131). The hierarchy of the Catholic Church and the mainstream press actively supported the government's anti-Republican policy. The biggest daily newspapers continued to offer representations of Republicans that reflected the views of the dominant elite in the new state.

In transgressing gender boundaries and participating in militarism, Republican women have presented feminists with some uncomfortable questions. Perhaps this may explain why there has been a tendency for so much feminist research and analyses to focus on the emblematic or allegorical woman within nationalist discourses and iconography rather than these controversial real women.

## Section 2: Militant Women in the Post-Civil War Period

> If you want to love Ireland pray for it and for its people daily. The only way to help was to leave politics alone. If I had a friend who had a tendency to take up politics I would pray for him and ask God to change his heart. If I had a little girl friend who took up politics I would give up praying for her. Women who go around taking despatches and arms from one place to another are furies. Who would respect them or who would marry them? Never join a Cumann na mBan or a Cumann na Saoirse or anything else. Do your work as your grandmothers did before you. (Bishop Doorley speaking at a confirmation ceremony in Castlerea, cited in the *Cork Examiner*, 18 May 1925)

*Introduction:*

After the Civil War ended in 1923 with the defeat and mass arrests of Republican men and women, the victorious Cumann na nGaedheal administration, under the leadership of William Cosgrave and strongly supported by the Catholic Church, set about defining the national identity of the newly established Irish Free State. Within this highly gendered ideology, women were ascribed rather limited traditional roles. As the quote from Bishop Doorley above demonstrates, women who continued to demand a role in politics and public affairs were treated with suspicion. Republican women, in particular, were represented as irrational public nuisances and as females who transgressed the boundaries of femininity but also as, 'furies' and 'die-hards' dangerous traitors to the state (Ryan 1999).

The high profile of many Republican women during the 1920s meant that they were easy targets for the government, the church and their allies in the mainstream press. While several Republican men, including Eamon de Valera, began to move away from militancy and redefine themselves as respectable politicians, organisations like Sinn Fein became increasingly associated with outspoken, politically extreme women, such as Mary MacSwiney. MacSwiney was a vocal defender of the Republican spirit and vehemently condemned all those, including de Valera, who abandoned Republicanism to work within the apparatus of the Free State (Fallon 1986). She was quoted in the *Cork Examiner*, 1 November 1926, as pledging that Republicans would consider 'no compromise and no surrender'.

The media's focus of attention on Republican women is interesting and worthy of further analysis. This was partly, in my view, a continuation of the way in which the Civil War had been reported in the daily press. Women's visible participation in the Republican movement, underlined by the large numbers of women incarcerated between 1922-1923, was used in the press to emphasise the irregularity of the entire Republican campaign. Later on as many Republican men either transformed themselves into Fianna Fail politicians, or emigrated to the USA or went underground, women's continuing visibility in both Sinn Fein and Cumann na mBan was used to highlight the illegitimacy and potential danger of Republicanism.

While Republicans were presented as the bogeymen, and especially the bogey-women, of the new nation-state, that is not to imply that they were constantly in the news. For much of the time, particularly in the mid-late 1920s, there was little mention of the Republican movement in the press. The implication might almost be that the movement no longer existed and that this part of Irish history was over. However, newspapers did suggest some of the underlying tensions in the country as every now and then a short report in the provincial press referred to some Republican gathering or commemoration or to some sinister occurrence involving the shadowy spectre of Republicanism. On several such occasions they are not referred to as Republicans at all but as 'an illegal military organisation'. Thus even the word 'Republican' took on dangerous and seditious undertones in the backlash which followed the civil war.

*'Up the Republic': Republican Women and the Cumann na nGaedheal Government:*

On 12 May 1928, the *Kerryman* newspaper, which appears to have been slightly more sympathetic to the Republican cause than most of the other provincial papers, printed a letter to the editor concerning the desecration of the Countess Bridge memorial. A plaque had been placed on the bridge in Killarney to commemorate the death of four IRA men in 1923. In fact, this had been a particularly controversial incident in which Free State troops were alleged to have executed IRA volunteers without trial. The letter, which was printed in a prominent position on the front page of the *Kerryman*, claimed that the plaque had been ripped off the bridge and thrown into the river. In a separate incident a well-known Republican activist, the Honourable Albina Broderick, had the windows of her house smashed. Neither of these incidents had been reported in any newspapers. Was there, the letter asked, a conspiracy of silence surrounding such attacks on Republicans? This sympathetic letter, although not unique, was relatively unusual, as most press reports of Republicans presented them as dangerous and potentially destabilising to the nation.

On 1 September 1928, the *Sligo Champion* reported 'Dump in a Wood'. This referred to an arms dump rather than a rubbish dump and the fact that the word 'arms' was not mentioned in the headline suggests that readers would be expected to share an interpretation of its meaning. As the finding of arms dumps was very common in the aftermath of the war years, (see for example *Cork Ex-*

*aminer*, 2 February 1925), it is likely that readers would have immediately realised the significance of the headline. Civic Guards discovered 24 rifles and 2,000 rounds of ammunition as well as an assortment of other weaponry in a Sligo wood. Although Republicans were not named in this short report, the implication of their involvement would have been apparent to readers in the 1920s. The IRA, following their defeat in the civil war, had dumped most of their arms around the countryside. The fact that these weapons still existed and were accessible helped to perpetuate the image of Republicans as dangerous and threatening.

The IRA and Sinn Fein were resented by the Cumann na nGaedheal government and presented as a threatening force primarily because they still refused to accept the Anglo-Irish treaty, especially the partition of North and South, and the partial independence of the southern Free State. In the editorial of the *Irish Independent* on 18 December 1926, the minister for defence, Kevin O'Higgins, was cited as saying that prior to Irish independence, resentment against the British was 'inevitable'. But things had now changed. 'So far as the Free State is concerned, the quarrel with Britain is ended'. The editorial supported minister O'Higgins in criticising 'the mischief' of those 'who still persist in shouting for a Republic'.

The adherence of the IRA and Sinn Fein to the Republican ideal underlined the view that the Free State administration had compromised on the Northern six counties and accepted a half-measure of sovereignty. Republicans took every opportunity to reiterate this point which may explain why the mainstream press was so reluctant to report their speeches. However, on 26 May 1928, in a somewhat unusual report, the *Wicklow People* reported in some detail on the commemoration of the IRA leader Liam Mellows, who was executed in December 1922 by the Free State army. Under the headline 'Late Liam Mellows: Pilgrimage to Castletown Cemetery', the *Wicklow People* described the event in great detail, noting that those in attendance included Maura (*sic*) Comerford. The orator Mr. Langley was quoted as urging Republicans to 'strive for unity as brothers in arms and fight against the common enemy 'til Ireland was free from the centre to the sea, not for 26 counties but for all of Ireland'. It is noteworthy that he should refer specifically to 'brothers' in arms, rendering Republican women invisible.

As I have argued at length elsewhere (Ryan 1999), Republican men were often deeply ambivalent about women's active and visible role in the military campaign. In reporting this speech, the *Wicklow People* may be seen as publicising the Republican cause. However, in reporting those particular words, it is equally likely that the paper was merely reinforcing the image of Republicans as dangerous, violent and threatening.

Although Republicans were frequently presented in the press as shadowy characters located on the murky margins of Irish society, several high profile court cases involving women helped to bring Republicans centre stage. However, while these cases received little attention in the local, weekly press, they were widely reported in bigger papers such as the *Cork Examiner* and in the national daily, the *Irish Independent*. These reports were usually brief but their frequency reinforced the strong association between women and a Republican movement that was being driven increasingly underground.

Throughout 1926, the *Cork Examiner* published, on virtually a monthly basis, accounts of court cases involving Republican women. For example, on 13 March the paper reported that two sisters aged 27 and 29, were found guilty of being in possession of a colt revolver and a Smith and Wesson revolver. They were fined £3 or one month in prison. Although this short piece did not explicitly describe the women as Republicans, the information that they refused to recognise the court clearly defined them as enemies of the State. On 22 April, the paper carried a short report under the heading 'Ladies with Paint Pots', which referred to two women who were charged with painting slogans on Dublin walls concerning a

Republican who was being mistreated in prison. They addressed the court in Irish, refused to pay the £4 fine and were sent to prison for 2 months. This report was also carried in the *Irish Independent* on 22 April 1926 under the heading 'Prison Treatment'. Comparing these cases it would appear that the penalty for painting slogans was greater than the penalty for carrying a gun. Perhaps Cosgrave's government viewed Republican propaganda as more dangerous than Republican arms. This suspicion is reinforced by a short paragraph in the *Examiner* just a few days later on 26 April under the equally artistic heading 'A Tin of Paste'. Two women were sentenced to one month's imprisonment for pasting posters on O'Connell Street, Dublin.

Attempts to draw public attention to the treatment and conditions of Republican political prisoners were carried out using a range of tactics. In addition to the poster campaign, there were also several public meetings. For example, on 21 December 1926, the *Irish Independent* published a very short report on 'a large meeting in College Green' presided over by Maud Gonne MacBride and also addressed by Hanna Sheehy Skeffington and Constance Markievicz. Gonne MacBride told the protesters that the Free State government was out-doing the British in the mistreatment of prisoners. Maud Gonne MacBride was the most vocal campaigner for prisoners' rights and, despite her advanced age, worked tirelessly to publicise prison conditions. She wrote a string of letters to the *Irish Independent* (see 23 April, 17 July, 23 August 1926). In printing these letters, the *Independent* newspaper, despite its obvious lack of sympathy for the Republican movement, did at least provide a forum in which prisoners' welfare could be aired and discussed. In that sense, the press was not simply the mouthpiece of the Catholic Church and the State but helped to provide a range of views and give some insight, albeit a limited one, into the processes of opposition and the processes of regulation at work in the country.

Republican women did not simply spend their time writing letters to newspapers and painting slogans on city walls. On 27 October 1926, the *Examiner* reported that 'a girl' was on trial for treason in Dublin. Roseen O'Doherty, described as 'a young, respectable looking girl', was charged with involvement in 'an illegal military organisation'. A search of her home had uncovered several incriminating documents. She was found guilty but the jury suggested she may have been unaware of the content of the documents which she was concealing. Perhaps the jury found it hard to believe that this 'young, respectable girl' could be involved in a military organisation, especially an illegal one.

The regular reports of court cases continued. On 10 November 1926, the *Examiner* carried the story of a 27 year old woman named Kathleen Kavanagh who was given a six month sentence for burning the Union Jack flag and attempting to burn down a premises where red poppy flowers were being stored. Republicans were vehemently opposed to British-style rituals such as Remembrance Sunday when poppies were worn to commemorate the dead from World War I. On 3 December 1926, both the *Irish Independent* and the *Examiner* reported that three women were sent for trial on charges of conspiracy. Mary (*sic*) Comerford, Sheila Humphreys and Helena Moloney were charged with attempting to influence juries in the trial of 'certain cases' at the Criminal Court. On 10 December the *Examiner* carried an up date report on proceedings against these three women. Ignoring all proceedings, the women kept up a constant conversation in the dock. They were found guilty and given three months imprisonment.

In 1928 the daily press reported several treason cases against Republican women. For example, on 12 April 1928, the *Independent* carried the rather dramatic headline – 'Cheers in Court'. This referred to the trial in Dublin District court of Miss Florence MacCarthy who was charged with 'taking part in, and assisting in, the formation and maintenance of a military organisation not established by law'. During the proceedings Sheila Humphreys, who was in the gallery, stood up and shouted 'Up the Republic'. Having been placed in the dock she would only speak in Irish and was reprimanded and dismissed. Meanwhile, Miss MacCarthy was remanded on £5 bail. On 23 April, the *Independent* reported that a further charge of embracery (attempting to influence jurors) had been brought against Miss MacCarthy. Speaking only in Irish, she refused to recognise the court. The paper quoted her as saying, presumably after translation, that 'as long as any British institutions remained in the country she would do what she could to pull down the reign of the Sassenach [English]'.

On the 4 May 1928, the *Examiner* carried the headline 'Silent Prisoners'. This lengthy article gave an account of three trials in Dublin. First was the treason trial of Sheila McInerney at Dublin's Criminal Court. She was charged with possession of an automatic pistol and 10 rounds of ammunition. She was also charged with 'assisting the formation of an illegal military organisation'. McInerney remained silent in court and after some legal discussion was deemed to be 'mute of malice' and was remanded in custody. The second trial involved two women, Lily MacDermott and Evelyn Jackson, charged with 'printing and publishing seditious libel against the Government of the Free State, its ministers and officials, and posting them outside the Mansion House'. The *Examiner* reported that they were also deemed by the court to be 'mute of malice'. In the third related case, Florence MacCarthy was charged with attempting to influence jurors by distributing intimidating leaflets. She also remained silent and was similarly deemed to be 'mute of malice'.

The *Examiner* went on to report the surprising twist in the trial of MacDermott and Jackson. Having heard the evidence against the two women, the jury retired but failed to reach an agreement. The judge sent them back to reconsider. They returned to court a second time still unable to reach agreement. The judge reiterated that one of the documents that the women had printed and circulated was clearly seditious. 'No document could be more so', he was reported as saying.

Clearly he was seeking a conviction against these women. The jury retired for a third time but later sent a message to the court that they had no possibility of agreeing on a verdict. The accused were put back. The *Examiner* made no comment on this interesting occurrence. One could suggest that jurors may have had some sympathy with the Republican cause and were reluctant to send the women to prison. One could equally suggest that jurors had been influenced in some way before the trial. On the same day the *Examiner* continued its detailed report on the trial of Florence MacCarthy who:

> was indicted for having on diverse dates conspired with others to induce jurors to disregard their oaths at the trial of prisoners at the Criminal Court, and to intimidate them....there was a second charge of aiding and abetting in the setting up of a Republican Army. (*Cork Examiner*, 4 May 1928)

This is unusual in naming the illegal military organisation. The report then quoted the prosecuting counsel, Mr. Carrigan, as saying that the object of embracery 'was to terrorise those who differed from them and to procure the collapse of the Free State courts'. After a short absence, the jury found Miss MacCarthy guilty on both charges but recommended leniency in sentencing.

On the following day, the 5 May, the *Examiner* reported the women's sentences. Miss McInerney got six months and shouted 'Up the Republic'. Miss MacCarthy protested against the jury's recommendation for leniency as she had only been doing her duty. She also got six months. The *Independent* also reported on the sentencing of the women under the heading 'Treason Act Charges: Dublin women sent to jail' (5 May 1928). However, it did not provide the sort of detailed coverage of the trial that the *Examiner* had given on 4 May. This is typical of the very patchy and inconsistent coverage which Republican trials received in the press. Hence Republicans continued to appear as suspicious spectres lacking any clear rationale or legitimate agenda. In fact, they were usually only mentioned in relation to the discovery of arms dumps, accusations of intimidation or acts of treason.

Republicans had a complex relationship with the mainstream media. Beyond their own narrow circles of supporters, Republicans could only reach a wider audience through the medium of the mainstream press. For example, although court appearances provided Republicans with an opportunity to publicise their cause, the accounts and images provided by the press were filtered through layers of representation. The Republican women described above were obviously conscious of self-representation. By keeping silent or speaking only in Irish, by refusing to recognise the court, by shouting 'Up the Republic', the women clearly took the opportunity to define themselves as patriotic Irishwomen, defenders of the Republican tradition and opponents of what they saw as an illegitimate state. However, in reporting these court cases to the wider public, journalists and newspaper editors were offering rather selective representations which contained the women in simple stereotypes.

On the 18 May 1928, the *Independent* gave a short report of the trial of Sheila Humphreys, aged 28, who was accused on a series of counts of embracery and taking part in the organisation of an illegal military force. Several women in court shouted 'Up the Republic'. The fact that women were repeatedly reported shouting 'Up the Republic' in court could be seen as reinforcing the image of unruly and unfeminine women, an image that had been regularly used in the mainstream press during the civil war. Such reports also highlighted the role which women played in 'organising' and 'maintaining' the illegal military movement. These images were clearly visible in the *Cork Examiner*'s coverage of Humphrey's very protracted trial. On 23 June 1928, the *Examiner* reported that she was accused of being 'an active agent of the Irish Republican Army'. This was an interesting choice of words as it not only gave the full, official name of the military organisation but also defined Humphreys as 'an active agent' rather than a mere supporter or sympathiser. This located women right at the heart of Republicanism, not just as vocal supporters but as hardened activists. That these women were so strongly associated with a treasonous organisation constructed an image of them as dangerous and disorderly and simultaneously constructed Republican militarism as irregular, illogical and hysterical.

But it is apparent that these women were not entirely without political support, however temporary and politically motivated that support may have been. On 8 June 1928, the *Cork Examiner* carried an article entitled 'Women Prisoners' which related to a discussion in Dail Eireann. The former Republican president and now leader of the opposition Fianna Fail party, Eamon de Valera raised a question about the five Republican women prisoners who were on hunger strike in their quest for political prisoner status. The women included MacCarthy, McInerney and Humphreys.

De Valera alleged that 'it had become common practice for detectives to arrest women, take them to prison and have them searched for documents'. He accused the Irish authorities of behaving exactly as the British had done and 'pretend[ing] now that they did not understand what these women were fighting for and what principle was at stake'. De Valera alleged that these women were held in solitary confinement and refused the right of association. A government minister denied that these allegations were true. This *Examiner* report is interesting for a number of reasons. Firstly, it publicised the women's hunger strike and their alleged mistreatment in prison. Secondly, by citing de Valera, the article gave voice to the view that the Free State authorities were behaving just as the British had done by imposing severe punishments on Republicans. Thirdly, the article again by citing the Fianna Fail leader, gave some political justification for the women's actions and referred to the principles that were at stake. In addition, by highlighting allegations that detectives were deliberately targeting women, the report reinforced the view of women as central to the Republican movement.

On 22 June 1928, the *Examiner* again reported political debates about the treatment of women political prisoners. Fianna Fail T.D.s once again raised questions in the Dail about the ill-treatment of women in jail. It was claimed that Mrs. MacDermott, 'one of the ladies recently on hunger strike in Mountjoy' had been transferred to hospital where she was visited by a Fianna Fail T.D. He witnessed several marks on her body where she had been physically mistreated. Denying any charges of mistreatment, the Cumann na nGaedheal minister claimed that all the women had been very difficult prisoners. He said they had barricaded themselves into their cells and kept the other prisoners awake by singing songs and shouting all through the night.

It is necessary to consider why the Fianna Fail party repeatedly called attention to the plight of Republican women prisoners. Of course, these men may well have had a genuine concern for the women's health and safety, after all many would have worked alongside these women during the War of Independence and the Civil War. However, Fianna Fail was also keen to assert itself as a legitimate political party, distancing itself from any association with dangerous, militant Republicanism. It could be argued that one reason why T.D.s raised questions about the alleged mistreatment of women political prisoners was in an attempt to discredit the Cumann na nGaedheal government, to present it as cruel to women, and to accuse it of using the tactics of the old enemy – the British. Thus the Republican women could be inscribed within a gendered rhetoric which constructed them as victims of official abuse. Hence, the government could be represented as violent and abusive, while Fianna Fail was the party of chivalry and fair play. However, the Fianna Fail attitude to Republicans was to change markedly.

The case involving Mrs. MacDermott not only attracted a good deal of publicity but also revealed the difficult position of Republicans in the Free State. On 16 July 1928, the *Independent* published a letter from Maud Gonne MacBride protesting about the rearrest of Mrs. MacDermott. Having been recently released from hospital, MacDermott had been rearrested almost immediately. Because the jury had failed to reach a verdict against her, she had not been convicted or sentenced. However, as she had not been acquitted, she remained on remand indefinitely and could be rearrested at any time.

In 1931 Cosgrave's government introduced legislation which led to the widespread arrest and imprisonment of Republican men and women. Republican prisoners were now tried by military tribunal instead of by jury. Accounts of the tribunals were published in the press on a fairly regular basis. One of the last women to be imprisoned under the old Cumann na nGaedheal regime was ubiquitous Sheila Humphreys. The military tribunal involving Miss Humphreys, Miss Maeve Phelan and Mrs. Kathleen Merrigan was reported in considerable detail in the *Irish Independent* on 16 January 1932. The three Dublin women were charged with possession of documents and membership of an illegal organisation. The prosecuting counsel referred to the 'childish nature' of the confiscated documents including one entitled 'Boycott British Goods'. Miss Humphrey refused to recognise the court but, unlike previous trials where Republican prisoners were 'mute', she appears to have been extremely vocal, continually berating the tribunal:

> You are a self-appointed clique of members of the British Army of occupation, making what I hope will be the final effort to hold this country for England. (*Irish Independent*, 16 January 1932)

She said that the military tribunal had been set up because the courts could not get twelve jurors to convict Republican prisoners. 'I am charged with being a member of Cumann na mBan, and I admit it. You are very foolish to try to suppress that organisation, for we thrive on suppression'. When the president of the tribunal warned her that this was not a political platform, she is reported as retorting:

indeed, I know it is more like a spectacular comedy than anything else. I don't know why you take yourselves so seriously. (*Irish Independent*, 16 January 1932)

The other two women were also quoted as referring to the proceedings as 'a farce'. While Mrs. Merrigan was found not guilty, the other two women were convicted and sent to prison.

Although this report was unusual not only in its length but also in reporting the actual words of a Republican prisoner, it still managed to represent the women, particularly Humphreys, as 'childish', disorderly, disruptive, disrespectful and aggressive. In general, newspaper references to Republican women are fragmented, partial and incomplete. The impact on the reader can be deeply confusing. Only by reading a range of newspapers over a lengthy period of time can one begin to piece together some of what was going on. It is difficult, if not impossible, to know how the contemporary reader might have interpreted these reports. It would be inaccurate and overly simplistic to say that there was a conspiracy of silence in the mainstream press in regard to Republicanism. But it would be fairly accurate to say that regular references to treason, hunger strike, arms dumps, intimidation and unruly women, did little to present a sympathetic or even balanced account of the Republican movement.

## *'Childish, Innocent and Rubbishy': Republicanism and the de Valera Government:*

In March 1932 Eamon de Valera and his Fianna Fail party won the general election and after ten years in the political wilderness, the former president of Dail Eireann regained his authority in the Free State. One of his election promises had been to release the Republican prisoners. Within a short time he had kept that promise and the prison gates were opened. On 11 March 1932, the *Independent* reported 'Prisoners Free: Remarkable Dublin Scenes'. 20 prisoners were released from Mountjoy and Arbour Hill. They received a rousing reception from the crowds of supporters. The prison releases led to a renewed confidence among Republicans, many of whom had been driven underground by the coercion policies of the Cosgrave government. On 14 March, the *Independent* carried the ominous headline 'Marching Men in Dublin'. 'For the first time for many years, battalions of the Irish Republican Army marched through the streets of Dublin yesterday'. They were cheered on by a crowd of 20,000. Cumann na mBan also participated in the march and Hanna Sheehy Skeffington and Maud Gonne MacBride were among those who addressed the crowd.

Cumann na mBan were again out in force for the annual commemorations of the 1916 Rising which were reported in the *Independent* on 28 March. Mary MacSwiney addressed the crowds in Cork. Her words were paraphrased as follows in the *Independent*:

> for ten years Ireland had lived in the nightmare of England's ministers, and the country had gone from bad to worse. They were paying England for Irish land, and the destruction done by English forces....Let us band together and tell England to get out. If she threatens tell her to come on. (*Irish Independent*, 28 March 1932)

Such fighting talk reveals the deep anger still felt by many Republicans. MacSwiney was not the only one making threats against continued English influence in Ireland. On 30 March 1932 the *Independent* reported 'Madame Gonne MacBride's Speech':

> We will have nothing less than a Republic for an Ireland one and undivided, as God meant our country to be, with equal right and equal opportunities for every child born on Irish soil. (*Irish Independent*, 30 March 1932)

Following the election victory of Fianna Fail, Maud Gonne MacBride shared the optimism of many Republicans. She disbanded her protest group Women's Prisoners Defence League as the problem of Republican prisoners now appeared to have been resolved for good and all. However, the de Valera government proved to have a very uneasy relationship with the Republican movement – both the political and military wings of that movement. Republican dissatisfaction with the Fianna Fail government led to a return to the military campaign in the mid-1930s. The murders of two men; Vice-Admiral Somerville in Cork (March 1936) and John Egan in Dungarvan (April 1936) led to widespread arrests and imprisonments of known and suspected Republican men. With so many men in prison, it was women who once again began to take a prominent role in the public demonstrations and debates around Republicanism.

The women on whom the press focused most attention were the veteran campaigners Mary MacSwiney and Maud Gonne MacBride, both of whom had experienced arrest and imprisonment for their beliefs. These women were very different in outlook, personality, appearance and family background. Although approaching 70 years of age, Gonne MacBride still embodied the elegance, charm and mystique that had made her the 'muse of Yeats' and the toast of literary and artistic society. She was nonetheless, a fearless, outspoken critic of the government. The weekly meetings she organised in Dublin's Cathal Brugha Street not only championed the rights of prisoners but challenged government policy on a range of social and welfare issues. The numerous raids on her home reveal the extent to which the government took her seriously. Aged in her 60s, MacSwiney was a devout Catholic, Irish-speaking, school teacher from Cork. A more hard line militant, she was less interested in social and economic issues than in remaining faithful to the true spirit of Republicanism. These two women came to embody the voice of Republicanism in the mid-1930s. Their regular public speeches and their constant flow of letters to the press enabled the newspapers to construct them as the extreme and uncompromising face of Republican politics and militarism.

On 6 May 1936, Mary MacSwiney, signing her name in Irish, *Maire Ni Suibhne*, wrote a letter to the editor of the *Independent* on the proclaiming of the IRA as an illegal organisation. In what was to become a familiar attack on Eamon de Valera, she said that when the IRA had been illegal 16 years earlier – at the height of the Anglo-Irish war – de Valera had been proud to be a member. She condemned the hypocrisy of politicians who celebrated the memory of the dead Republican heroes, like her brother the late Lord Mayor of Cork, Terence MacSwiney, while at the same time arresting young men on suspicion of membership of the IRA. Writing in the *Cork Examiner* on 5 May 1936, she said 'the family...cannot permit the hypocritical farce of people professing to honour the one brother who died for the Republic, while supporting the manacling and gaoling of the other brother for being loyal to the same Republic'. At the time of writing, her other brother Sean was among the many dozens of men who were being held on remand at Arbour Hill prison. In a further letter on 14 May she wrote that:

> Republicans have survived the Black and Tans, and the first Free State regime with its numerous Coercion Acts. They will survive the second Free State regime with its Coercion Acts. (*Irish Independent*, 14 May 1936)

On the following day, 15 May 1936, the *Independent* published a letter from Madame MacBride in which she pointed out that over 100 Republican men had been arrested in the recent roundup. Under the terms of the Public Safety Act they could be held for three days without the authorities having to supply them with food. This placed a great burden on families from around the country to buy food and transport it to Dublin prisons. The Women's Prisoners Defence League (which had been reformed in response to de Valera's crack down on Republicans) was endeavouring to buy food and bring it to the prisoners, and they were urgently appealing for donations. In subsequent weeks the press reported that the prisoners were charged, before a military tribunal, with membership of the IRA and were given sentences ranging from 6 months to 12 months. Republican women organised several open-air meetings around the country to protest about the arrest and imprisonment of Republican men. On 23 May 1936, the *Cork Examiner* reported a public meeting in that city's main street, Patrick Street, at which Mary MacSwiney 'was given a very cordial reception'. On the 26 May, the *Cork Examiner* reported that Mary MacSwiney addressed a protest meeting in Bandon, while her sister Eithne (Annie) addressed a similar protest meeting in Cobh.

Clearly women did not simply involve themselves in writing letters to the press and buying food for prisoners. Judging by the press reports, women took an increasingly active part in Republican protests. On 15 June 1936 the *Independent* reported that the annual Wolfe Tone commemoration ceremonies at Bodenstown cemetery were interrupted by women protesters. While de Valera and his ministers laid wreaths at the grave of the hero of the 1798 uprising, 'some women in the crowd' protested about the government's treatment of Republican prisoners. This brief report tells us nothing about the numbers or identity of the women involved but more was to come in the weeks and months ahead. In fact, Bodenstown cemetery was to become a major site of confrontation between Republicans and the forces of the State. On 20 June, the *Cork Examiner* reported that the IRA was to be proclaimed an illegal organisation and that the planned Republican ceremonies at Bodenstown were to be outlawed.

On 22 June 1936 several newspapers reported the dramatic events at the cemetery. For example, the *Independent* carried the banner headline 'Police and Troops at Bodenstown'. This provided a detailed description of the military operation which was put in place at the Wolfe Tone grave to prevent the IRA and other Republican groups from having their own commemorative ceremony. Over 1,000 troops and 500 police blocked off the roads around the cemetery. The *Cork Examiner* printed a two page report under the headline 'Military and Civic Guards in Occupation of Bodenstown'. The *Irish Press* carried the report under the front-page headlines 'Enforcing the Ban: Army Hold Bodenstown'. The *Press* reported that the army used 'full war equipment' including tear gas and machine guns, 'military armoured cars patrolled the roads'. But despite this display of military might some cars did manage to evade the blockades and approach the cemetery. Hanna Sheehy Skeffington arrived in a car with three other women marked 'Press' – ironically her press credentials were that she wrote occasional feature articles for the *Irish Press* itself. According to the *Independent*, 'Mrs. Sheehy Skeffington and members of Cumann na mBan wearing uniform held a meeting at Sallins Cross'. She told her audience 'keep a lookout and if you see the police or military tell me and I will read faster'. Her audience consisted largely of women including several who had long associations with the Republican movement, the *Independent* named Countess Plunkett, Eithne Coyle, Maire Comerford and Mrs. Brugha among others. According to the report in the *Irish Press*, about 100 people gathered to hear Mrs. Sheehy Skeffington read a speech in which she said 'I am glad for one thing...the mask is off the Fianna Fail government who can never more call themselves Republicans' (*Irish Independent*, 22 June 1936).

In its account, the *Examiner* carried a sub-heading entitled 'Cumann na mBan'. This described how a small group of women in uniform walked into Sallins village at about three o'clock. One of the women was heard to comment that they could walk where ever they wished. However, they were quickly approached by uniformed police and detectives 'who proceeded to escort them out of the village'. The *Examiner* concluded with the information that 'the women protested and made some attempt at resistance' (*Cork Examiner*, 22 June 1936).

According to the *Independent*, Mary MacSwiney, who had been due to make the graveside oration, 'made a dramatic appearance on the road leading to the cemetery' accompanied by Miss Barry sister of the martyred student Kevin Barry. However, police prevented them from entering the cemetery and they were sent away. Miss MacSwiney then apparently made her way to Dublin where she spoke at a Republican meeting in College Green outside Trinity College. She was joined by fellow veterans Maud Gonne MacBride and Helena Moloney, while members of Cumann na mBan held up the traffic. 'The Cumann na mBan girls, who were massed at this point, refused to allow [traffic] to pass'. However, the police quickly moved in to break up the meeting. 'With Miss MacSwiney still valiantly denouncing President de Valera at the top of her voice' the lorry on which she stood took off and drove away. Meanwhile, 'about fifty members of Cumann na mBan in uniform marched down Westmoreland Street, O'Connell Street and into Henry Street. They turned into Stafford Street and halted beneath the stone plaque that commemorates the birth place of Wolfe Tone'. There they were addressed by Mrs. Lawlor, Mrs. Brugha and Miss Lavery (*Irish Independent*, 22 June 1936).

Just a few days later on 27 June, the *Independent* again reported violent clashes involving Republican women under the headline 'Baton Charges at College Green: Wild Scenes at Meeting'. This referred to police efforts to prevent Republicans from heckling a Fianna Fail meeting in Dublin city centre. While Fianna Fail members addressed the meeting:

> several young women carrying banners bearing inscriptions relating to Republican prisoners marched along Church Lane into Dame Street towards the meeting place. The banners were seized by the Gardai and torn up and marchers were bundled up Trinity Street. (*Irish Independent*, 27 June 1936)

One of the women fell to the ground but she 'jumped to her feet and knocked off a garda's helmet'. Another woman fell in the melee and sustained an injury to her ankle. While some male protesters were arrested, there is no mention of any of the women being arrested. Confrontations such as these on the streets of Dublin and near Bodenstown cemetery at Sallins, illustrate the State's determination to prevent Republicans gaining access to the public realm. The fact that young women in uniform, marching in military formation, and older women speaking from the backs of lorries sought to defy the authorities, physically occupying prohibited spaces, reveals the audacity, commitment and fighting spirit of Republican women. However, the press reports also reveal the attempts to represent them as violent paramilitaries – disorderly bodies.

Meanwhile, MacSwiney and Gonne MacBride continued to bombard the press with angry letters. While the latter focused largely on the rights and conditions of Republican prisoners, particularly those being held on remand at Arbour Hill prison, the former launched a personal attack on Eamon de Valera and his hypocrisy towards Republicanism. In a fairly typical letter to the *Independent* on 20 July 1936, Mary MacSwiney wrote that:

> As far as injustice to, coercion and slander of Republicans go, there is no longer anything to choose between the first and second Free State governments...coercion does not become sacrosanct because the party enforcing it is called Fianna Fail instead of Cumann na nGaedheal. (*Irish Independent*, 20 July 1936)

Also on the 20 July 1936, the *Irish Press* carried a short report on the regular Sunday meeting in Cathal Brugha Street of the Women's Prisoners Defence League. Under the headline 'Madame MacBride: Invitation to the Government to Prosecute Her', she is quoted as saying that if her statements about the mistreatment of Republican prisoners were untrue then the government should bring her before the military tribunal for trial. On the following week, on the 27 July, the *Press* quoted her as saying that the government was creating a reign of terror by its campaign of raids and arrests. She also criticised the newspapers for failing to reveal the true extent of this reign of terror. While the *Irish Press* gave regular, brief coverage to these weekly meetings in Dublin, and to Maud Gonne MacBride's uncompromising opinions, that paper saved its most vicious attacks for Mary MacSwiney.

In the summer of 1936 MacSwiney became embroiled in a long battle of words with de Valera which was fought out largely in the pages of the *Irish Press*. Of particular note is the role played by the *Press* editorial. On several occasions the editor launched very personal attacks on MacSwiney, devoting entire editorial columns to denouncing her arguments. The Fianna Fail administration, strongly supported by the *Press*, took the view that the IRA had become a group of dangerous murderers who threatened to destabilise the state. MacSwiney sought to defend the organisation, pointing out that this was the same military organisation that boasted such proud heroes as Terence MacSwiney, Tomas MacCurtain, Michael Collins, Liam Mellows and even Eamon de Valera. Referring to the deaths of Somerville and Egan, she also argued that if the IRA had been involved in these shootings, which had not been proved, then these two men must have been spies. The *Press* editorial called her arguments 'extraordinary', 'hopelessly illogical', her statements were full of 'bluster and abuse'; her mood was dismissed as 'truculent' (*Irish Press*, 18 July 1936).

In August 1936 important by-elections took place in Galway and in Waterford. Republican women used both occasions to harass de Valera and Fianna Fail at every opportunity. The *Independent* carried the headline 'The Co. Galway By-Election Campaign: Madame MacBride in a Scene':

> There was a lively interlude at Salthill when Madame MacBride suddenly appeared near a meeting which was being addressed by Mr. O'Kelly, Minister for Local Government. She began to speak but was quickly moved some distance away by Civil Guards. Continuing her speech she attracted a large proportion of Mr. O'Kelly's audience. (*Irish Independent*, 3 August 1936)

This kind of incident afforded valuable publicity to the Republican cause and served as a constant reminder to the public and the politicians of that cause's continuing determination and energy. However, the fact that the campaign was now embodied largely by women may have played on the old civil war stereotypes of hysterical, wild, uncompromising women. The woman who could be most easily accommodated within that dangerous stereotype was Mary MacSwiney.

Speaking in Galway and reported at length on the front page of the *Irish Press* on 12 August 1936, Eamon de Valera responded very publicly to the arguments being made by MacSwiney. He attacked her claims that if the IRA had shot anyone then that person must have been a spy. He said that neither the elderly Admiral Somerville nor young Egan were spies. In any case, he argued, MacSwiney was merely attempting to justify murder and to encourage further crimes. He clearly differentiated between the IRA that had fought the War of Independence under the control of the democratically elected Dail, and this group who was accountable to no one. Now the IRA was engaged in 'murder naked and unashamed' and was threatening civil war. On 15 August, MacSwiney responded to de Valera and once again pointed out his sudden change of heart towards the IRA. When he had been in opposition just a few years ago he condemned the Cosgrave administration for holding 'secret tribunals' and for the 'maltreatment' of prisoners. He described the IRA as 'noble and good'. Now his approach was exactly the same as Cosgrave and his policy was purely coercive (*Irish Press*, 15 August 1936).

Once again the *Press* used Miss MacSwiney's letter as an opportunity to devote its editorial to attacking her. It accused her of avoiding the questions put to her by de Valera in his Galway speech. These questions were repeated in bold print: did she believe that the IRA had the right to commit murder, did she believe that the shootings of Admiral Somerville and John Egan were justified? The editorial then launched a direct attack on the IRA. 'What is the object which this armed body is intended to serve? What is the enemy which it is intended to attack? Who gave this armed body authority to drill, prepare and equip itself to levy war against the government?' The upshot will surely be 'civil war, chaos and anarchy' (*Irish Press* editorial, 15 August 1936).

The *Press* policy of using its editorial to attack MacSwiney seriously disadvantaged her; denied the last word, her letter was responding to the previous attack while the editor launched a new attack. Thus she always seemed one step behind in the argument. The authority of the editorial and its location in the paper, usually several pages before her letter, meant that by the time one came to read her letter one had already been given an answer and a new set of objections by the editor. Therefore, she was seen as not only challenging the President and his party but the editorial policy of the *Irish Press* as well. This is exemplified in the editorial and letters page of 19 August. Once again the editorial attacked MacSwiney, while her latest letter dealt with the previous editorial's comments. Under the heading 'Evading the Issue' the editorial once more repeated the questions put to her by de Valera in his Galway speech, she was accused of continuing to ignore and avoid answering these vitally important questions. Meanwhile in her letter she accused de Valera of being 'shameless' in his political practices. She said that Republicans would not be deceived and would 'carry on until every trace of English influence or control...is banished for ever'. On the 25 August, the *Irish Press* editorial 'No Straight Answer' dismissed her continuing refusal to answer de Valera's questions as 'cowardly'. 'We are sorry to see her place herself in this light before the public, but it is her own doing, and she has acted with her eyes open'.

Perhaps in an attempt to avoid the debate becoming too narrow and too personalised, or merely in an attempt to reach a wider audience, Mary MacSwiney also sent copies of her letters to the *Irish Independent* and the *Cork Examiner*. Thus, it was not uncommon for the same letter to appear in several newspapers (see 15 and 19 August 1936). However, the *Independent* did not attack the letters or their author in the same way or to the same extent. Like her elder sister, Eithne Mac-

Swiney also wrote several lengthy letters to the *Independent* defending the Republican tradition. These letters drew angry and very personalised replies from other readers of the paper. Thus unlike the *Press* which used its editorial to attack Republican women, the *Independent* allowed other letter writers do so instead. For example, on the 15 September, a letter written anonymously dismissed Eithne MacSwiney and other Republicans as 'childish, innocent and rubbishy'. A second letter published on 23 September and signed 'a working man' launched the following attack:

> Would it be too much to ask Miss MacSwiney and her other lady associates to attempt a real job and organise the teaching of our girls and women in the care of infants and good housekeeping, and in that way help to take care of the health of the nation...What would be the reaction of the militant ladies in this country if they were to find themselves in charge of one of our working men's homes with a large hungry family to look after? (*Irish Independent*, 23 September 1936)

He concluded by dismissing the militant women as 'soap box orators' and called for a 'return to sanity and [a] sense of true values'. Letters such as these constructed the MacSwiney sisters and other Republican women not only as deluded, childish and politically ignorant but also as women who had neglected their true roles in life as domesticated wives and mothers. If such women wished to be truly useful in society they should return to their proper sphere and contribute to child welfare and domestic economy. Thus once again, as in the civil war fourteen years previously, we see that militant Republicans were still being represented as unwomanly, and as falling far short of the ideal of Irish motherhood. The allegory of disorderly furies still informed images of confident, outspoken, ardent Republican women. These negative stereotypes were sufficiently flexible to be applied across a range of situations and a range of women: older, 'die-hard' Republican women who made passionate speeches and wrote fiery letters to the press as well as the younger uniformed women of Cumann na mBan. However, in the Free State of the 1930s, in particular, these images were not without some element of contradiction and ideological unease.

This is particularly apparent in an article on the front page of the *Irish Press* on 8 August 1936. Under the headline 'Procession dispersed: women's group in Arbour Hill March', the *Press* reported that gardai had dispersed a group of about 300 who were attempting to march to the prison where most of the Republican men were being held. 'Members of Cumann na mBan, led by Miss Nodlaig Brugha...arrived carrying a large banner on which was inscribed 'Open the Gaol Gates. Smash Coercion. On to the Republic'. The gardai formed a cordon blocking the road. Miss Brugha and her group, unable to proceed any further, called for three cheers for the Republic. 'A scuffle followed in which several persons were knocked down'. It is noteworthy that the report did not state who had knocked the women down. The report did say, however, that 'a young woman was later seen struggling on the ground', but it did not clarify with whom she was struggling. Thus the role which the gardai played in events remained vague and unclear. What is especially striking about this procession of uniformed women is that it commenced in Cathal Brugha Street, the same street where Maud Gonne MacBride held her weekly meetings of the Women's Prisoners Defence League. The significance and indeed the irony of a procession led by Miss Brugha beginning in the street named after her father appears to be lost on the gardai and the *Irish Press*. Brugha was a hero of the 1916 Rising where he sustained serious injuries, and he went on to play an active part in the formation of Dail Eireann in 1919. In a sense, therefore, Nodlag was merely continuing the Republican tradition of her heroic father, in the same way that Mary and Eithne MacSwiney were continuing the Republicanism of their martyred brother. In so doing these women were a thorn in the side of a Fianna Fail administration which, despite its close historical ties to the Republican movement, now sought to sever any connection with militant Republicanism. The 26 county Free State was built upon the symbolism, rhetoric and aspirations of a free nation. Yet the reality was very different from the ideal. Republicanism reminded the Free State not only that it was a partially independent, semi-autonomous state but also that it was partitioned. The dream of a 32 county Republic seemed to be no longer shared or even desired by the leaders and the people in the south.

The tensions between the government's celebration of a great Republican tradition and its unease with contemporary Republicanism was made painfully visible in the controversy over the commemoration of the two martyred Lord Mayors of Cork. In September 1936 the new City Hall opened in Cork replacing the old building which had been infamously burned down by the Black and Tans (British troops). Thus the official opening of the new building by President de Valera not only symbolised the recovery of Cork city but also the health and determination of the entire nation-state; like the phoenix emerging from the burning embers. The *Irish Press* carried a very positive account of the historic events in Cork under the front-page banner headline 'Mr. De Valera Opens Cork City Hall: Tribute to Heroic Mayors'. De Valera's speech was reported in detail:

> The wanton burning of your city and of the former city hall following the murder of Lord Mayor MacCurtain and the heroic sacrifice of his successor Tiorbhealach MacSuibhne, united the Irish people...and steeled their resolve to make good their right to govern themselves....The people of today are enjoying the fruits of the sacrifices then made. The Irish nation is being restored and developed. (*Irish Press*, 9 September 1936)

However, the headline in the *Irish Independent* suggested that paper's very different angle to the story – 'President in Cork Scene: Gardai remove women' (*Independent*, 9 September 1936). 'Two young women were ejected from Cork's new city hall today for interrupting during speeches at the opening ceremony'. One young woman 'rose in her seat but though only about 12 rows from the platform her voice was too weak to be heard clearly'. Perhaps this explains why the *Independent* did not inform readers precisely what the protester had said. 'Two gardai approached her. She stamped her feet indignantly and protested vigorously, but they hurried her out of the hall between them...A similar fate befell another young woman'.

Unsurprisingly, as the local paper, the *Cork Examiner* devoted most coverage, several pages in fact, to the grand opening of the city's new public building (9 September 1936). Amidst all the glowing accounts of the event's great success, the paper carried a short report under the heading 'Women Removed: Incidents at Opening of the City Hall'. 'A young woman in the audience created a scene by attempting to address the gathering'. The report stated that there was difficulty in hearing her but:

> she was heard to make reference to an insult to the memory of the Lord Mayor, when two Civic Guards hurried towards her and brought her, still protesting vigorously and stamping her feet, out of the hall....another young woman stood up and commenced to interrupt. She was immediately approached by detectives, who hustled her from the room. (*Cork Examiner*, 9 September 1936)

The women were protesting about the way in which de Valera was celebrating the images of MacCurtain and MacSwiney while imprisoning dozens of Republicans, including the son of MacCurtain and the brother of MacSwiney. But the press does not focus upon their arguments and instead falls back on the old stereotypes presenting the women as weak, ineffectual, childish and petulant figures of fun, while simultaneously representing them as disrespectful of authority, disorderly and in need of firm control. Nevertheless, such press reports are useful in suggesting the extent to which the women were speedily silenced by the physical force of the law and were once again denied any opportunity to publicly criticise government policy. Knowing that they would be removed from the hall, these young women were, nonetheless, determined to make some form of protest and attract some publicity for their cause.

The defiant attitudes of Cumann na mBan were again highlighted in a report in the *Cork Examiner* on 30 November 1936, under the heading 'Dublin Incident at Cumann na mBan Convention'. Although the convention began in a hotel, the delegates then marched 'in a body' to St. Andrew's Street where they occupied their old premises which had been sealed by the Gardai in June. Despite the protests of the guard on duty, the women entered the building and proceeded to hold their convention. 'A large force of uniformed guards and detectives arrived' but the women refused to move. They also declined to provide their names or addresses. When they had concluded their convention 'they left the premises in a body'. The gardai immediately sealed the building again. This brief account visibly demonstrates the determination of Cumann na mBan not only to defy the authorities but to physically occupy prohibited spaces. The fact that the women were nameless and moved 'as a body' illustrates their military organisation and their strength in numbers.

The state's ambiguous relationship with the trappings of Republicanism seems to be especially apparent in the official reactions to Republican women. This is particularly visible in the obituaries of Republican women who played an active part in the earlier militant campaigns. The *Irish Press* regularly carried short obituaries of this nature. For example, on 30 September 1936 under the headline 'Mrs. E. Bennett Dead: Her Services During the Anglo-Irish War', the paper briefly recounted how she had:

> with her husband and brother, rendered devoted service in the Anglo-Irish war. She sheltered and succoured men 'on the run' and her house was frequently raided by the military. (*Irish Press,* 30 September 1936)

Again on 21 October 1936, the *Press* reported the death of Mrs. O'Brien of Limerick who was described as a great loss to the Republican cause. 'Many soldiers of the Republic sought the refuge of her home in troubled times' all her sons took part in both the Anglo-Irish war and the Civil War. On the 28 October, the

*Press* similarly reported the death of Mrs. Anne McKenna of Clare. 'She played her part in the struggle for Irish Independence, her house in Tulla being a refuge for men on the run'. She was a personal friend of President de Valera. The deaths of such women were reported because they were deemed to have been important to the campaign for independence. They had fulfilled a number of varied roles. Several had provided 'safe houses' for men on the run. Others had played their part in the national struggle by giving their sons to the cause. For example, on 13 November 1936, the *Cork Examiner* and the *Irish Press* reported the death of Mrs. Loughnane. The *Examiner* headline 'Death of Mother of Murdered Brothers' and the *Press*'s headline 'Death of Heroic Mother' situate the woman in relation to her heroic sons. Her two sons had been shot by the Black and Tans. 'She was a woman of the great old national type who offered the sacrifice of her two sons to the nation' (*Irish Press*). The night after her sons were killed, the Tans burned down her house. But it was not just women who remained in the domestic sphere as heroic mothers or as providers of succour for men who were lauded by the *Irish Press*.

On 30 December 1936, the *Press* reported 'Woman Patriot Dead'. Miss Jennie Shanahan was described as 'a veteran' of the national and labour movements. She had worked with James Connolly in the Trade Union movement and participated in the Lock Out of 1913. As a member of the Irish Citizen's Army she had played an active part in the 1916 Rising. She was captured by the British and spent some time in prison. As a younger, unmarried, independent woman, Shanahan represented the more active and visible face of Republican women. Yet she was praised and lamented in the *Press*, while other Republican women were being condemned and mocked as childish and petulant. The one significant difference seems to be the passage of time. As active participants in conflicts from the past, even the recent past, Republican women, as well as Republican men, could be contained within the myths, symbols and stories of the good old days when the national struggle was fought and won. However, contemporary, active, 'die-hard' Republicans were vilified as dangerous and disorderly precisely because they argued that the national struggle had not been won and was not over. In a nation-state attempting to consign Republican militarism to a victorious past, 'die-hard' Republican women came to embody many of the contradictions underpinning the symbolism and ideology which was so important to de Valera's Ireland.

*Conclusion:*

The Republican women discussed in this chapter were members and supporters of illegal, outlawed bodies. At a time when women were being discouraged and even excluded from participation in the public realm, they physically occupied a diverse range of public spaces. Even though they were members of highly secretive organisations, these women courted publicity, taunting police and politicians, particularly at times when Republican men were either on the run or in prison. Through their regular letters to the press, Republican women aimed to air their views to the widest possible audience. Holding meetings in the streets, blocking traffic, defiantly marching up to Gardai blockades, they bore physical attacks and threats, endured arrest and incarceration, and took full opportunity of their court appearances to gain maximum publicity for their cause. Members of Cumann na mBan used their uniformed bodies not only to occupy public spaces but also to visibly demonstrate their organised militarism. However, in so doing, Republican women walked a fine line between demanding access to the public sphere and conforming to negative stereotypes of disorderly, truculent furies. This chapter has highlighted the various attempts by the press and the State to contain the women within such narrow, simplistic images.

As 'die-hard' Republicans and, in many cases, as the relatives of martyred heroes of the armed struggle, these women saw themselves as embodying the continuity of a tradition. However, this is not to imply that they were silent, passive symbols who were content to be the 'keepers of the flame', the 'guardians of tradition' (see Mosse 1985, Yuval-Davis 1997). These women were active agents, who refused to be silenced. If idealised, sanitised national icons like Roisin Dubh or Mother Ireland embodied all that was good and safe about the nation, 'furies' embodied all that was destabilising and politically/ militarily subversive; the enemy within. One could argue that these 'furies' and 'die-hards' legitimated the need for a vigorous police and judiciary and an army ever ready to defend the State. In addition, they represented an uncomfortable and an unwelcome reminder of an uncompromising and unfulfilled Republicanism. These women refused to withdraw from the world of political debate and activism, thus refusing to become the sort of passive, iconic figures which the State would have wished to honour and eulogise.

# CHAPTER SIX:

## CONCEALING BODIES: NEWSPAPER REPRESENTATIONS OF INFANTICIDE IN THE IRISH FREE STATE

*Introduction:*

> The last time I was holding a criminal sitting I stated that, in future I would deal with cases of infanticide with some severity. Infanticide has become a national industry in parts of this country. The number of newly born illegitimate children murdered is very great....an illegitimate child is entitled to the protection of the law....It must be brought home to all girls in this country that they are amenable to the law and must suffer for this crime. No doubt there is another person in each case who should suffer too, but he cannot be got. But someone must pay the penalty, not the penalty for being immoral, but the penalty for taking human life. (*Irish Independent*, 3 October 1928)

These words were spoken by Judge Kenny as he sentenced 'a young girl' to 12 months imprisonment for infanticide. As he makes very clear, infanticide was rampant throughout the society. In most reported cases, and certainly in the majority of cases which were prosecuted, the babies were illegitimate and the young mothers were charged as solely responsible for the crime. While there was some acknowledgement that for every illegitimate baby there was also a father, men were very rarely charged with complicity in infanticide. As Judge Kenny makes clear in his passionate speech, someone must be made to pay the penalty. Interestingly, he adds that the penalty is not for having committed an act of immorality but for killing the innocent baby. However, as we will see in the numerous cases reported in the newspapers throughout the 1920s-1930s, the situation was in fact highly complex and multifaceted. Infanticide raises many uncomfortable questions about how the newly established Irish Free State dealt with sex, unwanted pregnancy, the law, policing, family relationships and the various intersections of private life and public institutions. In addition, the press itself is interesting in playing a role both in reporting but also interpreting and containing this very sensitive but apparently pervasive issue.

On 22 February 1936, the *Examiner* reported a story that had also received attention in the national dailies (see *Irish Press*, 11 March). This incident only received publicity because it was unusual and thus deemed worthy of attention. Infanticide was so commonplace that it usually received only scant attention in the press. The *Examiner* reported the story under the heading 'Infant Found in Railway Carriage'. The story was quite complicated but in short it involved the discovery of a new-born infant (the body was 'still warm') in the toilet of a train near Glanmire Station. A Civic Guard was immediately sent for and he quickly became suspicious of a young woman passenger on the train. Approaching the woman the guard heard the cries of a baby and discovered that a second new-born baby was concealed in her suitcase. The baby was taken to hospital but seemed to be quite healthy. The other baby had died immediately after birth due to failure to establish complete respiration there were no marks of violence on the body.

This is a remarkable story. It seems hard to believe that a young woman, described in the article as 'unmarried', had quietly given birth to twins in the toilet of a train. Concealing the dead body in the toilet and the living twin in her suitcase she returned to her seat on the train. Women who worked hard to conceal their pregnancies for nine months had to be particularly careful about concealing the labour. They could not take the chance of seeking help, uttering loud cries or attracting any attention. Thus the process of concealment and deception begun in pregnancy, reached its dangerous climax in the act of giving birth. The final part of their secret ordeals was to conceal the evidence by hiding the body of the new-born infant. It was usually the discovery of the poorly concealed bodies that lead to the revelation of their secret.

This chapter concentrates on newspaper accounts of concealment and infanticide (or suspected infanticide) in the 1920s-1930s. Drawing on a range of national and provincial dailies, I will focus in particular on the years 1925, 1926, 1928 and 1936.

However, this is not to imply that infanticide was peculiar to the Free State in the 1920s-1930s. 'Infanticide has been practiced on every continent and by people on every level of cultural complexity' (Williamson 1978: 61). Nevertheless, the first two decades of the Irish Free State represent a particular legal, political and economic context within the project of nation-building. Cultural nationalism, political conservatism and the power of the Catholic Church combined together to create the circumstances in which women's bodies became the contested site of national good and national evil. Within the specificities of that social and cultural context, I argue, concealment and infanticide took on particular significance.

I suggest that concealed pregnancies and infanticide symbolise the complex relationship between women's bodies, 'deviant' sexuality, 'sin', regulation and gendered national discourses. Through their unwanted pregnancies these women embodied the evils of sex. Their dead infants embodied lost virtue and innocence. It is possible to interpret these women as tragic victims, helpless and alone, abandoned by families and lovers. It is equally possible to construct them as reckless, loose women who put pleasure before duty and honour. In addition, I argue that concealment and infanticide can be seen as symptomatic of the sexual hypocrisy underlying Irish society and the double standards that framed attitudes to sex, pregnancy and illegitimacy. These attitudes were not an aberration but a deep-rooted aspect of the Irish Catholic nation and its highly contradictory perceptions of the female body as the simultaneous embodiment of motherhood/life/goodness and evil/death/sin. Much of the unease caused by women who committed infanticide relates to their visible embodiment of these uncomfortable contradictions. The various reactions to them by the police, judiciary, the public and the press indicate complex negotiations of those contradictions.

Drawing on the arguments laid out elsewhere in this book, I suggest that attitudes towards concealment and infanticide indicate the conflict between power and authority in the new state as well as the individual autonomy of Irish women. However, it is important not to fall into a determinist trap and assume that Irish women crumbled into passive conformity under the constraints imposed by church and state. Women faced complex realities. In the context of the cult of celibacy and the absence of contraception, women's sexual experiences were underpinned by stark choices. While infanticide represents an extreme, though not uncommon, form of 'post-natal abortion' (see Fletcher 1989), it is also a significant indicator of social attitudes to sex, morality, religion and the law. In the context of gendered national and religious discourses, newspaper reports not only offer an insight into the prevalence of infanticide but also reveal how it embodies social and cultural contradictions.

In discussing the 1920s-1930s, we encounter one of the particular difficulties in studying Irish society – the gap between image and reality. Ursula Barry (1992) claims that the differences between the 'ideal' and the 'real' of Irish social life can lead to confusion and to accusations of hypocrisy. The impression is frequently given that Irish people live out their lives in accordance with the teachings of the Catholic Church (see for example Martin 2000). But Barry has argued that: 'while there is truth in this, it misses the divergence which exists in reality between social practices and social laws. This dislocation is key to understanding the Irish social system' (Barry 1992: 110). This view is echoed by Tony Fahey (1995). He argues that in spite of its considerable power to influence legislation in the 1920s-1930s, the Catholic Church was, at times, frustrated by the public apathy that greeted some of its more strident moral campaigns. While many lobby groups ardently supported Church policies, ordinary citizens were more ambiguous in their attitudes to religious teachings (see Horgan 1995: 61-67). Thus, despite its protests, it would seem that the Church was unable to prevent premarital sex and unwanted pregnancies; instead it may only have contributed to the secrecy and privacy that shrouded them.

Irish newspapers represent precisely this clash between image and reality. While ostensibly supporting the vision of the nation outlined by the new Irish government and the Catholic Church, by reporting day to day events the newspapers, perhaps inadvertently, revealed multifaceted realities of Irish life which were more diverse and complicated than the simple ideals advocated by those in power.

## *The Making or Marring of Catholic Ireland:*

As discussed in previous chapters, the press, both national and provincial, devoted a good deal of coverage to the views of the Catholic hierarchy. Sermons, lenten pastorals, letters and speeches by priests and bishops received regular press coverage. The following is a fairly typical example: On 22 November 1922, the *Cork Examiner* reproduced the text of Reverend J.S. Sheehy's speech to the Catholic Truth Society, under the headline, 'Influence of Women'. From the outset, Reverend Sheehy warned Irishwomen that 'you have the making or marring of Catholic Ireland in your hands'. He said that in former times Ireland had been renowned for the purity of its maidens and the holiness of its humble homesteads. Now, however, Ireland was facing many challenges; modern lifestyles were threatening to undermine virtue and purity. 'The future of the nation is in the hands of the mothers of the nation'. Women had the capacity to either protect or destroy the nation:

> Will you be the bane or the blessing of man; a ministering angel or a wily temptress....in your dress do not violate any commandment of God. Don't so dress that you may give scandal to all right thinking Christians. Exercise good sense and good taste as well as modesty. Don't be suggestive in dress or movement. (*Cork Examiner*, 22 November 1922)

Reverend Sheehy was adamant that women, particularly mothers, were largely to blame for the spread of new ideas and lifestyles. Through their influence over men, women were leading men away from the true path of Irishness and Catholicism. In reminding women of their duty to preserve Irish traditions, Reverend Sheehy advised mothers to learn Irish history and language and not be taken in by foreign styles of speech and education. He concluded his lengthy speech by urging women to be interested in Ireland and to 'reflect what you could do for the purification of the Irish stage and picture house'. Women had vital work to do 'in making Ireland a model Catholic nation'.

This is a significant speech encompassing the key elements of Catholic nationalist ideology of the period in which women embodied the Irish nation. Women have particular responsibilities not just as the biological reproducers of the nation but also as the guardians of cultural and traditional identity (Yuval-Davis 1997). However, as discussed earlier, women not only represented the potential good and purity of the nation but also its weakness and fragility. Through their bodies, fashions, lifestyles and influence over men, women had the ability to destroy the essence of the nation. Thus women are represented as untrustworthy and unreliable national icons. There is a constant need for vigilance. Women must be protected from their own base instincts and their susceptibility to foreign influences. This can only be successfully accomplished if women are contained within traditional roles and are denied the opportunity to experiment with modern trends and fashions:

> The separatist political vision of the creation of a Catholic, Gaelic nation-state was a profoundly misogynist vision based on the control of Irish women's sexuality. (Guilbride 1996: 86)

Women were circumscribed by contradictory images: the maternal ministering angel versus the non-maternal wily temptress. Both images framed their relationship to men; the blessing or the bane of men's lives and by implication the making or marring of the nation. In my view, while the image of the good, traditional mother was central to Catholic, nationalist ideology, the image of the evil, 'wily temptress' was equally important. The bad, sinful woman embodied all national weaknesses. She was not only a scapegoat for everything that went wrong, but also she demonstrated the need for effective controls not just on 'bad' women but on all women and girls. Thus the bad woman, just as much as the good woman, played a central role in defining national and religious discourses and policies in the early decades of the Free State. The punishments inflicted on bad, sinful women also reveal the attempts to simplify, explain and contain the extent of social and sexual deviance:

> The emphasis on rigid sexual repression for women, the banning of contraceptives, the legal sanctions put into place by a male dominated Oireachtas defined women as belonging to a different category of citizenship to men, in need of protection and control. (Maddock 1996: 116)

Women's sexuality had to be contained within marriage and motherhood. Unbridled sexuality would destabilise the idealised patriarchal family and thus undermine the nation and the entire social order. The unmarried woman was expected to be a celibate woman, 'any free expression of her sexuality was met with familial and communal condemnation' (Maddock 1996: 113). In the absence of widely available contraception, sex outside of marriage risked the shame and horror of unwanted pregnancy. To become pregnant in such circumstances was seen as a punishment for the sin of illicit sex. However, that was usually just the beginning of one's 'punishment'. The institutionalisation of 'fallen' women and girls in convents, for example in Magdalene laundries, was the ultimate form of control over female sexual freedom. But not all women accepted their fate and served their punishment. Many young women who found themselves pregnant opted for a different course of action:

> Throughout the 1920s and 1930s pregnant Irish women had been travelling to Britain in considerable numbers, either to have their pregnancies terminated by abortions which, although illegal, were more widely available in Britain than in Ireland at that time, or to have their babies there and give them up for legal adoption, which was available in England and Wales from 1926 onwards. (Guilbride 1996: 88)

Legal adoptions were not available in the Irish Republic until 1952. However, not all women and girls were in a position to travel abroad. For those who stayed at home and were unable or unwilling to marry the father of their child, options were limited. Deciding to conceal their condition, many women gave birth in secret, abandoning their newly born infants. These women were deemed particularly sinful and criminalised. This is an under-researched aspect of Irish history and to date relatively little is known about these women who committed concealment or infanticide. In her research on the topic, Alexis Guilbride (1996) found 91 recorded cases of infanticide going before the Central Criminal Court between 1922-1957. In all but two cases, the women were unmarried. In addition, many cases of concealment of birth went before the District Courts. Of course, these cases represent only those which were discovered and where there was sufficient evidence to prosecute. In that sense, these 91 probably represent only the tip of the iceberg.

Throughout the remainder of this chapter I will discuss some examples of infanticide cases in Ireland as they were reported in the daily press over four years: 1925, 1926, 1928 and 1936. Originally I had intended to concentrate on the 1920s and hence had analysed three years from that decade. However, in my research on the 1930s, particularly the provincial press, it quickly became apparent that infanticide remained a common occurrence and was reported with remarkable regularity; averaging almost two cases every month. Thus I have included several cases reported in 1936. I do not claim that newspapers represent an entirely accurate record of infanticide in Irish society. There are many difficulties involved in using newspapers as a source in historical research of this sort. One key problem is that newspapers merely reported those infanticides that were actually discovered and investigated. As it is probable that many went undetected, newspaper accounts do not offer reliable indications of the actual number of infanticides that were occurring. Nonetheless, newspapers do provide some valuable clues to the number of infanticides that were discovered and prosecuted and, in printing details about the accused women, the press also provides important information about the types of women most likely to come under suspicion. In addition, by reporting legal and medical perceptions and responses to infanticide, the newspapers usefully provide some insight into official attitudes, policies and practices.

The way in which infanticide cases are reported is important. Lionel Rose (1986) describes how, in Britain, reports were tucked away on inside pages of the newspapers, rarely meriting more than a few lines. In Ireland, too, press reports were often brief and low key, only very rarely achieving a main headline. Nonetheless, the fact that concealment and infanticide were reported in newspapers raises some questions about the shifting boundary of the public and the private as these very personal stories became public property, firstly, in the courts and secondly, in the press. Clearly, the press played a role in defining what was to be kept private and what was to be revealed. In addition, newspapers also played a part in labelling concealment and infanticide and in bringing knowledge of their existence to the wider public. While individuals may have heard rumours or suspicions about particular occurrences in their local communities or in their own families, the regular press reports probably generated a greater awareness of the frequency of infanticide. Perhaps, one could argue, the press gave some women the idea of how to go about committing infanticide and how to hide the body in a place where it was less likely to be found. While these are very difficult questions to answer, in raising them I am merely indicating the complex role which the press itself played in the dynamics of private agency, public scrutiny and representations of southern Irish social relations of reproduction.

*Uncovering Bodies:*

In the 1920s-1930s, while infanticide appears to have been fading as a social phenomenon in Britain (Rose 1986), this does not appear to have been the case in the Free State. To judge from the pages of the *Cork Examiner* and the *Irish Independent*, infanticide was a monthly if not weekly reality in Ireland (Ryan 1996). For example, during my research on the *Cork Examiner* for the period 1925-1926, I was startled by the frequency with which cases involving concealment and suspected infanticide were reported. In August 1925 there were four reports of alleged infanticide, in October of that year there were three reported cases. In both April and May of 1926 there were three cases, while in June there were references to four cases of alleged infanticide and during both November and December, the *Cork Examiner* reported a further two cases. Ten years later, in 1936, the reported rates of infanticide and concealment of birth showed no signs of abating. As in the 1920s, it was the provincial papers that were most likely to report local stories involving the discovery of infants' bodies. In 1936, the *Cork Examiner* reported over 20 cases of concealment, and while in at least two of these cases the babies were shown to have been still-born, in the vast majority of cases of concealment the infants died as a direct result of 'inattention at the birth'. In addition, the paper also reported two cases of child abandonment, in one case the baby survived and was deemed to be quite healthy, however, in the second case the baby was in a weak state and died soon after being discovered. In two further cases, babies were judged to have died from 'wilful neglect'. In both of these cases the babies were not new-born infants but several weeks old. These reports not only reveal the huge problem of unwanted babies/unwanted motherhood in Ireland, but the additional complexity of how to define the fate of these babies; abandonment, concealment, wilful neglect or actual infanticide. As will be discussed below, the use of these terms was at times confusing and at other times interchangeable.

The locations ranged from urban centres like Dublin City to the rich agricultural areas of counties Cork and Tipperary to remote parts of the Western seaboard. For example, on three occasions in 1928 the *Kerryman* newspaper reported the discovery of infants' bodies in the town of Tralee. 'Baby in a Bucket: Gruesome Finding in Tralee' (3 March) headed a report which outlined the discovery of a body and the subsequent arrest of a young domestic servant. 'Child's Body Concealed in Manure Heap: Gruesome Find in Tralee' (12 May) was the headline to a story of how a farmer discovered the body of a baby girl in his manure heap, a 25 year old domestic servant was subsequently arrested. 'Child's Body in Attache Case' (14 July) headed a report on the discovery of a badly decomposed body in a field, the body was wrapped in a newspaper dated 24 April. Each of these three reports, which were fairly typical of the many localised reports in other provincial papers, were brief and offered few background details to the case and little or no follow up information.

On 14 January 1936, the *Cork Examiner* reported an inquest into the death of a baby who had been abandoned in a Cork city church. The baby was discovered crying in the confessional but later died in hospital. The coroner remarked that there was an increase in illegitimate babies who were being disposed of in this manner: 'It is not a pleasant fact to have to comment upon'.

The vast majority of infants' bodies were discovered out-of-doors. For example, during 1936 the *Cork Examiner* reported bodies found in hedges and bushes (12 May, 25 June, 7 December), in bogs (24 March, 4 May), in rivers (15 January,

17 April), in fields buried in shallow graves (11 February, 7 December). The location and discovery of these bodies outside, in public spaces, represents the transgression of the 'normal' boundaries of sexuality and reproduction, for example, private, domestic spaces. This underlines the extent to which these unwanted babies were 'outsiders'. They did not belong inside the family, inside the home or inside the nation. The discovery of bodies, frequently wrapped in brown paper parcels, scattered around the countryside had become so common that one coroner remarked with some surprise when a body was actually uncovered in a shallow grave. In an inquest in Cork, the coroner's court heard how a labourer uncovered the body, wrapped in brown paper, buried in a shallow grave. The grave had been dug by hand and was probably only one day old. The coroner was quoted as saying: 'We are getting on in these matters. We are beginning to make graves now'. As was common in so many of these cases, the baby was found to have been born alive but died 'due to inattention' at the birth. The coroner concluded that he was 'sorry to say this type of case was increasing'. It was the second such case he had dealt with in six weeks (*Cork Examiner*, 11 February 1936).

The frequent discovery of infants' bodies, whether in make-shift graves or concealed in hedges and bogs, lead to some rather dramatic newspaper headings. The following are all taken from the *Cork Examiner* of 1936 but are remarkably similar to those cited in the *Kerryman* in 1928: 'Buried in Bog' (4 May), 'Body in Box' (8 September), 'Gruesome Discovery: Infant's Body found in Field' (3 October), 'Child's Dead Body' (7 December). The focus of attention on the body of the infant continued in the reports of the inquests which frequently involved some very technical medical evidence from the post mortem. Details were given about the level of decomposition, any marks of violence on the body, clothing or lack of clothing, and whether or not the baby had air in the lungs. This latter piece of evidence was usually crucial in determining if the baby had been born alive. Thus the bodies of these dead infants carried the secrets of their short lives and suggested something of the circumstances in which they died. As I have already argued, their bodies were highly significant in representing the concealed aspects of Irish society: pre-marital sex, the absence of contraception, unwanted pregnancy – issues which only came to the surface when these little bodies were uncovered.

Although scattered around the country, all of these stories shared many similar characteristics and usually began in one of two ways – either with the discovery of the body of an infant or when the suspicions of the local Civic Guards were alerted by an expectant mother who failed to deliver a healthy baby. In many cases the mother was an unmarried servant girl though in some cases she was a married woman who already had several children. Evidence suggests that married women were far less likely to be charged with committing infanticide (Guilbride 1996). One possible reason for this may have been that married women were viewed with less suspicion than single, supposedly celibate, young women.

The British Infanticide Act of 1922, which made a legal distinction between infanticide and homocide, did not apply to the newly independent Irish Free State where the law relating to infanticide still derived from the Offences Against the Person Act of 1861. Therefore, accused women usually had to stand trial for murder and the death penalty could be invoked. The persistent equation of infanticide with murder in the Free State framed the official responses of police, judiciary and also the juries.

This is clearly illustrated by a case reported in the *Cork Examiner* on June 4 1926. A woman from Co. Wicklow was brought to trial at the Central Criminal Court in Dublin. The woman, described as 'middle aged', was reported to be married with three children. She admitted killing her new-born baby and burying it in a field. The defence counsel argued that the woman had not been well for some time and she was, in any case, of 'low intelligence'. However, the judge is reported as saying that 'cases of infanticide unfortunately were appearing in that court more frequently than they should. The whole social fabric depended upon strict administration of the law'. The jury returned a verdict of guilty but with a 'strong recommendation' to mercy. The judge imposed the death penalty for 1 July 1926. However, on 26 June the *Examiner* reported that the woman's sentence had been commuted to penal servitude for life. This was quite usual during the period (Guilbride 1996). On 10 November 1926, the *Examiner* reported that another woman who had received the death penalty for infanticide also had her sentenced commuted to penal servitude for life.

Most of the inquests reported in the press concluded that babies had died due to 'inattention at the birth'. This was usually linked to the concealment of pregnancy and labour. However, it also raises the question of whether this could be seen as an unfortunate outcome of the need to preserve secrecy or if, in fact, the death of the baby was the desired outcome. It is difficult to guess the intention of the scores of women who, for a variety of reasons, felt compelled to conceal childbirth. However, it is likely that many hoped the pregnancy would not end in a living baby. Clearly they were not in a position to care for a child and, if the baby were to survive the birth, then they may have decided to abandon it to its fate. However, as many of the women were very young and probably ignorant about the process of giving birth, they are likely to have been ill-prepared and simply unable to assist their babies upon delivery. In short, it is impossible to say whether the failure to seek any attention during the birth of their babies was a deliberate act aimed at killing the baby, or an unforeseen consequence of the particular circumstances in which these women found themselves. This matter was alluded to by a coroner who urged the authorities to be vigilant and to do everything in their powers to track down those responsible for the deaths of infants:

> This inattention which results in death amounts to criminal negligence and they could find no excuse for any person or persons who, by deliberate negligence, blots out the life of another human being. (*Cork Examiner*, 29 July 1936)

While infanticide often followed the concealment of a pregnancy and birth, that was not always the case. In some instances young women were known to be pregnant and went to the local County Home or workhouse to give birth. Such deliveries were attended by a nurse or midwife. Only later when the baby died suddenly and unexpectedly did an investigation into suspected infanticide commence. Nevertheless, most reported infanticides followed from the concealment of pregnancy where women had succeeded in keeping their condition a secret from family, employers and the authorities. Concealment was not only a crime but it also involved the greatest health risks to the mother. The fact that so many young women chose, or felt compelled, to take this course of action suggests the extent of their desperation and fear of the consequences of discovery. From the press reports it would appear that those women who did conceal their pregnancies were determined to either abandon their babies or to commit infanticide immediately on delivery. The following case reported in the *Cork Examiner* on 28 January 1925 illustrates many of these points.

The article which unusually ran to a full column was boldly titled 'Infanticide Near Fermoy'. At the inquest the all-male jury was told how the 29-year-old servant woman had concealed her pregnancy from her employers and her family. However, having delivered her baby in secret she became seriously ill and died soon after. The doctor testified to the coroner's court that, according to a postmortem, her baby had been born alive but died from asphyxia. The infant's body was found hidden under the mattress. He added that the mother would have lived had she received proper attention at the birth. The coroner remarked that had she lived the woman would have been charged with murder. He described the case as being 'very sad' and 'regrettable'. This case is typical in many respects and highlights the terrible trauma of concealing a pregnancy and a birth. Despite her pregnancy, this domestic servant went about her daily routine as normal. Her fear of delivering the baby alone was obviously outweighed by her fear of discovery by her employers. At the inquest the woman's family denied all knowledge of her condition, though of course one cannot know for certain if this was, in fact, the case. Also at the inquest, there was some speculation about the father of the child. All the witnesses again pleaded ignorance although it was suggested that the young woman had frequented dances during the previous summer. The implication appears to have been that her pregnancy was a likely result of going dancing. As Jim Smyth (1993) has argued this was a connection regularly made by the Catholic clergy in their attempts to regulate dances and dancehalls.

The particular tragedy of this young woman from Fermoy was that having endured pregnancy and labour alone she then bled to death. Through her death the secret she had so closely guarded became open to official scrutiny and media publicity. In concealing her pregnancy and committing infanticide, the young woman must have considered the risks involved. Her decision to pursue this dangerous course suggests her rejection of the other 'options' available to her, for example, informing her family and her employers of her condition and having her baby with the appropriate medical attention. The 'option' of marrying the baby's father does not appear to have been possible. As a live-in domestic servant, this young woman stood to lose not only her job but also the roof over her head. Without a reference she would have found it extremely difficult to obtain another domestic post (Hearn 1993). Without the support of her family, her lover, her employer, this young woman would have been forced to turn to the workhouse, other charities or emigration. Entering an institution would have meant facing the stigma of being an 'offender' or a 'fallen' woman, it would also have meant likely separation from her baby.

While this Fermoy case is unusual in being reported in the newspaper at some length and in such detail, it does reflect many of the characteristics of other alleged infanticides. However, there was also some variation among the cases. For example, the privacy and secrecy that surrounded concealment and infanticide did, on occasion, include other close family members. On 27 August 1926 the *Cork Examiner* reported a case in which three members of one family, mother, daughter and son, were all charged with murdering a new born infant and concealing its body. In this case the young woman was widely known to be pregnant and the local Civic Guards became suspicious when her baby had not appeared. I will return to the role of the Civic Guards later.

But infanticide was not confined to rural areas. Child abandonment and infanticide were widely reported in Dublin City. For example, on 2 February 1925 the *Irish Independent* reported that a baby died having been abandoned on a Dublin train. On 15 May 1925 it was reported that a man (unusually) was charged with abandoning a baby in Dublin. On 14 August of that year the *Independent* reported that a baby died having been abandoned in Woolworth's department store in Dublin city centre and on the following day, 15 August, the paper carried a report of an inquest into the death of yet another baby who had been abandoned in the city. Because of the sheer number of such incidents in Dublin a well known lawyer, Miss Duggan, received the full backing of the *Independent* when she suggested that all babies born in hospitals should be immediately finger printed to facilitate identification of baby and mother if the child were later abandoned (*Irish Independent*, 20 August 1925).

### *Crime and Punishment:*

Those charged with committing infanticide were predominantly young, unmarried women from the lowest socio-economic groups. According to the *Cork Examiner* reports for 1925-26, half of all the unmarried women accused of infanticide were domestic servants. Similar characteristics are apparent in the cases reported in 1936, where there was a continuing preponderance of domestic servants among the young women arrested for concealment and infanticide (*Cork Examiner*, 3 March 1936, 1 May 1936). These women overwhelmingly pleaded not guilty, arguing that their babies had died of natural causes. The experiences of live-in domestic servants have been discussed by Mona Hearn (1993). Their specific vulnerability to exploitation by male members of the households may, in part, explain their high rate of infanticide. Alternatively, their lack of privacy may also explain their very high risk of getting caught trying to conceal newborn infants. In addition, as has been mentioned in previous chapters, working class young women, in both urban slums and remote rural areas were frequently suspected of deviant, lawless, immoral behaviour. They were particularly liable to official scrutiny. It is difficult to speculate about the extent of infanticide among middle class women. It is possible that these women may have had access to information about birth control, as, although censored in the Irish Free State, literature on contraception was available in Britain. But it is equally possible that 'respectable' middle class young women were simply less likely to attract the suspicions of the Civic Guards and other officials; they may have had a greater chance of getting away with concealment and infanticide.

The following case, which received 46 lines of coverage in the *Cork Examiner*, is fairly typical of those involving live-in domestic servants. Headed 'Infant Found in Well Near Kanturk', it reported that a farmer drawing water from his well near the north Cork town of Kanturk found the body of an infant floating on the water (31 August 1925). The matter was reported to the Civic Guards and a 'servant girl' in the farmer's employ was immediately arrested. She admitted that she 'had the child on Saturday' but added that it was stillborn and she had thrown the body into the well. The report went on to say that the medical evidence from the post mortem suggested death from haemorrhage due to inattention at the birth. After quarter of an hour's deliberation the inquest jury unanimously agreed that death was due to 'want of proper attention at birth'. That is the end of the newspaper article and the end of its interest in the case.

While most women accused of concealment were unmarried, and in their early to mid-twenties, some women were considerably younger. For example, on 7 May 1936 the *Examiner* reported that a 17 year old woman was arrested and charged with killing her male infant. On 27 May 1936, the *Irish Independent* reported that a 16-year-old domestic servant from Co. Sligo was charged with the murder her new-born baby. Occasionally older women were arrested. On 3 March 1936, the *Examiner* reported that a 40-year-old widow from Co. Limerick who already had several children was accused of causing the death of her new-born baby. The post mortem revealed that the baby was born alive but that when the body was discovered there was a piece of string tied around its neck. Although this may appear to have been a fairly clear case of infanticide, court decisions and jury verdicts were often very surprising in these cases. On 1 May, the *Examiner* reported that the woman had denied murder but pleaded guilty to concealment of the birth. She was sentenced to 12 months hard labour.

In addition to being short, newspaper reports were sporadic and rarely provided any follow up information on particular stories. This suggests that there was no further interest in the life experiences of these women, it also suggests a general reluctance to explore too deeply the underlying causes of infanticide. There was no obvious 'moral panic' about the frequency of concealment and infanticide. Despite the regular press reports and the angry comments of some coroners and judges, there is no evidence of a general outcry against these occurrences. Perhaps this was because the press reports helped to contain and rationalise infanticide and concealment within 'common-sense' notions of sin, deviance and pathological patterns of behaviour among particular types of women. Or perhaps many people simply accepted infanticide as a natural outcome of unwanted pregnancies. In any case, the press reports of inquests, investigations and court cases, although brief, reveal very varied interpretations of events – the conflicting perceptions of the accused, the witnesses, medical experts, barristers, judges, coroners and jurors. Doctors' testimonies on the cause of death were, in many cases, inconclusive. Nonetheless, even when juries were faced with very conclusive medical evidence suggesting infant death from violent causes, their verdicts were largely unpredictable. As the cases below illustrate, judges and prosecuting barristers frequently expressed their frustration at the high rate of acquittals.

In the case of infanticide, conflicting notions of the boundaries between private and public are apparent as the state institutions scrutinised the most intimate aspects of people's lives. A centralised, bureaucratic approach to infanticide meant that it was condemned as 'wilful murder', the 'massacre of the innocents'. However, its prevalence throughout the Free State suggests that many ordinary Irish people did not share that view (Guilbride 1996). While the state and the Catholic Church attempted to impose law and order, the clash between abstract institutional morality and private individual morality proved problematic. Perhaps it was not the massacre of innocent infants that proved so objectionable but the massacre of Irish innocence – shattering the illusion of a passive, obedient people who lived according to church doctrine. The courtroom provided an environment where the private worlds of desperate decisions, made in extremely difficult circumstances, encountered the public world of uncompromising law and order. As Tony Fahey has argued:

> conflicts over privacy will often entail competing views on what can and cannot be permitted within the private realm in question, so that privacy and competing ideological representations of what the private realm encloses often go hand in hand. (1995: 696)

The following example clearly illustrates the mechanisms through which individual (and family) privacy was subject to institutional regulation and public scrutiny. On the 15 April 1926, both the *Irish Independent* and the *Cork Examiner* reported on a murder trial involving a brother and sister from West Cork. The 18-year-old woman gave birth to her baby in the local County Home. However, the Civic Guards, aware she had been pregnant, became suspicious when the young woman returned home without the baby. On making enquiries they were informed that the baby had died. The police demanded to be taken to the grave and shown the infant's body. However, the family proved unable or unwilling to produce the corpse. A few days later the body of a baby was found in a nearby river but it had been partly eaten by dogs or otters so no post-mortem was possible. In court the woman's brother changed his earlier statement, now saying that the baby had died on the way home from the County Home and that they had decided to throw the body into the river. Their defence solicitor told the court that the baby had been in poor health and the journey from the County Home had been long and arduous exacerbated by bitterly cold weather. Brother and sister testified that they had done nothing to cause the baby's death. The jury found them not guilty and they were both discharged. This case is interesting for two reasons. Firstly, it was significant that the Civic Guards should have become suspicious immediately and begun to investigate the whereabouts of the baby. This was not an isolated incident. Such suspicion on the part of the police formed the basis of many investigations into suspected infanticide. Secondly, this case indicates that despite the suspicion of the Civic Guards and the courts, the jury, once again, refused to share the official opinion. Not only did the jury disagree with the powerful arguments of the prosecution but they arrived at their decision in just 35 minutes (*Irish Independent*, 15 April 1926).

Two cases reported in both the *Irish Independent* and the *Cork Examiner* during March and April 1926 offer particularly good examples of the many complexities and contradictions surrounding infanticide in the Irish Free State. The first case occurred in Nenagh, Co. Tipperary and involved the death of a seven-week-old baby. The mother was described as a 'young domestic servant girl' (*Cork Examiner*, 12 March 1926). Unlike the two servants referred to in the Fermoy and Kanturk cases above, this young woman did not conceal her pregnancy, instead she delivered her baby in the local workhouse. It would appear that she had lost her job and on leaving the workhouse was homeless. The press reported that the woman's sister had offered her accommodation but only on condition that the baby did not accompany her. What becomes apparent in all the stories involving domestic servants is that no male partner is implicated. The paternity of the child was rarely an issue in infanticide investigations. These unmarried young women were held entirely responsible for their predicaments.

In court, the Tipperary servant testified that her baby had died in her arms and she had then thrown its body into a nearby river. However, the other evidence contradicted this story. For example, the woman had told her sister that the baby was stillborn. In addition, the post-mortem revealed the baby had been in good health and had died from a fractured skull. The prosecution in a powerful speech told the jury that this was not a case of 'concealment of birth' but the 'wilful murder' of a seven-week-old child. This is a telling distinction and may explain some of the severity in prosecuting this case. He told the jury 'you will find this woman guilty to warn all others that there is such a crime as infanticide punishable, and that the massacre of the innocents, which takes place at present in this and other countries must be stopped, and it will be stopped' (*Cork Examiner*, 12 March 1926). What is of particular interest in this case is the finding of the jury – manslaughter – a verdict that the judge found surprising, describing it as 'rather unfortunate'.

A second case reported in the *Examiner* on 1 April 1926 reveals a similar disparity between individual and official attitudes to infanticide. This concerned a woman who gave birth in a County Clare workhouse. The baby who had been in perfect health died mysteriously during the night. The mother and her baby had been sleeping in a dormitory along with many other mothers who testified that they had neither seen nor heard anything suspicious during the night. The young woman was reported as being 'very fond' of her baby and had looked after it well. A post-mortem showed the child had died of asphyxia but there was no bruising of any kind on the body. The jury found in accordance with the medical evidence that the baby had died of asphyxia attaching no blame to anybody. However, despite the decision of the jury the police later arrested the young mother. She was charged at a special court held in Kilrush barracks with the murder of her baby.

These two cases indicate that while private individuals, including jurors, may have had a sympathetic attitude to infanticide or suspected infanticide, the legal authorities took a very harsh line. This suggests an attempt to impose not just legal but moral social controls on a population which tended to deal with things quietly in their own way. Although women were frequently sentenced to a term of imprisonment, sentencing in concealment cases was not only unpredictable but it also contained an unusual option not available to other prisoners. Women, particularly younger women, often had their sentences suspended if they agreed to enter a convent for a prescribed period. For example, a 22 year old domestic servant found guilty of concealment had her one year sentence suspended on condition that she enter a convent for 2 years (*Cork Examiner*, 1 May 1936). A judge sent a 24 year old woman from Co. Mayo to a convent for two years 'to be subject to the control of the Mother Superior' (*Irish Independent*, 29 May 1936). A woman from Limerick had her sentence suspended on condition that she enter the local Good Shepherd convent for 12 months (*Cork Examiner*, 9 July 1936). The implication seems to have been that these women were in need of moral reform and this could be best achieved not in prison but in a convent. Thus the women were not treated like ordinary criminals but as a special case of deviant and disorderly behaviour. They were treated primarily as sinners. They had strayed from the path of morality and needed to be punished and made to repent. One could argue that their great sin was not so much the killing/concealing of their babies but the shame of having had inappropriate sexual experiences that resulted in pregnancy and disgrace. Thus despite Judge Kenny's pronouncement cited at the start of this chapter (*Irish Independent*, 3 October 1928), I believe that girls and women were being punished as much for sexual 'immorality' as for concealing the births of their infants.

## Contextualising Infanticide:

In my view, the moral restraints imposed on young Irish women need to be located within the context of religious orthodoxy and cultural nationalism that showed a marked intolerance of sexually 'deviant' women. The rigorous prosecution of cases involving suspected infanticide represents just one of the ways in which church and state sought to restrict private and personal ways of dealing with social problems. Mark Ryan says:

> The church took to policing the most intimate details of people's lives, embarking on one of the most remarkable campaigns of moral engineering ever attempted....The Irish people, and women in particular, have paid a terrible price for the moral straitjacket imposed by church and state. (1994: 91)

The definition and imposition of a strict moral code of Catholic, Irish behaviour was influenced by lay groups as well as by religious bodies. In 1926 at a meeting of the influential lobby group, the Catholic Truth Society, a speaker told his audience that 'the basis of morality is the fact of the existence of God...it is impossible for a Christian to admit a solid and complete moral system which abstracts from the existence of God' (*Cork Examiner*, 16 October 1926). He attacked the liberal Protestant tendency to allow individual private judgements instead of the undeniable authority of religion. He concluded by praising the legislators for their efforts in curbing modern habits especially the 'craze for amusement and pleasure'.

As mentioned in earlier discussions of flappers and modern girls, the press, both local and national, played a key role in reproducing and reinforcing Church teaching on sex, sin, shame and pregnancy by reprinting sermons, speeches and pastorals from the Catholic hierarchy. The connection between dance halls and sexual immorality was repeatedly made by the Catholic hierarchy. For example, Bishop O'Doherty was quoted in the *Connacht Sentinel* on 22 May 1928, under the headline 'Dance Hall Dangers'. Speaking at a Galway parish church he said:

> There have been four cases of illegitimate births in this parish and six cases of forced marriages. That is altogether an undue proportion for a Catholic parish like this. We are all ashamed of it. (*Connacht Sentinel*, 22 May 1928)

He blamed unsupervised 'company keeping' between young men and women and urged parents and employers to exert more control over their charges. The main danger, however, was the dance hall. Dancing without the 'proper control' and dancing which is of a 'dangerous and lascivious kind', he argued, had 'often led to damnation'. This point was reinforced in a report carried by the *Sentinel*'s sister paper, the *Connacht Tribune* on 8 December 1928 under the heading 'Village Dance Halls: Girls who make the Acquaintance of Strangers'. A speaker addressing a Galway charitable organisation claimed: 'From statements made to me by some unmarried mothers there can be no doubt that dance halls all over the country are a great source of evil to girls'.

On 24 April 1926, the *Wicklow People* carried a report on a local temperance meeting. In a lecture entitled 'Drink and Dancing', a speaker told the meeting: 'Dancing without drink was dangerous enough but dancing with drink was still more dangerous to morals. Every public dance should be the charge of a conscientious M.C. and committee.' All-night dances were particularly worrying. 'Women, as well as men, indulged in stimulants to keep on dancing until morning'.

On 24 February 1936, the *Cork Examiner* devoted extensive coverage to the lenten pastorals of the Church hierarchy. Bishop O'Brien of Kerry railed against dance halls as 'the plague spot of moral rot'. He argued that the 'craze for pleasure, especially dancing, is weakening parental authority and lowering the standard of morality'. He went on to cite a letter from a 'rescue worker' who had written to him on the subject of pregnant Irish girls emigrating to England:

> Scarcely a day passes that I do not receive an application from one of these Irish girls who come over here to hide their shame and to transfer the burden of the coming child to us. (*Cork Examiner*, 24 February 1936)

The bishop used this letter as evidence of the falling standards of morality among young people and took the opportunity to attack unsupervised dance halls and the consumption of alcohol at dances after which people would walk home along dark country roads. The bishop did not mention the young men who were partly responsible for young girls getting pregnant. Nor did he address why girls found it necessary to travel to England to 'hide their shame'. His argument seems to have been that once girls had sinned they deserved all they got. His solution was that girls should not sin in the first place.

The fact that several bodies of infants were not so much concealed as abandoned in public places, especially in churches, where they were sure to be quickly discovered is worthy of comment. A woman may have abandoned a living baby in a church in the hope that a responsible person would find it, but it seems strange to abandon the body of a dead infant in a church, yet it appears to have been a fairly frequent occurrence (*Cork Examiner* 29 July 1936, *Irish Press* 18 September 1936). It may well be that after the birth of her baby the woman went to the church to pray and ask for guidance or to confess her 'sin': one baby was found in the confessional. In my view, by leaving the body in the church, these women raised many uncomfortable issues about the role of religion and the Catholic

Church in defining and constraining sexuality and reproduction in the Irish Free State. The body of an illegitimate baby in the 'house of God', the focal point of Catholic power and authority, can be seen as a visible demonstration of the complexities and contradictions of sexual mores in society. Despite church teaching, women did have premarital sex and did give birth to unwanted babies. The church did nothing to help these women but merely judged them as sinners to be punished. Thus abandoning a dead infant in the church may have been simply a desperate cry for help or an indictment of the failure of church teaching.

As argued at the start of this chapter, infanticide needs to be located within its specific cultural and historical context. In order to fully appreciate this point let us briefly examine the position of unmarried mothers in southern Ireland. The census results of 1926 revealed that the rate of illegitimacy was 30.7 per thousand births. Illegitimacy provoked much reaction from the Catholic Church who blamed it variously on a breakdown in morality, lack of parental control, foreign cultural influences, sinful books, cinemas and dance halls (J. Smyth 1993). But it was not only the Church that was concerned about the levels of illegitimacy in the state. In July 1925 the *Irish Times* began reporting on the Committee on Child Welfare which had been set up to investigate poor law reform and the workhouse system. On the 15 July the paper reported the numbers of unmarried women who were giving birth in Dublin workhouses. In her evidence to the commission, Mrs. Power from the Dublin Union (workhouse) testified that in the period 1924-1925, 161 unmarried mothers went to the Union for their confinement. Of that total 103 claimed they were 'first offenders'. In her opinion 'first offenders' should be segregated from other unmarried mothers. In 1925 the Dublin Union had boarded out 180 babies. In the absence of legal adoption, 'boarding out' (fostering) was widely practised in Dublin. The newspaper article further reported that, as it was largely unregulated, this was an unsafe and an unsatisfactory arrangement. For example, of 274 children fostered in Dublin 94 had died. These children were frequently fostered by people living in unhealthy and over-crowded conditions. A lump sum was paid to the foster family in advance making it a very lucrative enterprise. Mrs. Byrne, a former member of the Dublin Board of Guardians, was quoted as saying that in one slum area of Dublin 110 children were being fostered (*Irish Times*, 15 July 1925).

As the Committee on Child Welfare continued to take evidence on the conditions of unmarried mothers and their illegitimate babies, the *Irish Times* devoted an editorial to the subject, entitled 'Unwanted Children', on 16 July 1925. According to the editorial, the committee's investigation was revealing 'a nefarious trade in unwanted children practised in Dublin'. The editorial added that 'evils are rampant in the Irish underworld which call for the pen of a Dickens for their adequate exposure'. Children should be adopted properly into decent homes where they would learn to live a better, healthier life than in an institution and they might gladden the hearts of their adoptive families. In such an atmosphere of love 'the handicap of an unhappy origin' could be forgotten.

In the same issue the *Irish Times* continued to report on the work of the committee under the headline 'Poor Law Relief'. According to the evidence given by Miss Kenney, Local Government Inspector for boarded out children (since 1902), first time 'offenders' should be strictly segregated and repeat 'offenders' should be sent to a state penitentiary for seven years. On the following day, 17 July, the *Irish Times* once again used the heading 'Unwanted Children'. This report focused on the evidence given to the committee by Miss Cruise, founder of St Patrick's Guild in Dublin. She said that the Guild was used mostly by unmarried mothers who did not wish to enter an institution. The majority of these women were domestic servants. She reported that of 227 births at the home in the previous year only 35 were legitimate. Miss Cruise declared – 'The problem of the unmarried mother is a very big one, but so far we in Ireland have closed our eyes to it'. All the children who came under her care were boarded out in 'respectable homes'. However, she admitted that in 1923, 54 of the 86 children boarded out in Dublin City had died.

On 17 September 1925, the *Irish Times* returned to the findings of the committee under the headline 'Unmarried Mother Problem'. Miss Desmond, who worked at a home run by nuns in Liverpool, had some enlightening things to report. She claimed great success in 'reforming' girls who came to the home. However, she added that it was best for some of the 'weak minded girls' to remain in the home after their confinement because if they left the institution they would surely 'fall' again. She did not approve of unmarried mothers going to a workhouse. Miss Desmond reported that pregnant Irish women tended to travel to the Liverpool home to ensure greater secrecy.

The newspaper accounts of the evidence given to the Committee on Child Welfare offer a rare insight into what the editor of the *Irish Times* called the 'nefarious underworld'. However, while the newspaper reports and the committee were ostensibly concerned with the fate of 'unwanted children', what they actually highlight is the tragedy of unmarried mothers. As one witness told the committee, these women were usually domestic servants whose precarious economic and social position forced them to turn to institutional support. They were faced with a limited range of bleak 'choices'; the workhouse, the nuns or the boat to England. The construction of these women as 'offenders' informed the subsequent official responses of punishment or reform. Both measures were predicated upon separating mother and child. One could argue that this was done to protect the child and give it a secure start in life. However, the stark reality of huge infant mortality among these children suggests that genuine concern for their welfare was not the primary motive in enforcing separation from the mothers. Instead, I would argue that the rationale behind separation was more moral than practical. It was underpinned by a need to maintain social order and deny the possibility of single-parent families. Society could, in some way, tolerate 'fallen' women as offenders or as victims but to acknowledge them as real mothers caring for their children seemed impossible. Perhaps it would have represented a challenge to the norms of marriage and the taboo of conception outside marriage. It is within this context that Irish infanticide must be understood.

*Family Values:*

As I have mentioned earlier, men were rarely implicated in the conception or concealment of babies. However, on rare occasions men were held accountable for their actions in getting young women pregnant. On 30 October 1936, the *Cork Examiner* carried a report under the headline 'Wronged Girl'. This referred to a court case in which a father was awarded £60 damages because his 20-year-old daughter had been made pregnant and then abandoned by a local farmer aged 25. The judge said 'the seduction of a girl by a man is a very immoral thing'. However, the judge seemed to be even more annoyed by the fact that the young man refused to accept responsibility for the baby. The judge commented that in his 30 years experience of such cases men hardly ever accepted responsibility for their illegitimate babies.

Although the image of the single young woman alone in the dock is the dominant representation of suspects in newspaper accounts of infanticide trials, there were some notable exceptions. Interestingly, these cases usually involved other family members, both male and female. Involvement of families in concealment and infanticide frequently added to the complexity of the story and also added to the level of newspaper attention. Perhaps because these stories were more unusual than the average, run of the mill 'lone woman in the dock', they tended to receive more coverage and to attract the attention of national dailies as well as local provincial papers. In 1928 there were two cases of infanticide that had all the right ingredients to be sensational news as opposed to simply mundane cases of infant abandonment and concealment of birth.

On 6 July 1928, the *Cork Examiner* carried the headline: 'Found in a Bog: Cork Woman Charged with Murder'. A baby's body was found in a bog hole by a passer-by. The body had several knife wounds and its internal organs had been removed. A local woman aged 19 years was arrested and charged with the murder of her baby. At first she denied ever having had a baby but she later admitted giving birth to the baby on New Year's Eve at her grandmother's house. At the trial in the Central Criminal Court, Dublin, she denied killing the baby saying that her grandmother had taken charge of the situation immediately the baby was born, sending the young woman to bed where she remained for several days. The woman alleged that it was her grandmother who must have killed the baby and disposed of its body. The judge instructed the jury that the 19-year-old woman appeared to be 'dominated' by the older woman. The *Examiner* reports that, after only a few moments deliberation, the jury found this young woman to be not guilty.

On 12 July 1928, the paper reported that the 67-year-old grandmother had now been arrested and charged with murder. On 14 July the paper provided further gruesome details of this case. The baby's lungs, heart, liver and intestines had all been 'scientifically' cut out. This, it was alleged, had been done to prevent any evidence as to whether or not the baby was born alive and also to hinder a medical diagnosis as to the actual cause of death, however, the baby did have a fractured skull. The removal of internal organs could have been expertly done by 'a person accustomed to killing table fowl'.

This case attracted widespread press coverage. For example, the *Kerryman* devoted two columns to the case against the grandmother (21 July 1928) under the headline 'County Cork Trial: Old Woman Sent for Trial'. Part of the evidence against the woman was that she had tried to bribe the Civic Guard who came to her house by offering £1 to stop his investigation. The trial of the grandmother also received coverage in the national dailies. On 1 December 1928, the *Irish In-*

*dependent* carried the headline 'Woman Sentenced to Death: Murder of Great Grandchild'. When asked by the judge if she had anything to say:

> the prisoner clutched the iron rails of the dock with a muscular hand, and declared in a firm tone – 'I have nothing to say except that I had nothing to do with it and I know nothing about it' (*Irish Independent*, 1 December 1928).

This description presents the grandmother in a rather interesting light. Despite being 67 years of age, she is represented as strong, muscular and speaking in a firm voice, all usually masculine characteristics. In this way the paper suggested her ability to commit such a crime which required strength of character and determination, as well as clear thinking and precision. She is not presented as an elderly pathetic grandmother. She appears to transgress the 'normal' feminine and maternal traits associated with idealised Irish womanhood. As was usual in reporting murder trials the paper describes the evidence in a straightforward and apparently impartial manner. The journalistic style is matter-of-fact and unquestioning. However, in summarising very lengthy and complex testimony the invisible hand of the court reporter was obviously taking a decisive role in editing and rationalising information for the reader. For example, the newspaper article reports that although the woman shared a bedroom with her 19-year-old grand daughter, she claimed not to know that the younger woman had a baby on New Year's Eve. She was aware that her grand daughter was unwell and had stayed in bed for a few days but she accepted the explanation that this was due to earache. The fact that this account was written after the jury's verdict of guilty and the passing of the death sentence must have helped to frame the way the unnamed journalist subsequently reported the evidence. The allegation that she tried to bribe the civic guard, her testimony that she was unaware of her grand daughter's pregnancy or child birth, the previous judge's view that she dominated the 19 year old, plus the woman's strong physical appearance, all pointed towards her likely guilt.

However, the story did not end there. On 19 December, the *Independent* reported that an appeal was being launched against the conviction because the judge had not allowed for the possibility that the grand daughter may have acted with the older woman as an accomplice or an accessory. On the following day, the paper reported the argument being put forward by the woman's barrister that there was no medical evidence against her. The case was built largely on the testimony of her grand daughter and she had previously been found to have lied, when she had originally denied having had a baby in the first place. The only medical evidence in the entire case was against the young woman, she had definitely been proven to have given birth to the baby. On 21 December the *Independent* reported that the Court of Appeal had quashed the original verdict against the grandmother because the judge should have warned the jury not to simply accept the uncorrobated testimony of a possible accomplice.

This case is fascinating because unlike most infanticide cases that were treated as fairly straightforward by the police, judiciary and the press, it had the added dimension of more than one suspect. Usually, a young woman was arrested very quickly after the discovery of a body. She was seen as acting alone and thus singled out for punishment. The complicity of other family members not only made the case more complicated but also made it more difficult to secure a conviction. This point is highlighted by another case which also came to light in 1928 and which was also widely reported in the press over a period of months.

On 31 May 1928, the *Independent* reported that a man from Co. Wexford was accused of the murder of a three-day-old female infant born to his daughter. The source of the accusation was the young woman's employer, a farmer, whose son was the father of the baby. The farmer alleged that after the woman had given birth on his farm he had brought the baby to her family home where her father had been determined to get rid of it. Her father had hit the baby on the head with a poker and then concealed the body. However, as in the case above, there was a dispute between the parties as to who had actually killed the baby. The young woman was adamant that her father had not harmed the baby. She claimed that a few hours after she had given birth on the farm, the farmer approached her and removed the baby. She did not see the child again. Her allegations appear to have been strengthened by the fact that the body of the infant was discovered not near her father's house but on the farmer's property. The case against her own father now appeared to have collapsed and the farmer was arrested and charged with murder (*Irish Independent*, 21 September 1928). In this case there was no doubt that the young woman had given birth to a baby on the farm. There also appears to have been no suspicion that she had harmed the infant. The father of the child, the farmer's son, does not appear to have featured very strongly in the case. Suspicion was focused entirely on the two male grandparents, shifting from the woman's father to her employer. Finally, on 12 December the *Independent* reported the verdict in this complex case. The farmer eventually pleaded guilty to manslaughter and received a 12 month sentence. The judge took advantage of the opportunity to make a statement about infanticide: 'Mr. Justice Sullivan said that no more distressing feature in that court arose than the number of cases in which infants had been done to death' (*Irish Independent*, 12 December 1928).

These cases involving various family members are interesting for a number of reasons, not least because they raise questions about how 'deviant' families were represented in the press. As has been mentioned in earlier chapters, while the idealised Irish family was the bedrock of the nation, particular types of families were especially liable to official scrutiny and sanction. Images of the wild, unrestrained family who showed no respect for authority, and the poor inadequate, dirty, diseased family were clearly apparent in both the national and provincial newspapers. These deviant, immoral or pathological families could be used as scapegoats for a wide array of social problems, ranging from infanticide to the illegal poteen trade. Thus a 'common-sense' notion of the idealised, married Irish mother, the patriarchal family and the 'cosy homestead' could be perpetuated and maintained in opposition to the immoral unmarried mother and the 'deviant' family.

*Conclusion:*

Although infanticide can be seen as an extreme reaction to unwanted pregnancy, there is evidence to suggest that in the absence of safe abortion, contraception and legal adoption, it was widespread in the Irish Free State (Guilbride 1996, Ryan 1996). The extent of infanticide demonstrated several aspects of life in southern Irish society in the 1920s-1930s. Firstly, it embodied the hypocrisy of deep-rooted sexual double standards; while mothers were stigmatised and punished by incarceration in institutions, fathers simply abdicated responsibility and avoided sanctions. Secondly, the policing and prosecuting of infanticide revealed official attempts to contain women's sexuality. Rather than admitting the extent of sexuality within the society, the cult of celibacy on the one hand, and of idealised married motherhood on the other hand, were protected by demonising all means of birth control. Thirdly, it indicated the contradictory attitudes towards illegitimate babies. While concealment, abandonment and infanticide were treated as very serious criminal offences, the extremely high rate of infant mortality within charitable institutions suggests that no great value was attached to the health and safety of illegitimate children. Hence the criminalisation of women who abandoned or killed their new-born infants was probably fuelled more by an outrage against illicit female sexuality than by a concern for the welfare of their unwanted babies. Finally, however, the frequency of infanticide also embodied the failure of the state and the church to successfully control attitudes and behaviour in Irish society. Rates of infanticide were clearly influenced by official policies. For example, while in Britain rates of infanticide were falling in response to changing government policies in the 1920s (Rose 1986); in southern Ireland, the extent of infanticide represented the impossibility and impracticality of state policy and church teachings. The reaction of jurors in frequently refusing to convict accused women suggests an appreciation of some of these complexities.

As I have argued in this chapter, the dead bodies of babies, so regularly discovered throughout the Free State, could be interpreted as a threat to constructions of Irishness in the 1920s-1930s. These concealed and abandoned infants embodied the many complexities and contradictions of the newly established nation-state. Despite its obvious prevalence, the fact that infanticide did not provoke a widespread public outcry needs to be understood in terms of the official state, church and media responses. The newspapers in particular played an important role in publicising the nature and extent of concealment, abandonment and infanticide. While the regular press reports were short and apparently quite factual, they offered specific representations of young women (and occasionally their families) which framed them in terms of immorality, sexual deviance and sin. Thus, in my view, newspapers played a dual role in both publicising and containing these issues. Unlike the heated debates which took place in the press concerning flappers, Republican women, and the role of working women or female emigrants, infanticide remained an ever present but marginal, taken-for-granted issue. The many potentially complex and uncomfortable questions which infanticide raised about Irish society were never addressed in any of the national or provincial newspapers that I have studied.

# CONCLUSION

This book has drawn upon and, it is hoped, contributed to theoretical analyses of the gendered nature of national rhetoric and the processes of representing the nation. As narrators of the nation, newspapers offer an interesting and under-researched insight into the ways in which the nation represents itself. With a wide circulation and a very wide readership (Russell 1999), the press was probably the second most significant influence on public opinion after the Catholic Church. This study of the Irish press from 1922-1937 has demonstrated the ways in which particular gendered symbols, archetypes and images were used to embody notions of Ireland and Irishness.

I have argued that newspapers can be read on a number of different levels. On one level they offer particular accounts of social events, trends and phenomena. In that sense they present a snap shot of the nation, they highlight the viewpoints, arguments and priorities of the period. But, on a deeper level, newspapers offer a partial, fractured and somewhat distorted view of complex and contradictory social realities. Hence, the newspapers in my study can be used in three ways: firstly, to show the prevalence of national icons such as Tailte and Mother Ireland, secondly, to highlight the varied, heterogeneous and competing discourses in the Free State, and thirdly, as a tool to deconstruct national rhetoric, images and symbols.

Focusing on the mainstream national dailies and on a range of provincial papers, I have attempted to highlight the role of the press in both reporting and reproducing certain categories of idealised womanhood. While images of the idealised woman – mother-of-the-nation – are important in all nationalist repertoires (Anthias and Yuval-Davis 1993, McClintock 1993), I have argued that images of demonised womanhood are of equal significance. Thus while particular types of female figures were repeatedly used in the Irish press to represent evil, lawlessness, immorality and deviance, male figures were rarely used to represent these phenomena. Hence, the flapper, the feminist, the fury, the bachelor girl, the unmarried mother, the inadequate mother, the emigrant girl, the woman in industry, etc., stood as a shorthand, simple explanations and scapegoats for the problems underlying the newly established Free State. In most of these cases there was no male equivalent. The emigrant male or the unmarried father did not figure to any great extent in media discourses. There was no male equivalent of the flapper or the feminist. The bachelor girl and the woman in industry were constructed in direct opposition to the male bachelor and the man in industry, which were the taken for granted and unquestioned norm. Only the fury had a male equivalent – the Republican gunman. In the post-1922 period, both figures were presented in the mainstream press as dangerous and threatening to the status quo. However, unlike her fellow Republican, the fury, as an inherently female figure, was subject to specific processes of representation which framed her as hysterical, ridiculous, illogical, mad, and a frustrated spinster.

But, as I have argued at length in this book, these archetypal female figures were not simple, one-dimensional characters. There was often a high degree of ambiguity in relation to figures such as the flapper, the feminist, the bachelor girl, the woman in industry and even, to some extent, the fury. While frequently attacking these symbols of modern womanhood, both national and provincial newspapers also carried some competing and opposing viewpoints. For example, as Church leaders railed against the flapper and the woman in industry, other sources such as advertisers, trade unionists, feminists and some journalists offered more sympathetic and supportive opinions. Hence, despite censorship, the press does not represent a single, monolithic, narrow, conservative and Church-ridden medium in the Irish Free State. As I have tried to suggest in this book, newspapers are far more complex and at times even contradictory, as is particularly apparent in relation to flappers who were simultaneously condemned and celebrated in the press. In fact, as an analysis of the letters' pages suggests, some young women even embraced the flapper archetype in a self-affirming way. Thus my research concurs with the recent findings of Caitriona Clear (2000), that the attitudes, opinions and ideologies that existed in the early years of the Free State were rather more intricate and diverse than has been assumed by historians.

Of course, this study cannot and does not claim to be exhaustive in its analyses of the Irish press. Taking 1922 and 1937 as my parameters, I have attempted to keep my study manageable by focusing on particular years and, in the case of provincial newspapers especially, selecting particular newspapers. In addition, it was beyond the scope of this study to examine the press in Northern Ireland or to undertake a comparative analysis with the press in Britain. Because so little research has been done on the press in the 26 counties of the Irish Free State it was necessary, in my opinion, to focus solely on that topic before widening the field of study.

It is my contention that newspapers serve as a complex and fascinating source in historical investigation and analyses. They did not merely report events and information, they actively participated in interpreting, supporting and attacking specific viewpoints, individuals and interest groups. As was apparent in relation to the Constitution of 1937, the press lost all claims to impartiality and neutrality, firmly nailing its colours to particular political masts. In that specific context the debates not merely about the draft Constitution *per se* but also about the nature of Irish society focused around three female figures: the woman in the home, the woman citizen and the woman worker. This offers a clear example of firstly, the ways in which national discourses and policies were gendered and secondly, of the role of the press in reflecting and reinforcing those gendered images and rhetoric. In addition, the coverage of debates on the Constitution also highlights a third point; the role of the press in publicising the other, opposing and competing voices, for example those of the feminist campaigners.

Infanticide and concealment visibly represent the role of the press in not simply reporting the problems in Irish society but also in interpreting, explaining and containing these problems. Although it was widespread, reports of infanticide were kept fairly un-sensational, brief and matter of fact. The simple explanation that infant abandonment and death resulted from female immorality was usually made abundantly clear. The lonely young woman in the dock was the obvious scapegoat who substituted for a more probing exploration of the problems underpinning unwanted pregnancy. National morality and purity were framed almost entirely in terms of female purity and morality. Women's behaviour was reported and interpreted within very narrowly defined notions of moral codes. Women who were seen to deviate from these codes were punished more as sinners than as law-breakers. Nevertheless, as I have argued throughout this book, newspaper reports do offer the possibility of alternative readings. Taken as a whole, the frequent reports on infanticide, concealment and infant abandonment begin to suggest the more complex and multifaceted realities that underlie the simple newspaper stories. Thus while it is possible to interpret infanticide, family violence, emigration, unemployment, lawlessness, immorality, etc. in terms of deviant, sinful, naïve and disobedient women, it is equally possible to use these female figures to unravel the tightly woven strands of life in the Irish Free State.

The existence of such female figures as the flapper, the fury, the emigrant girl, the inadequate mother, the woman in industry, etc., and the frequency with which they appeared in the press is, to some extent, merely a reflection of the wider discourse register in Irish society and abroad. In other words, one could argue that the press did not invent these archetypes but merely reported what politicians, the Catholic hierarchy and other social commentators said about them. Images such as the flapper were common in many countries and embodied similar concerns about modernity and the apparent collapse of traditional values (Melman 1988). However, I believe that such figures take on specific national characteristics and need to be located within cultural, social and economic specificities. Hence, the emigrant girl, for example, was a particularly Irish figure representing the uniquely Irish phenomenon of wide scale female emigration. This archetypal figure, therefore, represented the reality of high levels of emigration by young women in rural Ireland. However, the figure was also circumscribed within particular ideological constructions that used the emigrant girl as a scapegoat for the causes and consequences of emigration. On one level, of course, the press did report the views of political and religious leaders on such figures as the emigrant girl and the flapper. However, on another level, it is apparent that the press was far more than simply the mouthpiece of the Church or the Government.

The juxaposition of competing viewpoints within the pages of the same newspaper indicates many internal contradictions. However, that is not to simplify the power dynamics that clearly operated within the press. As we have seen, the views of editors, religious leaders and political allies were usually given priority over the letters and articles of opponents.

Only in the last two decades has there been serious academic analysis of the ways in which nationalism and nation-building are gendered projects (Mosse 1985, Parker *et al* 1992). In that short time, feminist scholars in particular have developed a very important body of work. Many writers have explored the role of female symbols within nationalism in many diverse countries including Ireland (for example, Innes 1993, Meaney 1993). However, there has been a tendency for such studies to concentrate on literary and cultural studies deconstructing well-known national icons such as Mother Ireland. My work has attempted to show not only the diverse range of female figures within the national repertoire but also their varied and ambiguous nature. Using a sociological perspective, I have analysed how several female archetypal characters were used simultaneously to represent various aspects of Irish society: from emigration to unemployment, from Republicanism to the jazz age. The use of these female figures as scapegoats attempted to simplify and obscure the many social and economic problems underlying the newly established state. This book has attempted to go beyond these simple female archetypes to uncover some of the complex realities that lay behind the myths. Hence, it has highlighted not only the varied ways in which women were constructed and contained within the nation-building project, but also the ways in which women contributed, confronted and challenged that project.

# BIBLIOGRAPHY

Akenson, D. (1993) *The Irish Diaspora: A Primer* (Belfast: Institute of Irish Studies).
Anthias F. and Yuval-Davis N. (1993) Racialised Boundaries (London: Routledge).
Arensberg, C. (1937) *The Irish Countryman* (London: Macmillan).
Anderson, B. (1991) *Imagined Communities* (London: Verso).
Augusteijn, J. (1996) *From Public Defiance to Guerrilla Warfare*, (Dublin: Irish Academic Press).
Augusteijn, J. ed (1999) *Ireland in the 1930s* (Dublin: Four Courts Press).
Barry, T. (1997) *Guerrilla Days in Ireland* (Dublin: Anvil Press).
Barry, U. (1992) 'Movement, Change and Reaction' in A. Smyth. ed *The Abortion Papers* (Dublin: Attic).
Beale, J. (1986) *Women In Ireland: Voices of Change* (Dublin: Gill and Macmillan).
Beaumont, C. (1997) 'Women, Citizenship and Catholicism in the Irish Free State.' in *Women's History Review*, Vol. 6 No. 4 pp.563-584.
Benton, S. (1995) 'The Militarisation of Irish Politics' in *Feminist Review*, No. 50 pp.148-172.
Bhabha, H. (1994) 'Narrating the Nation' in: J. Hutchinson and A. Smith eds *Nationalism* (Oxford: Oxford University Press).
Blake, F. (1986) *The Irish Civil War* (London: Information on Ireland).
Boase, W. (1979) *The Sky's the Limit* (London: Osprey).
Boland, E. (1989) *A Kind of Scar* (Dublin: Attic Press).
Breen, D. (1997) *My Fight for Ireland's Freedom* (Dublin: Anvil).
Brennan, M. (1980) *The War in Clare* (Dublin: Four Courts Press).
Brown, T. (1987) *Ireland: A Social and Cultural History* (London: Fontana).
Buckley, M. (1938) *The Jangle of the Keys* (Dublin: James Duffy Press).
Byrne, L. (1980) *The History of Aviation in Ireland* (Dublin: Blackwater Press).
Clarke, K. (1991) *Revolutionary Woman* (Dublin: O'Brien Press).
Clear, C. (2000) *The Women of the House* (Dublin: Irish Academic Press).
*Commission on Emigration and Other Population Problems* (1955) Irish Government Publications, Dublin.
Conboy, M. (1996) 'Communities and Constructs: National Identity in the British Press', in S. Stern-Gillett *et al* eds *Culture and Identity: Selected Aspects and Approaches* (Katowice: Wydawnictwo Uniwersytetu Slaskiego).
Conlon, L. (1969) *Cumann na mBan and the Women of Ireland* (Kilkenny: Kilkenny Press).
Coogan, T. P. (1993) *Eamonn De Valera* (London: Hutchinson).
Clancy, M. (1990) 'Aspects of Women's Contribution to the Oireachtas Debates in the Irish Free State', in: M Luddy and C Murphy eds *Women Surviving* (Dublin: Poolbeg Press).
Daly, M.E. (1995) 'Women in the Irish Free State, 1922-1932', in: J. Hoff and M. Coulter eds *Irish Women's Voices* (Bloomington: Indiana University Press).

Dempsey, D. (1939) 'Facts and Figures About Ireland's Population' in *Irish Monthly Magazine*, vol. 67, pp.529-535.
Enloe, C. (1983) *Does Khaki Become You?: The Militarisation of Women's Lives*, (London: Pluto).
Fahey, T. (1995) 'Privacy and the Family' in *Sociology* Vol.29 No. 4 pp.687-702.
Fallon, C. (1986) *Soul of Fire: a Biography of Mary MacSwiney* (Cork: Mercier Press).
Fielding, S. (1993) *Class and Ethnicity: Irish Catholics in England 1880-1939* (Buckingham: Open University Press).
Fitzpatrick, D. ed (1990) *Revolution? Ireland 1917-1923* (Dublin: Trinity History Workshop).
Fletcher, J. (1978) 'Infanticide and the Ethics of Loving Concern' in Kohl, M. ed. *Infanticide and the Value of Life* (New York: Prometheus Books).
Gardiner, F. (1993) Political Interest and Participation of Irish Women 1922-1992, in A. Smyth ed *Irish Women's Studies Reader* (Dublin: Attic Press).
Gibbons, L. (1996) *Transformations in Irish Culture* (Cork: Cork University Press).
Goldring, M. (1993) *Pleasant the Scholars Life: Irish Intellectuals in the Construction of the Nation State* (London: Serif).
Gray, B. and Ryan, L. (1996) 'Gendered Constructions of Irishness: stagnation or change in Irish society since Independence', in S. Stern-Gillett *et al* eds *Culture and Identity: Selected Aspects and Approaches* (Katowice: Wydawnictwo Uniwersytetu Slaskiego).
Gray, B. and Ryan, L. (1997) '(Dis)locating 'woman' and women in Representations of Irish nationality' in A. Byrne and M. Leonard eds *Women and Irish Society* (Belfast: Beyond the Pale).
Gray, B. and Ryan, L. (1998) 'The Politics of Identity and the Interconnections between Feminism, Nationalism and Colonialism' in R. Roach Pierson ed *Nation, Empire and Colony* (New York: Indiana University Press).
Guilbride, A. (1996) 'Mad or Bad? Women Committing Infanticide in Ireland' in R. Lentin ed *In From the Shadows* (Limerick: University of Limerick).
Hearn, M. (1993) *Below Stairs: Domestic Service Remembered* (Dublin: Lilliput).
Hobsbawm, E. (1992) 'Inventing Traditions' in: E. Hobsbawm and T. Ranger eds *The Invention of Traditions* (Cambridge: Cambridge University Press).
Horgan, J. (1995) 'Saving us from Ourselves: contraception, censorship and the evil literature controversy of 1926' in *Irish Communications Review* Vol 5 pp.61-68.
Innes, C.L. (1993) *Woman and Nation* (Hemel Hempstead: Harvester Wheafsheaf).
Innes, C. L. (1994) 'Virgin Territories and Motherlands: Colonial and Nationalist Representations of Africa and Ireland' in *Feminist Review* 47, pp.1-14.
Jackson, J. (1963) *The Irish in Britain* (London: Routledge and Kegan Paul).
Jones, M. (1988) *These Obstreperous Lassies: A History of the Irish Women Workers' Union* (Dublin: Gill and MacMillan).
Kandiyoti, D. (1996) 'Women, Ethnicity and Nationalism' in J. Hutchinson and A. Smith eds *Ethnicity* (Oxford: Oxford University Press).
Katrak, K. (1992) 'Indian Nationalism, Gandhian Satyagraha and Representations of Female Sexuality' in A. Parker *et al* eds *Nationalisms and Sexualities* (New York: Routledge).
Kelly, A. (1999) 'Cultural Imperatives: the Irish language revival and the educational system' in J. Augusteijn ed *Ireland in the 1930s* (Dublin: Four Courts Press).
Kennedy, R. (1973) *The Irish: Emigration, Marriage and Fertility* (Berkeley: University of California Press).

Keyes McDonnell, K. (1972) *There is a Bridge at Bandon: A personal account of the Irish War of Independence* (Cork: Mercier).
Layoun, M. (1992) 'Telling Spaces: Palestine Women and the Engendering of National Narratives' in A. Parker *et al* eds *Nationalisms and Sexualities* (New York: Routledge).
Lee, J. J. (1988) 'State and Nation in Independent Ireland' in The Princess Grace Irish Library ed. *Irishness in a Changing Society* (Gerrards Cross: Colin Smythe).
Lee, J. J. (1990) 'Emigration: A contemporary perspective' in Richard Kearney ed *Migrations: The Irish at Home and Abroad* (Dublin: Wolfhound Press).
Lentin, R. (1998) 'Irishness, the 1937 Constitution and Citizenship' in *Irish Journal of Sociology* vol. 8 pp.5-24.
Litton, H. (1997) *The Irish Civil War* (Dublin: Wolfhound).
Lomax, J. (1986) *Women of the Air* (London: John Murray Publishers).
Lyons, F. S. L. (1989) *Culture and Anarchy in Ireland* (Oxford: Oxford University Press).
Maddock, E. (1996) 'Citizenship, Protect, Control, Resistance' in R. Lentin ed *In From the Shadows* (Limerick: University of Limerick).
MacEoin, U. ed (1980) *Survivors* (Dublin: Argenta Publications).
Markham, B. (1988) *West with the Night* (London: Virago).
Martin, A. (2000) 'Death of a nation: transnationalism, bodies and abortion in late twentieth century Ireland' in T. Mayer ed *Gender Ironies of Nationalism* (London: Routledge).
McClintock, A. (1993) 'Family Feuds: Gender, Nationalism and the Family' in *Feminist Review*, No.44. pp.61-80.
McCoole, S. (1997) *Guns and Chiffon: Women Revolutionaries and Kilmainham Gaol* (Dublin: Government Publications).
McDevitt, P. (1997) 'Muscular Catholicism: Nationalism, Masculinity and Gaelic Team Sports, 1884-1916' in *Gender and History* vol. 7 no. 2 pp.262-284.
Meaney, G. (1993) 'Sex and Nation' in A. Smyth ed *Irish Women's Studies Reader* (Dublin: Attic).
Melman, B. (1988) *Women and the popular imagination in the 1920s* (London: Macmillan Press).
Miller, K. (1990) 'Emigration, Capitalism and Ideology in post-famine Ireland' in R. Kearney ed *Migrations: The Irish at Home and Abroad* (Dublin: Wolfhound Press).
Mosse, G. (1985) *Nationalism and Sexuality* (London: University of Wisconsin Press).
Moser, P. (1993) 'Rural Economy and Female Emigration in the West of Ireland, 1936-1956' in *UCG Women's Studies Centre Review*, Vol. 2 pp.41-51.
Newspaper Press Directory (1925) (London: Mitchell and co. Ltd.).
Nash, C. (1993) 'Remapping and Renaming: New Cartographies of Identity, Gender and Landscape in Ireland' in *Feminist Review* 44, pp.39-57.
Nava, M. (1995) 'Modernity Tamed? Women Shoppers and the rationalisation of consumption in the interwar period' in *Australian Journal of Communication* vol. 22 no. 2 pp.1-18.
Nava, M. and O'Shea J. eds (1996) *Modern Times: Reflections of a Century of English Modernity* (London: Routledge).
O'Brien, John A. ed (1954) *The Vanishing Irish* (London: W.H. Allen Press).
O'Callaghan, M. (1984) 'Language, Nationality and Cultural Identity in the Irish Free State, 1922-27' in *Irish Historical Studies*, No. 94, pp.226-245.

O'Donoghue, F. (1986) *No Other Law* (Dublin: Anvil).
O'Malley, E. (1992) *The Singing Flame* (Dublin: Anvil).
O'Malley, E. (1994) *On Another Man's Wound* (Dublin: Anvil).
Peteet, J. (1997) 'Icons and Militants: Mothering in the Danger Zone' in *Signs*, Vol 23 No 1 pp103-129.
RadhaKrishnan, R. (1992) 'Nationalism, Gender and Narrative' in A. Parker, *et al* eds *Nationalisms and Sexualities* (pp77-95), New York: Routledge.
Rao, S. (1999) 'Woman-As-Symbol: The Intersections of Identity Politics, Gender, and Indian Nationalism' in *Women's Studies International Forum*, Vol.22, No.3, pp.317-328.
Rose, L. (1986) *The Massacre of Innocents: Infanticide in Britain 1800-1939* (London: Routledge).
Ryan, L. (1994) 'Women without Votes: The Political Strategies of the Irish Suffrage Movement' in *Irish Political Studies*, 9 pp.119-139.
Ryan, L. (1995) 'Traditions and Double Moral Standards: the Irish Suffragists' critique of nationalism' in *Women's History Review*, Vol. 4 No. 4 pp.487-503.
Ryan, L. (1996) 'The massacre of innocence: Infanticide in the Irish Free State' in *Irish Studies Review*, No.14 pp.17-20.
Ryan, L. (1997) A Question of Loyalty: War, Nation and Feminism, in *Women's Studies International Forum* Vol.20, No.1 pp. 21-32.
Ryan, L. (1998a) 'Negotiating Modernity and Tradition: newspaper debates on the Modern Girl in the Irish Free State' in *Journal of Gender Studies*, Vol.7 No. 2 pp.181-198.
Ryan, L. (1998b) 'Constructing Irishwoman: Modern Girls and Comely Maidens' n *Irish Studies Review* vol.6, no. 3 pp.263-272.
Ryan, L. (1999) 'Furies and Die-Hards: Women and Irish Republicanism in the early twentieth century' in *Gender and History*, Vol 11 No 2 pp.256-275.
Ryan, L. (2000) 'Drunken Tans: Representations of Sex and Violence in the Anglo-Irish War 1919-1921' in *Feminist Review*, No. 66 pp.73-94.
Ryan, Mark. (1994) *War and Peace in Ireland* (London: Pluto).
Ryan, Meda (1986) *The Real Chief: The Story of Liam Lynch*, (Cork: Mercier).
Russell, E. (1999) 'Holy Crosses, Guns and Roses: themes in popular reading material' in J. Augusteijn ed *Ireland in the 1930s* (Dublin: Four Courts Press).
Sharkey, S. (1994) *The Iconography of Rape* (London: University of North London Press).
Scannell, Y. (1988) 'The Constitution and the Role of Women' in B. Farrell ed *De Valera's Constitution and Ours* (Dublin: Gill and Macmillan).
Sheehan, A. (1990) 'Cumann na mBan' in D. Fitzpatrick ed *Revolution? Ireland 1917-1923* (Dublin: Trinity History Workshop).
Smyth, J. (1993) 'Dancing, Depravity and all that Jazz' in *History Ireland*, Summer, pp.51-54.
Taillon, R. (1996) *When History was Made: The Women of 1916* (Belfast: Beyond the Pale Publishers).
Thapar, S. (1993) 'Women as Activists, Women as Symbols: A study of the Indian Nationalist Movement' in *Feminist Review*, No 44 pp. 81-96.
Tinkler, P. (1995) *Constructing Girlhood* (London: Taylor and Francis).
Travers, P. (1995) 'There was nothing there for me: Irish Female Emigration, 1922-1971' in P. O'Sullivan ed *Irish Women and Irish Migration* (London: University of Leicester Press).

Valiulis, M.G. (1995a.) 'Power, Gender and Identity in the Irish Free State' in J. Hoff and M. Coulter eds *Irish Women's Voices* (New York: Indiana University Press).
Valiulis, M.G. (1995b.) 'Neither Feminist nor Flapper: the Ecclesiastical Construction of the Ideal Irish women' in M. O' Dowd and S. Wichert eds *Chattel, Servant or Citizen* (Belfast: Institute of Irish Studies).
Walsh, A. M. (1999) 'Root them in the land: cottage schemes for agricultural labourers' in J. Augusteijn ed *Ireland in the 1930s* (Dublin: Four Courts Press).
Ward, M. (1989) *Unmanageable Revolutionaries* (London: Pluto).
Ward, M. (1995) *In their Own Voice: Women and Irish Nationalism* (Dublin: Attic).
Ward, M. (1997) *Hanna Sheehy Skeffington: A Life* (Cork: Cork University Press).
Webster, W. (2001) 'Representing Nation: Women, Obituaries and National Biography' in A.M. Gallagher, C. Lubelska and L. Ryan eds *Changing the Past: Women, History and Representation* (London: Longmans).
Williamson, L. (1978) 'Infanticide: An anthropological Analysis' in M. Kohl ed *Infanticide and the Value of Life* (New York: Prometheus Books).
Wilson, E. (1985) *Adorned in Dreams: Fashion and Modernity* (London: Virago).
Yuval-Davis, N. (1997) *Gender and Nation* (London: Sage).

# INDEX

Abbey Theatre, 198
Adoption, 260, 279, 287
Advertising, 38, 62, 63, 64, 65, 66, 68, 162
Arbour Hill jail, 235, 237, 241, 246
Aviation, 70, 71, 72, 75, 78, 80, 82, 83, 87, 89
Batten, Jean, 86, 87
Bennett, Louie, 103, 104, 108, 113, 143, 249
Birth control see also contraception, 167, 270, 287
Black and Tans (British soldiers), 237, 247, 250
Bobbed hair, 19, 57, 61, 63, 65, 67, 68, 72, 80
Bodenstown cemetery, 238, 240
Bowles, Mary, 209, 218
Britain, 9, 25, 40, 41, 70, 78, 84, 91, 94, 96, 110, 111, 112, 114, 115, 118, 132, 192, 212, 224, 260, 261, 262, 270, 287, 291, 296, 298
Brugha, Nodlaig, 246
Buckley, Margaret, 106, 208, 220, 295
Cars, 58, 62, 64, 67, 68, 85, 208, 217, 239
Catholic Church, 3, 4, 7, 10, 12, 22, 27, 28, 29, 42, 43, 47, 51, 54, 65, 68, 112, 126, 143, 147, 152, 183, 188, 190, 213, 220, 221, 226, 255, 256, 257, 272, 279, 289
Catholic Truth Society, 43, 66, 151, 257, 276
Celtic, 13, 14, 16, 17, 18, 20, 21, 22, 23, 24, 28, 29, 32, 34
Censorship, 3, 7, 43, 138, 153, 188, 189, 206, 210, 213, 219, 290, 296
Census, 115, 117, 279

Charities, 119, 122, 123, 124, 268
Children, 2, 17, 23, 30, 109, 111, 120, 141, 145, 146, 153, 157, 158, 159, 160, 162, 163, 164, 165, 166, 167, 170, 172, 173, 175, 176, 178, 179, 180, 189, 190, 201, 216, 253, 265, 271, 279, 280, 281, 287
Church of Ireland, 166
Cigarette smoking, 19, 43, 48, 52, 53, 58, 61, 62, 63, 67, 68
Cinema, also see films, 30, 40, 50, 58, 65, 66, 67, 68, 95, 112, 125, 189
Citizenship, 128, 129, 130, 131, 136, 138, 139, 141, 143, 145, 146, 147, 148, 151, 164, 166, 192, 257, 259, 291, 295, 297
Civic Guards, 28, 46, 54, 177, 180, 181, 182, 224, 238, 248, 265, 269, 270, 272
Civil Service, 3, 93, 97, 98, 104, 142
Civil War, 3, 7, 11, 31, 32, 41, 52, 54, 205, 206, 207, 209, 210, 211, 212, 213, 214, 217, 218, 219, 220, 221, 222, 223, 224, 230, 232, 242, 243, 244, 245, 249, 295, 297
class, 3, 7, 11, 22, 41, 45, 46, 67, 93, 94, 102, 109, 117, 121, 161, 162, 163, 169, 174, 176, 270
Colonialism, 1, 15, 296
Comerford, Maire, 208, 217, 218, 224, 227, 239
Committee on Child Welfare, 279, 280, 281
Concannon, Helena, 161, 162
Concealment, 12, 254, 255, 256, 260, 261, 262, 266, 267, 269, 271, 274, 275, 282, 287, 288, 292
*Connacht Sentinel*, 7, 31, 32, 33, 39, 50, 77, 172, 174, 179, 277

301

*Connacht Tribune*, 7, 39, 46, 51, 64, 65, 72, 73, 76, 77, 78, 94, 173, 176, 178, 184, 185, 277

Constitution of 1937, 10, 92, 109, 126, 127, 129, 131, 132, 133, 134, 135, 137, 138, 139, 140, 141, 142, 143, 144, 145, 146, 148

Consumerism, 40, 59, 63

Contraception, 3, 259, 265, 270, 287, 296

Convent, 122, 275

*Cork Examiner*, 7, 29, 30, 38, 42, 45, 58, 61, 73, 75, 84, 85, 86, 87, 95, 96, 112, 115, 116, 117, 142, 151, 152, 175, 209, 210, 214, 215, 217, 218, 219, 221, 222, 224, 225, 229, 230, 231, 237, 238, 239, 244, 248, 249, 250, 257, 258, 262, 263, 264, 265, 267, 269, 270, 272, 273, 274, 275, 276, 278, 282, 283

Cosgrave, William, 213, 216, 221, 226, 233, 235, 243

Costello, John A., 130, 131, 135

Cottages, 11, 154, 156, 157, 161

Court reports, 12, 26, 27, 46, 95, 170, 172, 173, 174, 175, 176, 177, 179, 180, 181, 185, 187, 209, 225, 227, 228, 230, 233, 251, 264, 266, 267, 271, 273, 274, 275, 282, 284, 286

Cuchulain, 13

Cumann na mBan, 144, 145, 207, 208, 209, 211, 212, 214, 220, 221, 222, 233, 235, 239, 240, 245, 246, 249, 251, 295, 298

Cumann na nGaedheal, 33, 79, 217, 220, 221, 223, 224, 232, 233, 241

Dail Eireann, 128, 129, 134, 138, 140, 141, 142, 147, 161, 212, 231, 232, 234, 243, 246

Dance halls, 181, 183, 184, 186, 188, 277, 278, 279

Dancing, 16, 19, 23, 27, 28, 29, 30, 59, 61, 66, 67, 179, 181, 183, 184, 185, 186, 188, 268, 277, 278, 279, 298

De Blacam, Aodh, 104, 105, 106, 107, 156

De Valera, Eamon, 10, 20, 27, 31, 33, 87, 110, 128, 129, 131, 132, 133, 134, 135, 136, 137, 138, 139, 140, 141, 143, 145, 146, 147, 148, 157, 194, 195, 196, 197, 199, 200, 201, 222, 231, 234, 236, 237, 238, 240, 241, 242, 243, 244, 247, 248, 250, 251, 295, 298

Depopulation, 91, 112, 113, 115, 118, 164

Divorce, 3

Domestic servants, 10, 94, 118, 269, 270, 274, 280, 281

Domestic service, 94, 107, 110, 124, 127

Domestic violence, 11, 168, 172

Domesticity, 9, 91, 99, 109, 116, 142, 148, 151, 165, 185, 190

Earhart, Amelia, 9, 70, 71, 72, 73, 80, 81, 82, 83, 84, 87, 88

Easter Rising of 1916, 192, 206

Economic war, 91

Embracery, 228, 229, 230

Emigration, 9, 91, 92, 94, 105, 106, 108, 109, 110, 111, 112, 113, 114, 115, 116, 117, 118, 124, 125, 126, 132, 139, 155, 157, 159, 160, 181, 268, 290, 292, 294, 295, 296, 297, 298

Erin, 1, 14

Eucharistic Congress of 1932, 26

Famine, 114, 118, 297

Farms, 87, 92, 109, 110, 113, 136, 159, 170, 173, 179, 263, 270, 282, 285

Fatherhood, 157, 158, 159, 166, 170, 173, 175, 176, 193, 211, 246, 253, 260, 268, 282, 285, 290

Feminine, 1, 9, 34, 39, 42, 43, 45, 47, 52, 53, 68, 71, 72, 75, 80, 91, 95, 100, 108, 126, 144, 152, 161, 202, 215, 284

Feminism, 10, 92, 101, 105, 131, 140, 141, 143, 144, 145, 148, 149, 221, 290, 292, 293

Fianna Fail, 20, 79, 104, 114, 115, 138, 142, 145, 146, 157, 161, 162, 163, 193, 196, 222, 231, 232, 234, 235, 239, 240, 241, 242, 246

Films, see also Hollywood, 41, 62, 65, 80, 111, 152, 169, 189

Fine Gael, 133, 140, 141, 161
Fitzmaurice, Colonel James, 69, 70, 73, 79, 88
Flapper, 8, 9, 19, 37, 38, 39, 40, 41, 42, 45, 46, 49, 56, 58, 59, 65, 66, 67, 68, 73, 162, 290, 292
Foreign fashions, 8, 19, 37, 48, 50, 55
Freemasons, 50
Furies, 11, 206, 212, 221, 245, 251, 252, 298
Gaelic Athletic Association, 28, 31, 183
Gaelic League, 50, 66, 198
Gaeltacht, 116, 156
Gaffney, Gertrude, 100, 101, 118, 119, 120, 121, 122, 123, 124, 125, 126, 127, 131, 132, 135, 142, 145
Gambling, 177, 178
Gilmartin, Archbishop, 51, 111, 124, 152
Gonne MacBride, Maud, 226, 232, 235, 236, 240, 241, 246
Gregory, Lady Augusta, 13, 198, 199, 200
Hayden, Professor Mary, 100, 136, 139, 143
Heath, Lady Mary Sophie, 9, 73, 74, 75, 76, 77, 79, 83, 88
Hibernia, 1, 14
Hitler, Adolph, 131, 132, 135
Hollywood, 22, 41, 50, 57, 58, 95
Housing, 4, 157, 165
Humphreys, Sheila, 208, 218, 227, 230, 231, 233, 234
Illegitimate children, 220, 222, 230, 253, 255, 263, 277, 279, 280, 282, 287
Industrial schools, 172, 173, 175, 176
Infant mortality, 4, 163, 164, 281, 287
Infanticide, 12, 122, 253, 254, 255, 256, 260, 261, 262, 265, 266, 267, 268, 269, 271, 272, 273, 274, 275, 276, 279, 282, 285, 286, 287, 288, 292, 296, 298, 299
Inquest, *see also court reports*, 263, 264, 266, 267, 269, 270, 271
*Irish Independent*, 7, 8, 10, 17, 19, 23, 24, 25, 26, 28, 29, 30, 43, 47, 48, 52, 53, 54, 55, 56, 57, 63, 69, 70, 71, 72, 74, 76, 80, 81, 82, 83, 84, 85, 86, 87, 91, 96, 97, 99, 100, 101, 104, 105, 107, 111, 113, 114, 115, 117, 118, 124, 126, 128, 130, 132, 135, 136, 138, 142, 146, 149, 152, 158, 159, 161, 177, 178, 179, 185, 187, 188, 196, 198, 209, 210, 215, 216, 217, 219, 224, 225, 226, 227, 233, 234, 235, 237, 239, 240, 241, 242, 244, 245, 247, 253, 262, 269, 271, 272, 273, 275, 284, 286
Irish language, 22, 24, 50, 100, 116, 198, 200, 296
Irish National Teachers' Organisation, 96
*Irish Press*, 7, 10, 17, 20, 26, 27, 31, 84, 85, 86, 101, 102, 103, 104, 105, 106, 117, 128, 129, 132, 133, 134, 135, 136, 137, 138, 139, 141, 143, 144, 148, 154, 155, 156, 157, 158, 162, 163, 164, 165, 166, 180, 181, 192, 193, 194, 195, 196, 197, 198, 199, 200, 238, 241, 242, 243, 244, 246, 247, 249, 250, 254, 278
Irish Republican Army, 206, 207, 208, 211, 212, 223, 224, 230, 235, 237, 238, 242, 243
*Irish Times*, 7, 17, 18, 19, 22, 25, 26, 28, 31, 57, 58, 215, 216, 217, 219, 279, 280, 281
Irish Women Workers' Union, 104, 113, 124, 136, 137, 141, 143, 296
Jazz, 50, 66, 183, 186, 294, 298
Jews, 50, 120, 121, 122
Johnson, Amy, 9, 82, 83, 84, 86, 87
Kerryman, 7, 16, 37, 39, 58, 59, 60, 61, 74, 77, 96, 183, 197, 198, 200, 201, 223, 263, 264, 283
Kettle, Mary, 105, 134, 135, 137, 143
Kilmainham jail, 217, 297
Lenten pastorals, 7, 43, 112, 119, 257, 278
*Limerick Leader*, 7, 38, 47, 65, 66, 74, 76, 77, 171, 183, 188
Lindbergh, Charles, 70, 73, 80, 87, 89
Logue, Cardinal, 213
London, 10, 22, 58, 60, 67, 74, 76, 84, 86, 110, 120, 121, 124, 154, 295, 296, 297, 298, 299

Lugh Lamh Fhada, 16, 19, 20, 21, 23, 26, 27
Macken, Professor Mary, 100, 139, 143
MacRory, Cardinal, 27, 28
MacSwiney, Mary, 137, 222, 235, 236, 237, 238, 239, 241, 243, 244, 296
Manhood, 23, 27, 29, 30
Manly Gael, 13, 16, 24
Markham, Beryl, 85, 86, 87, 297
Markievicz, Countess Constance, 226
Marriage, 2, 45, 51, 74, 86, 91, 93, 96, 98, 99, 100, 102, 103, 105, 106, 107, 108, 109, 112, 116, 118, 131, 139, 146, 148, 160, 259, 277, 282, 296
Marriage rate, 91, 105, 109, 112, 131, 139, 146, 160
Masculinity, 1, 23, 28, 29, 31, 34, 205, 297
Maternity, see motherhood, 119, 148, 151, 190
Modern girl, 8, 9, 37, 42, 52, 53, 57, 58, 60, 61, 62, 63, 65, 66, 67, 68, 162, 184, 276
Modest Dress and Deportment Crusade, 47, 48, 49, 66
Mollison, Jim, 82, 83, 84, 85, 86, 88
Moloney, Helena, 227, 240
Mother India, 14
Mother Ireland, 10, 24, 198, 252, 289, 293
Motherhood, 10, 23, 30, 45, 91, 107, 108, 132, 142, 153, 160, 165, 177, 184, 191, 194, 195, 197, 202, 203, 245, 256, 259, 263, 287
Mountjoy jail, 217, 232, 235
National identity, 2, 3, 5, 13, 15, 23, 24, 28, 38, 41, 42, 43, 49, 68, 78, 89, 128, 154, 221
National Society for the Prevention of Cruelty to Children, 170, 172, 173, 174, 175, 176, 182
Nationalism, 1, 2, 7, 8, 11, 12, 13, 14, 15, 19, 20, 22, 28, 30, 32, 35, 37, 40, 41, 42, 43, 47, 53, 59, 67, 153, 169, 182, 183, 191, 192, 193, 196, 198, 200, 201, 202, 205, 221, 255, 258, 259, 276, 290, 293, 295, 296, 297, 298, 299
Nazi, 121
New York, 82, 84, 86, 87, 154, 200, 201, 296, 297, 298, 299
Northern Ireland, 2, 7, 39, 67, 82, 138, 145, 224, 291
Nuns, 51, 122, 281
Obituaries, 11, 153, 191, 192, 203, 249, 299
Olympic Games, 16, 30
Paris, 22, 50, 57, 58, 65, 74, 154
Pearse, Margaret, 11, 153, 192, 193, 194, 195, 196, 197, 198, 199, 201
Pearse, Padraic, 193, 194, 198
Pope, 42, 54
Poteen, 178, 179, 180, 181, 190, 286
Poverty, 4, 11, 103, 118, 120, 124, 167, 174, 183
Pregnancy, 12, 120, 160, 254, 255, 257, 259, 260, 265, 266, 267, 268, 271, 273, 275, 277, 284, 287, 292
Prostitution, 119
Protestant, 7, 199, 200, 276
Rape, 1, 169
Redmond, Bridget, 141
Republican women, 11, 137, 205, 207, 208, 209, 210, 211, 212, 213, 214, 215, 218, 219, 220, 221, 222, 225, 227, 230, 231, 232, 234, 238, 240, 241, 242, 245, 249, 250, 251, 288
Republicanism, 7, 144, 205, 214, 222, 223, 231, 232, 234, 236, 241, 246, 247, 249, 252, 294, 298
Rock, Nancy, 18, 19, 26
Roisin Dubh, 1, 14, 49, 50, 197, 252
Rural, 8, 11, 38, 48, 62, 64, 67, 91, 94, 105, 109, 110, 111, 112, 113, 115, 117, 118, 119, 122, 124, 153, 154, 155, 156, 157, 158, 160, 161, 162, 163, 164, 169, 173, 181, 182, 183, 186, 190, 203, 215, 269, 270, 293
Sexual violence, 168, 171
Shebeens, 179, 180, 181, 182
Sheehy Skeffington, Hanna, 135, 143, 226, 235, 239, 299
Sinn Fein, 31, 222, 224

*Sligo Champion*, 7, 20, 39, 49, 51, 62, 63, 170, 223
Spinning wheels, 11, 154, 155, 156, 181
Suffrage, 41, 136, 139
Synge, John Millington, 13, 200
Tailte, 8, 13, 15, 16, 18, 19, 20, 21, 23, 24, 26, 27, 30, 35, 78, 289
Tailteann Games, 12, 18
Teachers, 93, 96, 99, 142, 236
Travellers, 177
Unemployment, 4, 92, 103, 105, 106, 108, 112, 115, 124, 126, 127, 131, 155, 175, 292, 294
Unionism, 2
University, 75, 93, 99, 100
Unmarried mothers, 119, 122, 277, 279, 280, 281
urban, 7, 8, 11, 38, 46, 48, 62, 67, 95, 102, 109, 110, 112, 153, 157, 160, 162, 163, 164, 169, 190, 203, 263, 270
Urban slums, 11, 153, 157, 163, 164, 165, 166, 167, 270
Virgin Mary, 152, 167, 194, 198

War of Independence, 2, 11, 199, 205, 206, 207, 208, 209, 210, 211, 212, 217, 218, 219, 232, 237, 243, 249, 297
Wheelwright, Mrs. Catherine nee Coll, also Mrs de Valera, 200, 201
*Wicklow People*, 7, 31, 32, 33, 39, 42, 44, 45, 50, 186, 188, 224, 225, 277
Wild West, 11, 153, 174, 182, 203
Wolfe Tone commemoration ceremony, 238, 240
Womanhood, 2, 3, 8, 12, 23, 35, 37, 39, 50, 53, 57, 59, 68, 73, 99, 100, 104, 130, 144, 147, 152, 154, 193, 197, 284, 289, 290
Women Graduates Association, 142, 143, 144
workhouse, 267, 268, 273, 274, 279, 281
Working woman, 9, 92, 95, 104, 131, 195
World War I, 40, 192, 227
World War II, 192
Yeats, W.B., 13, 199, 200, 236